Praise for THE ANGLO FILES

"Because [Sarah] Lyall is rather witty and understated herself, as well as a dogged, meticulous reporter, the result is a book that is both funny and illuminating." —Laurie Hertzel, *Minneapolis Star Tribune*

"It should be handed out, as a public service, in the immigration line at Heathrow." —Malcolm Gladwell

"When Sarah Lyall married an Englishman and moved to London . . . few around her realized she was a modern-day Tocqueville— otherwise they would have been much more guarded." —Graydon Carter

"Sarah Lyall is the wittiest observer of the English and their curious habits. Now she's written a book that takes her game to an entirely new level. It's funny, it's delightful, and anyone with even a passing interest in these strange people should read it." —Michael Lewis

"By turns wry, mordant, affectionate, bitter, and sweet. I never miss any of Sarah Lyall's dispatches because, while they manage to remind me why I left, they also contrive to make me feel occasionally homesick." —Christopher Hitchens

"Sarah Lyall brings all the virtues of the best American journalism, including accuracy, to the task of analysing all the vices of British society, including hypocrisy, venality, and hopeless confusion about sex. In addition to its importance as a sociological treatise, *The Anglo Files* is an indispensable guide to all the best true stories about the country to which she has emigrated, and in which she will now be hailed as one of its supreme analysts, preparatory to her being executed on Tower Green." —Clive James

"An entertaining, indeed delightful, book. If the exchange rate makes going there impossible, read this. It's cheaper and almost as much fun." —Jeff Simon, *Buffalo News*

"A superb social and cultural anthropology by a reporter who has lived among her subjects without losing her sense of wonder for them. It is beautifully written, always insightful, and often hilarious. Imagine Margaret Mead channeling Jon Stewart and you have Sarah Lyall." —Eric Lax

"A witty, incisive collection of essays . . . on everything English, from soccer to aristocrats to Scotch eggs." —*Elle*

"A good, funny book." —*Bookforum*

"Although this book may shatter your illusions about our charming, well-spoken cousins, at least it will make you laugh. That's high praise in these parts." —Kevin Walker, *Tampa Tribune*

"A hilarious, poignant, and beautifully observed account of two cultures permanently separated by a common language . . . no one headed across the pond should even consider leaving home without it." —Charles Kaiser, *Radar Online*

"Tartly provocative. . . . [Lyall] writes about Britain not as a neutral foreign observer but as someone who'd dearly like to set the place to rights with a course of psychotherapy."
—Jonathan Raban, *New York Review of Books*

"Sarah Lyall tracks the odd and endearing behaviors that help us measure our own quirks and cultural obsessions."
—*Los Angeles Times*

"It's hard to imagine a sharper or more compulsively readable guide to the British, who emerge here as unexpectedly exotic, and endearing. . . . I have lived in these rain-lashed isles for roughly twice as long as the author, but reading her book I was continuously surprised, enlightened, and entertained. With her wit and energetic need-to-know, Sarah Lyall is part Isabel Archer and part Nancy Drew, and her Britain is altogether riveting."

—Isabel Fonseca

"Amusing and well-written." —*USA Today*

"A delightful read." —Kim Crow, *Cleveland Plain Dealer*

THE

ANGLO FILES

A FIELD GUIDE TO THE ENGLISH

SARAH LYALL

W. W. NORTON & COMPANY
Independent Publishers Since 1923

For information about permission to reproduce selections from this book,
write to Permissions, W. W. Norton & Company, Inc.,
500 Fifth Avenue, New York, NY 10110

For information about special discounts for bulk purchases,
please contact W. W. Norton Special Sales at
specialsales@wwnorton.com or 800-233-4830

Manufacturing by LSC Communications, Harrisonburg
Book design by Judith Stagnitto Abbate / Abbate Design
Production manager: Anna Oler

The Library of Congress has cataloged a previous edition as follows:

Lyall, Sarah.
The Anglo files : a field guide to the British /
Sarah Lyall.—1st ed.
p. cm.
Includes bibliographical references and index.
ISBN 978-0-393-05846-8 (hardcover)
1. Great Britain—Social life and customs—21st century.
2. Americans—England—History—21st century. I. Title.
DA589.4.L93 2008
941.086—dc22

2008019440

ISBN 978-0-393-35379-2 pbk.

W. W. Norton & Company, Inc.
500 Fifth Avenue, New York, N.Y. 10110
www.wwnorton.com

W. W. Norton & Company Ltd.
15 Carlisle Street, London W1D 3BS

1 2 3 4 5 6 7 8 9 0

FOR ROBERT AND OUR ENGLISH GIRLS,
ALICE AND ISOBEL

CONTENTS

PREFACE TO THE NEW EDITION

n 2013, several years after *The Anglo Files* was published and eighteen years after I moved to London, I returned home to New York. It had been an eventful whirlwind of a time. I had married a man who believed "blimey" to be a plausible exclamatory word. I had produced two children who unexpectedly sounded like tiny female versions of Little Lord Fauntleroy. I myself had started saying things like "shirty" and "nappies" when I meant "annoyed" and "diapers." I had traveled up and down the country writing about the Brits and their strange ways, covering (among other things) four different prime ministers, a couple of royal weddings, a terrorist bombing, and the spectacular implosion (at least it seemed that way at the time) of Rupert Murdoch's tabloid empire. Having an English family at the same time gave me a double lens through which to observe as both outsider and, sort of, insider.

Yet even after all that time, I never really knew where I stood with the English. Why did they keep apologizing? (Were they truly sorry?) Why were they so unenthusiastic about enthusiasm? When were they being ironic, and how could you tell? When they said "quite," did they mean "very" or "not very"? Why did rain surprise them? Why were they still obsessed with the Nazis? Why did they behave as if Scotland was on another planet, when in fact it was only four hours away? Why were they so nasty about Europe, when they traveled to Europe all the time and had flourished under the open borders and liberal trade policies of the European Union? Could they ever relax without alcohol? And—this was the hardest thing— what lay beneath their default social style, an indecipherable mille-feuille of politeness, awkwardness, embarrassment, irony, self-deprecation, arrogance, defensiveness, and highly articulate deflective humor?

On a personal note, it turned out that trying to re-Americanize after so much Anglicization was unexpectedly challenging. I had thought I was returning home, but I am not sure if a place can be truly home when you have been away from it for so long.

After living among people who were physically incapable of unironic excitement (unless they were drunk), I was discomfited to find that in America, "awesome," once a risible word used only by stoners and surfers, had somehow become a ubiquitous modifier, the Starbucks of adjectives. Though it was thrilling to be back in a city that had the cultural advantage of having a garbage can on every corner, it was sad to leave one in which they were called "rubbish bins." After years of enjoying the heft and feel of the U.K.'s sturdy pound coins, I found American dollar bills to be flimsy and idiotic, even if they were increasing in relative value. The varied drinking cultures bewildered me in reverse, too. My friends in London, by American standards, would be considered functioning alcoholics; after all that time in the pubs of London, I found that my American friends seemed unnecessarily abstemious and puritanical.

In London I had often felt like a Labrador among cats, as loud and gauche as if I had rocked up to a wedding in a garish green pantsuit and forced everyone to answer inappropriately intrusive questions about their sex lives. In New York, on the other hand, I felt tentative and ineffectual, loath to draw attention to myself. I had become an expert in the art of the meaningless exchange, the anodyne weather discussion. I cringed in inward embarrassment when people asked me how much money I made, whether I rented or bought, and how much I paid. I was, it appeared, chronically sorry.

"Sorry," I said to a train conductor soon after moving back home. I wanted to ask him if my dog, Hershey, was allowed on the train, but I did not want to bother him or risk being caught doing the wrong thing. "Why are you sorry?" the conductor asked, whereupon I apologized again, for apologizing. "He's not a very big dog," I added, as if that mitigated Hershey's possibly felonious presence under the seat. I had not understood. "Dogs of any size are welcome on Metro-North!" the conductor said.

Later I went to the Apple Store on the Upper West Side to conduct some iPhone-related business. It was enough to make anyone's head spin. I tried not to take up too much space or thrust myself forward, but you can wait there all day if you use that approach in New York City, where patience and modesty do not bring their own rewards. I told the customer service person that I had to change my official address, since I'd just moved back. I am sorry to be so difficult, I tried to say.

But he had plenty of time, though he talked fast. He asked me a million questions, not even related to technology: Where had I been? Why had I returned to the city? Where was I going to live? How about my family? How did I feel?

I explained, a little. He looked so psyched on my behalf. He considered the whole thing for a moment—me, the joys of globalization, the forces that propel us from one place to another, the excitements of New York City, life itself.

"Awesome!" he said.

I didn't really belong anywhere, or maybe I belonged in more than one place, but that is part of what it is like to be a newspaper reporter. It's better if you live apart from or to one side of what you are covering. For a while I missed London—the pace of life, the beauty of the skyline, the un-nosiness of the neighbors, the way the light looks in midsummer, the old-fashioned uniforms my daughters wore to school, how you could be private in the midst of all those people and all that energy—so much that thinking about it was almost too painful. But just as America had in some ways seemed clearer to me when I was abroad and viewing it from a new perspective, so England began gradually to drift back into focus through a new lens sharpened by the distance of an ocean and the passage of time.

As I write this now, America is well into the administration of its first reality TV president. Things are changing everywhere. Britain has willingly set itself up on a collision course with history, having voted— almost on a whim—to leave the European Union and go it alone in the unpleasantly named process known as Brexit. Half the country is currently furious at the other half, and everyone—even the people who voted to go—is flummoxed about what it will all mean.

Many of the stories I covered when I lived in London came back to the same two questions, the questions this rupture from Europe was meant to solve, the questions the English, and the British, have asked themselves incessantly since their empire fell: Who are we, and what is our place in the world? No one can really put their finger on it, but the thing that summed it up the most for the most came during the 2012 Olympics, held in London. There had been a lot of grumbling beforehand about the cost and what seemed to be a lack of preparation, but in the end the Olympics was a stunning success. It was during the bonkers opening ceremony, with its music medleys and dancing National Health Service nurses and quotes from Shakespeare and references to Mary Poppins and sly inclusion of the queen and depictions of the Industrial Revolution and compendiums of key moments in British television history, that the country seemed to have found some sort of answer to its perennial quest for self-definition.

The opening was a bold, ecstatic celebration of so many things—individuality, creativity, quirkiness, sense of humor, playfulness, rebelliousness, and competence in the face of potential chaos—and more than anything I have ever seen, it seemed to sum up what was great about the country and its people. And that felt like enough.

SARAH LYALL
NEW YORK, 2019

THE

ANGLO FILES

INTRODUCTION

LUNCH WITH AN EARL

Soon after I moved to London I was invited, through some mutual friends, to have lunch with an earl—a real one, as opposed to someone like James Earl Jones or my Uncle Earl back home. I looked it up. Earls, it turns out, are better than viscounts, barons, and knights, but worse than marquesses or dukes, who themselves are not so exciting as monarchs. But in a world of title inflation and cheap celebrity, an earl is still an impressive thing to be.

The lives of many British aristocrats have been diminished by crippling taxes, exorbitant heating costs, and the inconvenient disappearance of the feudal system. Some old lords are rattling along in indigent splendor in crumbling castles; many have had to sell off their furniture, their paintings, and even their houses (they still get to keep their titles). But my host was not one of those. He was still rich, and he had made his massive estate work for him, attracting tens of thousands of visitors a year who paid to look around its most prominent feature, a 460-year-old mansion that rose like some unwieldy palace in the middle of the Wiltshire countryside. Its treasures included a room where George III slept before sending his troops off to quell (or at least that was the plan) the American Revolution; a room full of Chippendale bookcases; and a portrait of Rembrandt's mother, by Rembrandt himself.

Due to the length of the corridors and the swarms of visitors and the army of guides and the labyrinth of rooms with their velvet ropes and their signs telling you Do Not Touch and This Way Please, it was hard to locate the inhabitants of the house, our hosts. But we finally found them, the earl and the countess and their small aristocratic children, reading the daily papers like any other family in an exquisite room the length of a football field, every inch of whose walls were adorned with ancestral portraits by such artists as the seventeenth-century court painter Anthony Van Dyck. We were going on a picnic. I thought: wicker baskets, smoked salmon, asparagus, strawberries, a babbling brook, weeping willows. I thought of the picnic scene in *The Wind in the Willows*.

But then we went out back, and I saw the car.

An ancient Jeep that was now a skeletal husk of its former self, it threatened to fall apart as we climbed aboard and folded ourselves in to what was left of the seats. Doors were missing. Hooks swung from the ceiling, festooned with scraps of animal carcasses and deceased-bird by-products matted with dried blood. Wellington boots jostled for floor space with decrepit gardening implements; insect carapaces; muddy, torn, country-pursuits magazines, and broken-off sections of farm machines. It smelled really bad, a noxious mixture of dead things, stale things, and oil.

The earl was driving; the countess piloted a second, equally clapped-out vehicle of indeterminate vintage. We jolted and lurched past hills covered in wildflowers, rolling meadows and vast fields of crops. It soon became clear that the earl owned all of it. Not just this part here but the part straight on to the horizon in all directions, too: literally everywhere the eye could see, fourteen thousand acres in all. It was that rare thing, a beautiful spring afternoon; the sun was shining, and we were bathed in warmth.

The Jeeps stopped, which was good, because I was pregnant and queasy from all the buffeting. With a world of lovely places to choose from, our host had selected as his preferred picnic spot a decrepit, semi-burned-down barn with most of one of the walls missing. The temperature seemed to fall thirty degrees, following the unwritten law that says that on warm days, old buildings in Britain are always freezing.

We sat on bales of hay, skirting the bird droppings, and listened to the earl discuss his latest quixotic scheme, investing in obscure British films, few of which had yet made it to the cinema. I helped unpack the food. Hot canned cream of tomato soup in a Thermos, poured into Styrofoam cups. Make-your-own sandwiches of processed supermarket ham on white, Wonder-style bread. A bottle of orange-flavored sugar water, known as orange squash, for the children. And some very nice wine for the grownups, which immediately rendered the food a nonissue, except for those of us who were not supposed to drink.

What did I learn about my newly adopted country? That assumptions were made to be unmade. That true aristocrats are perhaps the only people in Britain secure enough not to care how others view what they drive, wear, or eat. That some aspects of British life would likely remain forever beyond the grasp of my feeble colonial understanding. And that when invited to a picnic in the country, you should bring an extra sweater, and possibly also some extra food.

I had heard it a million times: Britain and America are two nations separated by a common language. But anyone who doubts the truth of it should have been in Boston, Massachusetts, a few years ago, when my extremely English husband, Robert, tried to rent a car.

He telephoned Avis.

"Hello," he said, sounding like Hugh Grant in *Four Weddings and a Funeral*. "I'd like to high-ah a cah."

"Huh?" said the Avis operator.

"I'd like to high-ah a cah."

"What?" she repeated. Robert immediately adopted a Prince Philip-addressing-the-peasants approach, which meant that he enunciated with exaggerated slowness and increasing volume, as if the operator were feeble or deaf, rather than just American.

Eventually he got her to understand that he had said "hire," and that "hire" did not mean "employ," but "rent," and we got our car. Our vacation was saved. But multiply this little exchange by a million, imagine me as the ignorant peasant surrounded by people like my husband, and you will have an idea of what my early days in London were like.

I moved for love. In the early 1990s, I got a job covering the publishing industry for the *New York Times*, a big change from my earlier assignments at the paper, when I covered things like Long Island (major themes: garbage, traffic, and taxes) and state government (major theme: health insurance). The publishing beat meant that instead of eating my meals in a subterranean Albany cafeteria and spending the evenings listening to legislators bicker about the mysterious formulas used to determine the size of New York City's mass-transit subsidy, I got to swank around at fancy Park Avenue publishing parties and talk to famous authors. I also got to take editors out to lunch at expensive restaurants and to go to the Frankfurt Book Fair, the world's largest and most exciting banquet of books, held annually in Frankfurt, Germany.

Tall, boyish, and answering to the exotic name of Robert McCrum, my future husband appeared on the first night of my first trip to the fair, at a dinner given by Morgan Entrekin, a New York publisher and book-fair bon vivant. Robert was a friend of Morgan's; I had been invited along in case I wanted to write an article about what Morgan got up to in Frankfurt, as *Times* publishing reporters generally do.

Robert was like something out of *Brideshead Revisited*, or at least that's what I thought, not knowing very many British people and not yet having read a lot of Evelyn Waugh. I could barely understand half of what he said, but I was hooked by his charismatic arrogance, glinting brown eyes, and expert way around the English language. For his part, he liked my raw New World enthusiasm and the fact that I was credulous enough to believe pretty much anything he told me about the UK.

We commuted between London and New York for a year, exchanging torrid, illegible letters—this was just before e-mail—and spending hours on the phone laughing delightedly at each other's accents and quaint worldviews. When it came time for one of us to move so that we could live in the same place, we decided that it would be me.

I had only one friend in London, my old college roommate Lily, who had also married an English person, and the transition was much harder than I expected. Sometimes the gloomy weather made me feel gloomy. Sometimes it seemed as if nobody believed I was even speaking English, so hard was it to make them comprehend what I was trying to say. And sometimes, despite my desire to keep an open mind and look past the stereotypes, I ran smack up against a wall of clichés that, annoyingly, turned out to be true.

British people really are more reserved and repressed than Americans. They really do say "Sorry," all the time, even when it is not their fault, such as when they trip and fall down, or when someone knocks into them in the street. They actually do admire the fact that they have no written constitution. And yes, they believe that baked beans are a vegetable, that the loathsomeness of the French is exceeded only by the loathsomeness of the Germans, and that it is better to shiver in the dark than to swelter in the light.

Other things came as a shock and made the transition harder, because I was so ill prepared. Even in the twenty-first century, for instance, many British people still ride the subway during the evening rush hour without benefit of deodorant. Their nursery-rhyme spider is incy-wincy, not itsy-bitsy. When they sneeze, they say "ah-tishoo," not "ah-choo." They have something called salad cream, a squirtable mayonnaise product that can be slathered on their food to obscure its unpalatability. When they do the dishes, they appear to believe that the part where you are supposed to rinse off the soap is optional.

Also, they are not as impressed by Americans as they might be, which was a bit of a blow.

I arrived in the mid-1990s, just as eighteen years of Conservative Party rule were starting to crumble away. Out of the ruins emerged a new Labour government and a new prime minister, Tony Blair, whose youth, idealism, and energy promised to sweep aside the tired platitudes of yesterday for a better tomorrow. At home, my husband fell spectacularly ill, and as he recovered, we had a baby, and then another one. The country felt reborn, too, poised for something better, even if no one knew exactly what.

It's been an eventful time, and I have spent much of it trying to adjust to, or at least get the measure of, the customs and peccadilloes of my adopted country. Because of my reporting job, I've been allowed to be professionally nosy in a place where the truth beneath the surface is not always readily apparent.

Britain is an impossible subject, as impossible to grasp as quicksilver, and God knows, people have tried. Things here are so coded, so unstraightforward, so opaque, so easy to misinterpret. At the same time, my experience has naturally been subjective: you can't help observing through the prism of your own culture, interests, and environment. I live in London and work for a newspaper; this would be a different book if I lived in Skegness and worked in a pub. I have found Britons everywhere to be a touchy group, especially when outsiders try to pin them down. But, as I explain to interviewees who become defensive and say, "Well, it's hardly better in America, is it?"—it's not a competition. The two countries are just different from each other. Really different.

Opposites, in some ways. We look to the future; they look to the past. We run for election; they stand for it. We noisily and proudly proclaim our Americanness; they shuffle their feet and apologize for their Britishness. We trumpet our successes; they brag about their failures. When they say they are pleased to meet you, they often mean nothing of the kind. Unlike Americans, they do not want to tell you their life story minutes after making your acquaintance; it takes some time to get that far, but if you do, it means you're friends for life.

I came at a singular period of change, one of those great transitional eras in the life of a country. Some of Britain's most ancient institutions, like the House of Lords and the monarchy itself, suddenly seemed up for grabs. So did the old mindset of low expectation and downtrodden self-denial. Money poured in, and London went from being an almost provincial town to a truly international city, awash in riches. There was more greed, more emotion, more hurrying, more selfishness, less deference.

But underneath it all, it seemed to me, the British character remained essentially the same.

When I first moved here and had a certain amount of free time to devote to cultural studies of my new home, I took a deep breath and set about reading *Clarissa*, Samuel Richardson's classic eighteenth-century novel about a virtuous young girl whose seduction and ruin lead her, inevitably, to death. From an anthropological point of view, what is interesting about *Clarissa* is not only that it is more than one million words long and that reading it without skipping the dull bits demands a particularly British-style stoicism and patience, but also that it is an epistolary novel, written in the form of letters between its characters.

It is a quaint custom, all that letter writing, and at first, I assumed it was peculiar to the British gentry from centuries past. In Richardson's time, educated Britons regularly sent letters in the morning, received replies at lunchtime, and responded again in the afternoon. But it was not as unusual as I thought.

Ever since we moved into our house, in west London, my husband and I have carried on a purely epistolary relationship with our neighbors, an older couple the husband of which was knighted by the queen, which means you are meant to call them "Sir" and "Lady." But we never have occasion to call them anything. These are people with whom we share a wall and a bit of sidewalk, and with whom, in all this time, we have had fewer than a dozen conversations. Even saying, "Good morning," which I did once or twice in the 1990s, seems like an act of aggression, a violation of their zone of privacy.

But we write to each other all the time. We are intimate pen pals. When we moved in, we got a letter welcoming us to the neighborhood. When we wrote to notify them of some work we planned to do on the house, they sent a note back inquiring about the common drywall and the potentially creeping damp—subjects that haunt the imaginations of British homeowners. Every year, we get a letter asking us to contribute a bottle of alcohol to the annual church bazaar. Every year, even now, the letters begin, "Dear Mr. and Mrs. McCrum."

I haven't been here long enough to unravel the layers of meaning in all this. Clearly, they don't want to talk to us. But their reserve can't simply be xenophobia, because my husband's respectable pedigree ought to mitigate the dubiousness of my own. Maybe it's one of those things that's a mixture of rudeness and politeness—discourtesy disguised as courtesy, or vice versa—that the British do so well.

It could also be a way to maintain a relationship without the mess and bother of distressing face-to-face intimacy, or simply a reflection of a formality and adherence to convention that still manifest themselves at odd times in social situations. I have constantly been surprised, for instance, at the way it is considered rude at a party to introduce yourself to someone you don't know—the rule is, you're supposed to wait to be formally introduced, preferably by your host.

I am useless at making introductions, since names tend to fly out of my brain when I am confronted with more than two people at a time. But the old American standby, where you take your two friends whose names you can't remember and say, "Do you two know each other?" and wait for them to chime in helpfully, simply doesn't work here.

"Do you two know each other?" I'll ask.

"No," they'll say, followed by silence.

I tried a little experiment with my British friend Stephen. We were at a cocktail party, and another guest, a college professor, was coming down the stairs. I briefed Stephen on what an American might say.

"Hi, I'm Stephen Bayley," Stephen said forthrightly, sticking his hand out. "What do you do?"

The professor looked defensive—stricken, almost. You could see him searching for the angle. "Is that supposed to be some sort of a joke?" he said.

I have now lived in Britain for more than a decade. I have two daughters who, despite the New World blood in their veins, think that the American Revolution was called the War of American Independence and that it had to do with British domestic politics rather than the legitimate grievances of the oppressed. I tend to write more letters than I used to. I try to be less boisterous and not wave my arms around so much. I have worked hard to adjust to the puzzling way things can seem the same but be slightly off—the Hoover instead of the vacuum cleaner, the bin liners instead of the garbage bags, the aluminium-with-an-extra-*i* foil, the football that means soccer. I have tried not to be one of those tedious foreigners who cleaves to other expatriates, whining and reminiscing about Back Home, forcing unbearable traditional food like dumpling stew (or, if you are American, Lucky Charms and boiled red hot dogs) on your mortified, eye-rolling children.

Of course I am still noticeably American. I have an exaggerated can-do spirit and a tendency to alarm the natives by suggesting that psychotherapy might help. I dislike Marmite, Cornish pasties, unheated houses, and drinking outside pubs in the rain, and I don't see the point of Mr. Bean and his silly movies. I have clung to my native accent as a shipwrecked sailor might clutch at a piece of driftwood in the ocean. But I have definitely begun to change. It's a matter of self-preservation, but also a matter of coming to love and perhaps almost to understand my adopted country.

Not that I'd ever be so American and emotional as to put it that way in public.

In the spirit of David Letterman, here are the top ten signs that I am beginning to adjust to life in Britain:

10. I greet people by kissing them twice, once on each cheek, and asking, "How was your journey?"

9. I care whether the English soccer team wins the World Cup (not that it ever does), and sometimes, if I am concentrating, I can explain the offside rule.

8. I recognize that Dick Van Dyke's fake Cockney accent in *Mary Poppins* was a travesty and a disgrace.

7. I am no longer afraid that if I cross the street a car will suddenly emerge from the wrong direction at one hundred miles per hour and mow me down.

6. I recoil when people in social situations ask direct questions about one's salary or the price of one's home.

5. I sometimes use the word "one" as a first-person singular.

4. I often call dishtowels "tea towels" and math, "maths," and I once wrote an article in which I used the phrase "to scupper an agreement"—"scupper" being the British equivalent of "scuttle"— having forgotten what people say back home.

3. I cushion my statements with qualifications, disclaimers, apologies, unnecessarily modifying adverbs, and backhanded ironic remarks. I am "quite upset," "slightly depressed," "a little unhappy"; I think that Hitler was "not exactly the nicest person in the world." When I dislocated my shoulder and lay in a heap at the bottom of a flight of stairs at the hairdresser, with hair-dyeing foil all over my hair, feeling pain that was worse than anything I have ever felt before—not even when I had the children—my overwhelming emotion was embarrassment. I said, "Sorry" in a meek little voice. Then, "I think I'm in a bit of pain," and: "I might possibly at some point need an ambulance."

2. I realize that history did not start in the year 1492.

1. No matter what happens—I come home; the telephone rings; there is a lull in the conversation; nuclear war is declared—I put the kettle on and start making tea.

Still, do I ever eat baked beans for breakfast, believe that it is okay to leave the suds on the clean dishes, or announce my intention to hire a car? No. But give me time.

ONE

NAUGHTY BOYS AND RUMPY-PUMPY

JONATHON COWAP: If someone is described as hirsute, what are
they?
CONTESTANT: Erm.
COWAP: Here's a clue. Most men are, and most women would like
us to think they are not.
CONTESTANT (*after long pause*): Is it gay, Jonathon?

—exchange on BBC Radio York,
quoted in *Private Eye*

Just as some women are inexplicably attracted to prison inmates, so others yearn above all for Englishmen, with their thrilling accents, rumpled boyish hair, and ability to make even pointless banalities sound like brilliant repartee. Find one of those, you think, and you will never be lost for conversation. Madonna, so keen on the genre that she successfully acquired first a strangulated faux English accent and then a real-life English husband, is perhaps the most prominent contemporary example, but there are others. Gwyneth Paltrow married an Englishman. So did Wallis Simpson, and look what happened to her.

I have a personal interest in this issue, of course, on account of the fascinating domestic specimen currently at work at home upstairs in his study (which could be the sunniest room in the house, except that he keeps the curtains pulled shut even in summer, toiling away like Bob Cratchit by the weak light of a small desk lamp). But never mind that now. The point is that while Englishmen present an impeccable facade—capable, articulate, charming and, best of all, ripe for emotional awakening at the deft hands of a clever foreigner—underneath, things are much more complicated than they appear.

There are many reasons, I believe, but we might as well start with their sex education.

When I was in sixth grade in New York back in the 1970s, our science syllabus included *Love and Sex in Plain Language*, a paperback bulging with lurid drawings of naked teenagers in the full sprouting bloom of puberty. The lessons themselves were not particularly useful—"What is it like to have sex with your husband?" I remember a classmate asking our horrified teacher—but at least we got an idea of what we were in for.

Relegated to single-sex education or shipped off to unheated boarding schools with no girls for miles, my British male contemporaries, meanwhile, were learning either nothing, or information so bizarre as to be permanently crippling. My friend Jon was informed, along with his classmates, that he would soon find a "golden seed" in his bed in the mornings. At the age of twelve, the writer John Mortimer was told by his headmaster, "You will probably have dreams, and in the morning you will wake up thinking what a rotter you are. My advice is to have a very cold bath or go for a run to get it out of your system." Ben Macintyre, a columnist for *The Times* of London, said, "My entire sex education consisted of being shown enormous six-foot pictures of diseased private parts."

For my friend Ed, it happened when he was eight and hunting grouse on the moors with his father, an activity that covered a lot of important father-son ground. They were spending time together. They were engaging in an invigorating outdoor pursuit. They were having a heart-to-heart talk. And, on account of having to pay attention to what they were doing, or else they might shoot the wrong thing, they could look at the birds instead of at each other.

"You'll soon be going away," Ed's father remarked, peering at the potential grouses concealed in the brush. He fired a shot.

"Boys will want to interfere with you."

He fired again.

"Don't let them."

One of my in-laws had an off-the-syllabus sex lesson on his last day of prep school, when he was about twelve. The headmaster gathered the departing class in his study and *pulled down his pants*. He took out his penis. He announced to the assembled boys that when they got older, theirs would grow larger and have hair, too.

Another relative was sitting innocently in school one day when his teacher said that the time had come to talk of sexual intercourse. Oh, goody! he thought. But the lesson consisted of a fifteen-minute nature video of two racehorses copulating in a field. There were no follow-up questions, and he was filled with emotional anxiety, particularly about the film's relevance to the human experience. Were women similarly standoffish? Was it over that quickly, and was it okay for the man to trot off afterward for lunch and a drink with his friends?

"It was a long time before I realized that you didn't always have to do it from behind," he said.

In his memoir *Stand Before Your God*, the novelist Paul Watkins describes late 1970s sex education at Eton, taught by the notorious Dr. Twombley, so creaky, vague, and rackety looking that at first the boys mistook him for an ancient member of the custodial staff, kept on for sentimental reasons. Until then, everything Watkins knew about sex he had gleaned from a contraband copy of *Big Tits* magazine that he concealed inside a *New Statesman* cover.

After successfully arriving at the blackboard, Dr. Twombley drew a diagram of a male stick figure lying atop a female stick figure. "Why do you suppose people lie on top of each other when they are having sex?" he barked.

> *Dr. Twombley drew the answer in the air with his chalk, speaking slowly so the writing would catch up with his voice.*
>
> *"So they can talk to each other!"*
>
> *I saw a look spread on Wittingham's face, but it was too late to stop him.*

"But, sir. Surely if you just raised your voice a bit, you could do all the other styles and still talk as much as you wanted to."

Wittingham spent the next couple of hours on punishment duty, which we called On the Bill, picking moss from between the flint cobblestones of the main school courtyard.

Monty Python sent all this up in *The Meaning of Life* in a scene where John Cleese, playing a teacher, has sex with his wife in a bed at the front of a classroom of bored boys, by way of pedagogical demonstration. "Now, did I or did I not do vaginal juices?" he muses aloud. His naked wife lying underneath him, he prepares to dispense with the preliminaries and get right down to it. "We'll take the foreplay as read, if you don't mind, dear," he says. You get the impression that this is how it usually goes at home. "Of course, dear," she murmurs back.

Girls did not necessarily fare better. Instructed to turn to the "Reproduction" chapter in their religious education book at a convent school in the 1980s, the writer Alice Miles and her classmates received some sharp advice from a nun named Sister Catherine, gleaned from her lifetime of virginal inexperience.

"Girls," she intoned gravely, glaring over her spectacles, "soon you will begin to visit discos. At these discos there will be boys."

The word "boys" hung threateningly over the classroom.

"There will not be enough chairs for everybody," Sister Catherine continued, in a tone implying male conspiracy. "You will be expected to sit on the boys' laps."

Her tone dropped even lower. "Girls. Put a newspaper on it first."

My daughters go to a small private school in the middle of London whose teachers several years ago introduced government-mandated sex-ed classes, otherwise known as "sex and relationships education," into the curriculum. As unsubstantiated rumors about the possible topics swept through the ranks of the worried parents, the teachers called an emergency meeting to outline the proposed lesson plan. It was pretty mild stuff, it seemed to me. The illustrations, such as they were, were mainly Twombley-esque diagrams of sexually active stick figures, so that if one did happen to be lying on top of another one, it would look like a pile of sticks. The foreign parents—the ones from the United States, South America, and Continental Europe—thought it was about time, already. But many of the British parents were appalled.

"Do we really want our children exposed to this?" one demanded rhetorically. One father got up, and knock me down if he didn't say, "I don't want to have to come down to have my breakfast and hear my daughter using the word 'vagina.'" He put vagina in quotes, so as to disassociate himself from it—the word, the body part, the implications.

It felt as if a small war was developing, the promiscuous foreigners-of-ill-repute vs. the respectable Britons-with-proper-values.

But all this talk about the proper place for vaginas in the home raised an interesting issue. Britain is the land of bodily-function euphemism. No one has gas, they have "wind." When older people go to the hospital, they do not say that it hurts to pee, let alone urinate. Instead, they say they are having problems with their "waterworks," as if the urinary tract were a utility in Monopoly, along with the electric company.

Australians, who are a forthright lot, like to tell a joke about an Aussie who goes to an English doctor, complaining of hemorrhoids. The doctor gives him a week's worth of suppositories.

"Just put one of these in your back passage each night," says the doctor.

The patient comes back a week later. "Doctor, I did what you said— I put them all out the back door—but nothing happened," he says. "Wouldn't it have been better if I'd just shoved them up my ass?"

British people do their best to glide over the messy stuff. When I had my first child, I rented a breast pump from a company in London that delivers to your door. Along came a young man dressed in dark pants and a white shirt, like a missionary from the Church of Jesus Christ of Latter-Day Saints, carrying the pump in the kind of discreet attaché case in which one might keep one's Bibles. I stood there in my bathrobe in the hallway, unwashed, wild eyed, and sleepless. He did his best not to look at me. He pulled out a device that looked like something you would see in an industrial dairy farm, minus the rows of cows, and explained how it was to be operated—the workings of the pump and the tubes and the cups and the pulling-and-tugging action. It was a tour de force of circumlocution: he did it all without once saying "nipple," "milk," or "breast" (or even "cup" or "pump").

I once visited a distinguished gynecologist at a London hospital for a routine procedure. Wearing the pin-striped suit of a private banker, the doctor smoothly sidestepped any discussion of what it was he proposed to do to me, exactly. He mumbled something about "the womb," flinched when I countered with "the uterus," and hastily returned to his mini lecture, *while he was examining me*, on the fascinating new book he had just read about the life and times of the nineteenth-century adventurer Henry Morton Stanley. Stanley was exploring deepest darkest Africa while the gynecologist was exploring . . . well, I would rather not say.

He swanned in later to see how I was doing.

"How are you getting on?" he asked grandly.

It seemed too embarrassing to discuss my actual symptoms, so I said I felt okay. "Jolly good!" he said, before swanning out.

My American friend Michael was visiting and imagined that this was part of the regular hospital service, part of some sort of customer-satisfaction program. But he found it puzzling. "Who *was* that man?" he asked, after the doctor left.

At home the euphemisms only get sillier: "private parts" for genitals, "willies" for penises, "front bottom" for the dread vagina, "naughty bits" for the whole package (unless you are talking specifically about a man's whole package, and then you can say "dangly bits"). Or they use random pet words. "She kept tugging on his batteries," a friend related, apropos of a traumatized dog and an aggressive toddler, and it took me some time to understand that he was referring to the dog's testicles. Not even serious people seem comfortable with using real words for real sex, known popularly as "shagging," "bonking," or "having it off." *Private Eye* magazine calls it "discussing Ugandan affairs," a reference to a woman journalist who, when caught in flagrante with a Ugandan politician, claimed they were just talking about Uganda.

The Labour politician Denis Healey, interviewed when he was chancellor of the exchequer, in charge of the country's finances, complained that he was too busy to spend much time with his wife. "Pity we've no time left for rumpy-pumpy," he sighed.

When I put my confusion about these nonword words to one of the English mothers at the school sex education meeting, she peered at me disapprovingly.

"I'm a rumpy-pumpy kind of girl, myself," she said.

They like rumpy-pumpy; they also, it seems, like buttocks, which count as quasi-naughty bits. People in Britain are always going on about other people's bottoms, and even using the word brings with it a certain titillation, whether you are speaking to your husband or your children, whether you are six or sixty, whether you are at a Christmas pantomime or a production of *A Midsummer Night's Dream*, where Bottom is the rudest of the rude mechanicals, the one who turns into the ass. I'm not sure why this is so. It may be that it is a way of referring obliquely to sex in a nonthreatening way, since bottoms are located "down there" with all those pesky bits and unmentionables. On the other hand, it may be because British people never advanced beyond the anal stage of their Freudian development. Or it may be because of spanking.

Spanking, or "smacking," is associated with a shameful sexual thrill, the kind of humiliation laced with pleasure that British people are said to particularly enjoy. "Le vice anglais," the French call it. It can evoke nostalgic reveries of one's nanny, a source of severity and punishment but also of security as she snuggled you inside the safe confines of her large soft bosom. When he returns to his family's huge estate from college in *Brideshead Revisited*, Sebastian Flyte bypasses his distant mother and heads straight for the nursery, where the aged nanny who raised him is thrilled, as ever, at the appearance of her favorite boy. Britain is a good place to go for establishments like the Hush-a-bye Club in London, where grown men who are into infantilism can dress in giant diapers, suck on giant pacifiers, and sit up on giant high chairs while Mummy feeds, changes, and disciplines them. James Bond, at least in the books, was an eager spanker, as was his creator, Ian Fleming. (In one priceless scene, Bond threatens to throw his secretary, Miss Moneypenny, over his knee for a good spanking.)

Spanking in the extreme becomes beating, which has its own sexual undercurrents. Beating was officially made illegal in 1999, and most schools had abolished it by then, but it was once a fact of boarding-school education: All those stories you hear are true. It shouldn't matter so much, because boarding-school students make up such a small percentage of the total population in Britain. But they are disproportionately important: they tend to be the people who now run the government, the judiciary, the military, and many of the major institutions in the country. The weapons once used on friends of mine include cricket bats, pool cues, belts, straps, and birch sticks.*

Like victims of Stockholm Syndrome, not all schoolboys were bitter about their punishments. In 1994, a debate broke out on the letters pages of *The Times* of London about the late Anthony Chevenix-Trench, who as headmaster of Eton in the 1960s was famous for getting drunk, flogging the pupils, and then breaking down and tearfully begging their forgiveness. Legend had it that, in what must have been an amateur record, he once beat an entire divinity class of twenty-one students in a single afternoon.

But was it really wrong?

One mitigating factor, some said, was that Chevenix-Trench had been a prisoner in a Japanese POW camp, a sadistic, discipline-filled ordeal bound to confuse anyone about the proper links between authority, pain, and relief.† Some of his former students were actually quite fond of him. An Old Etonian named Christopher Hourmouzios remembered Chevenix-Trench as "a fine teacher who taught me Latin," even if he "flogged the living daylights out of me." Another former student, one

---

* In *The Eye in the Door*, part of Pat Barker's *Regeneration* trilogy about World War I, she describes how Winston Churchill, then the home secretary, spent an afternoon with his chief of staff at the Home Office "beating each others' buttocks with a plaited birch" to test whether it conformed to government regulations.

† It works both ways. In a joke set in a Japanese prison camp, one of the prisoners has a terrible night, sweating, crying out, thrashing around.
He wakes up. "Oh, God!" he sobs. "I dreamed I was back at Eton!"

Nard B. Camber, recalled how the headmaster, on the verge of beating him, would suddenly stop, pull two ceremonial sabers down from the wall, and engage him in an impromptu fencing match.

Camber failed to ask the obvious question: What kind of school administrator decorates his walls with sabers?

"He was an expert swordsman," Camber wrote, "and a very kind and understanding master."

Was this a homoerotic exercise? You bet it was. The most graphic illustration I have seen comes in the BBC's 1971 version of Thomas Hughes's *Tom Brown's Schooldays*, set in Rugby School in the 1830s. The hero, Tom, is wrongly accused of improper behavior, and sentenced to be publicly flogged. The head of his house, a handsome Apollo-like student who shines splendidly over the younger boys (and doesn't appear to go to class much), leads Tom to the headmaster for the punishment and then himself leans forward across a table. Tom then *lies facedown on top of the other boy's back and legs* during the beating, so that every stroke of the lash is felt, in a way, by both of them, the older boy's buttocks being pressed against by the younger one's, er, batteries.

Men my age and from my husband's background of educational privilege may be the last ones to have gone to all-male boarding schools whose halls were suffused with sexual undercurrents, but it has had a lasting effect on them. The masters leered at the boys; the older boys leered at the younger ones. Robert's school had a teacher known popularly as "Homo Holmes," who used to hang out and watch the wet naked boys emerge from the shower. At his Catholic prep school, one man I know used to have to sit on the lap of one of the priests so that the priest could stick his hand down my friend's pants while pretending he wasn't (at that school, the boys were required, after being beaten by the headmaster, to shake his hand and say, "Thank you, sir"). An older man once told me how, on his first night at prep school, he was ordered to get into bed with an upperclassman, and did.* Another said that one

---

* The two met again some years later, when the younger man was an admiral in the Royal Navy, and the other man was his boss—one of the navy's three top commanders.

of his teachers lectured to the assembled class: "Boys, if you must play with someone's genitals, make sure they are your own!"

My friend Ian went to a school where every year all the boys had to stand naked in a line as a teacher lifted their testicles with a tablespoon and inspected them with a flashlight, apparently to see whether "our balls had dropped," he explained. I have countless acquaintances who were harassed and groped, if not forced to have sex, by teachers and other boys. Even now, in the way the culture works, they are supposed to make light of it, as the blustery drunken banker in *Four Weddings and a Funeral* does when talking about the brother of the groom, an old schoolmate.

"Buggered me senseless," he hiccups, "but still, taught me a thing or two about life." A man in his fifties said to me, when I asked about this: "Christ, I looked forward to being fondled by the choirmaster each Sunday!"

Is it any wonder that Englishmen—particularly British men of a certain class—are so mixed up about sex?

Is it any wonder, either, that so many of them still harbor erotic fantasies about former prime minister Margaret Thatcher, who managed to hit all their buttons at once—femininity laced with masculinity, firmness laced with seductiveness, pleasure interwoven with pain? For the men who worked for her, nothing could surpass the exquisite humiliation of a Thatcher "handbagging," as they called it when she was cross with them. Alan Hollingurst's *The Line of Beauty*, about life among the Tories during the Thatcher era, has a long scene in which all the men at a party, including the gay ones, melt in the electric presence of the prime minister. In his diaries, the late government minister Alan Clark refers to her as "the Lady," flirts shamelessly with her, and lusts after her in the House of Commons.

Christopher Hitchens wrote an enthusiastic article about Thatcher's sex appeal in the *New Statesman* back in the late 1970s, when Labour was still in power and Thatcher was merely the leader of the opposition. He met her in person soon afterward, and he fancied he felt a frisson passing between them—perhaps she had read his piece and found him sexy, too? They bantered flirtatiously about Rhodesia, as Zimbabwe was still called. He told me what happened next:

A point of fact came up, and she said, "That's wrong," and I said, "I think you'll find that I'm right," and then I finally conceded and I bowed as if to acknowledge my concession.

She said, "No, bow lower," and then she said, "much, much lower," and then, as if I had no will of my own, I found myself doing it. She'd been meanwhile rolling up a House of Commons order paper, and she gave me a smart thwack on the behind.

And then she looked over and said, "Naughty boy!"

There is of course another "vice anglais": homosexuality. Unfairly or not, many British men of a certain class and type are often suspected—if you look at sexuality as a spectrum, with pure heterosexuality at one extreme and pure homosexuality at the other—of flouncing around on the gay side of the divide.

"English culture is basically homosexual," declared Germaine Greer, who arrived in Britain from Australia in 1964, "in the sense that the men only really care about the other men." Before getting into bed with her, one English lover said: "Let's pretend you're dead."

Édith Cresson, who was prime minister of France in 1991 and 1992, once told an interviewer that she believed that in Anglo-Saxon countries, as many as one-quarter of the men were homosexual. The English? Particularly gay.

"I remember from strolling about in London—French girls still make the same observation—that men in the streets don't look at you," she said. "In Paris, the men look at you. A workman, or indeed any man, looks at passing women. For a woman arriving in an Anglo-Saxon country, it is astonishing. She says to herself, 'What is the matter?' It is a problem of education, and I consider it something of a weakness. A man who isn't interested in women is in some way a little maimed."

The English took her remarks personally, as if she had come into their houses, flung open their closets, and mocked their secret stashes of frilly floral dresses. The tabloids, seizing the welcome opportunity to disparage a French person, took to calling Cresson "the Frog Prime

Minister" or "Mrs. Frog." Tony Marlow, a Tory MP, considered proposing a Commons motion: "This House does not fancy elderly Frenchwomen."

Their sensitivity suggested, in fact, that maybe she was onto something. In a satirical cartoon in one of the papers, the angry British ambassador depicted lodging a formal complaint in Paris wore a lovely dress and high-heeled pumps—and was a man. Englishmen do seem unusually enthusiastic about cross-dressing. Men in drag feature in every sort of comedy, from *Twelfth Night* and Monty Python to the annual Christmas pantomime featuring the Dame, played by a man, to the contemporary television series *Little Britain*.* When I have played charades (still a post-Christmas amusement) at the houses of friends and relatives here, I have been struck by how eagerly the men volunteer to play the part of women, and how quickly any old scarf can become an elegant makeshift frock for a guy with an eye for that kind of thing.

The *Guardian* advice column once featured a letter from a puzzled Australian woman. She said she had been seeing an English guy for six months: "The relationship is going well, apart from one thing: he has started to wear my clothes and it is becoming increasingly embarrassing. Not to mention the fact that he stretches everything. . . . He says it is a cultural thing, something that English men like to do." (A reader wrote in with another explanation: "I think that this is an example of a much more common form of English male behavior: the inability to break off a relationship," he said.)

In *Brideshead Revisited*, Waugh portrays between-the-wars university life as a big camp party in which lovesick men bring one another flowers and decorate their rooms as if auditioning for inclu-

---

* I had an unsettling experience at the Christmas pantomine the first time I came to London, aged nine. I didn't understand the broad sexual innuendos that underpin these annual entertainments, which are meant to appeal to all age groups; I also didn't notice that the enormous, hairy woman playing the Dame was, in fact, an enormous hairy man. But then he took off his clothes—layer after layer after layer—until he got down to his (enormous) bra. He peeled it off to reveal two large lightbulbs affixed to his chest, twinkling merrily. It was an unfortunate introduction to British sexual culture.

sion in *World of Interiors* magazine. One of the most confusing components of the whole are-they-gay debate is that Englishmen of a certain public-school background can be the first to suggest that, yes, maybe they are.

"I'm in costume—I've dressed as a homosexual!" one guest—who calls other men "darling" and pats their bottoms when he greets them—said to me when he and his wife arrived at our front door for a cocktail party. (He was wearing a loud seersucker suit. "I'm gay in everything but the sex!" he once merrily explained.)

My *New York Times* colleague Mark Landler had a jarring experience when a British banker he had interviewed for an article invited him out to dinner at the Garrick Club, a bastion of maleness in the center of London (they let women in sometimes, but only in a few of the rooms; they take the rule so seriously that you worry that they will call in the antifemale SWAT team should you mistakenly penetrate the perimeter of the wrong sector of the building). They sat at the communal table—the idea is that any member of the Garrick Club should be able to be friends with any other member, especially with no girls around—and it happened that Mark was seated near several men from Oxford University, including the master of one of its grandest colleges. Mark asked how the new university chancellor, Chris Patten, the distinctively heterosexual former governor-general of Hong Kong, was doing in the job.

"I have no idea," the master said, "but when he was an undergraduate, I certainly wanted to get him into bed!"

His friends, alarmed at the incorrect impression their colleague had given of Patten's sexuality, tried to move the subject along. "He's been very busy," said one, about Patten's work as chancellor.

"Yes, dishy!" the master said. "He was very dishy!"

The hint that the groom is hooking up with the wrong gender is a standard feature of the best man's speech in some English weddings. (The speeches take some getting used to. At American weddings, we have heartfelt, sloppy tributes to the couple's benign excellence. "He's one of the best people . . . on the planet!" the beaming best man said at a wedding I once went to, practically crying with affection. In Britain, they have acerbic, hyperarticulate speeches attacking the groom in as offensive a manner as possible).*

For foreign women hoping to endure one of these rituals in an effort to bring home an Englishman, literature offers little solace. Is your future husband a brooding, violent Heathcliff? A pedantic Casaubon, the tedious and emotionally arid husband in *Middlemarch*? A Scarlet Pimpernel, daring on the inside, a mincing fop on the outside? Does he sympathize with Henry Higgins in *My Fair Lady*, with his lament about the chaos women bring, not to mention their tendency to lower the cultural tone?

Perhaps your man identifies with the clueless heroes in P. G. Wodehouse novels, who romanticize women as concepts but run screaming for a drink the moment they are confronted by real-life examples. They much prefer each other, and you can't really blame them, since Wodehouse's female characters might as well live on another planet, the Planet of Bizarre Notions. "She holds the view that the stars are God's daisy chain, that rabbits are gnomes in attendance on the Fairy Queen, and that every time a fairy blows its wee nose a baby is born, which, as we know, is not the case," Bertie says of Madeline Bassett in *Stiff Upper Lip, Jeeves*. In Wodehouse's work, the happy ending is not the engagement but the breaking of the engagement. His characters embody the famous saying by the Hungarian-born writer George Mikes that "Continental people have a sex life; the English have hot-water bottles."

There is also Daphne du Maurier's Maxim de Winter, sexy, rich, and condescending, whose ideal wife is inexperienced, timid, socially inferior, and so colorless that no one—not even the author—seems to know her first name. Or Charlotte Brontë's Mr. Rochester, who talks a good game but is sarcastic, self-pitying, and moody, and who stashes his first wife up in the attic just because she has gone inconveniently bonkers.

In a pinch, they have the royal family. But any woman for whom a

---

* When an American friend married an Englishman some years ago, the speeches at the rehearsal dinner were so appalling that the bride's mother burst into tears, her grandmother walked out, and her father took her aside and assured her he would not hold it against her if she decided to call the whole thing off.

theoretically dashing prince was once the ultimate erotic fantasy has likely had her illusions shattered by Prince Charles, whose standard for romance has been generally poor. First there was his response to a reporter's question of whether he was in love with his future wife, Diana, after the couple announced their engagement. "Of course," she started to say, mock-offended, getting all coy and gooey, but the prosaic Charles seemed to find the question puzzling. "Whatever 'in love' means," he said.

Even more disconcerting was the leaked transcript of a telephone conversation between Charles and the woman he actually did love, Camilla Parker Bowles, who would go on to become his wife after they had successfully divorced their troublesome spouses (and after Diana had died). The conversation was recorded in December 1989, when the divorces (and the death) had not yet taken place and Charles and Camilla were enjoying their long extramarital romp.

Few of us, I imagine, would be happy if our own bedroom chat was recorded and released to the world. But few of our erotic fantasies are likely to feature Tampax and toilet bowls in quite the way Charles and Camilla's did. Although the entire transcript—in which Camilla says that her greatest achievement has been to love Charles and eagerly asks him to send her a copy of his forthcoming speech on "Business in the Community"—is well worth reading, here is the best part, when they talk about sex:

CHARLES: What about me? The trouble is I need you several times a week.

CAMILLA: Mmmm, so do I. I need you all the week. All the time.

CHARLES: Oh, God. I'll just live inside your trousers, or something. It would be much easier!

CAMILLA: (laughing) What are you going to turn into, a pair of knickers?

Both laugh.

CAMILLA: Oh, you're going to come back as a pair of knickers!

CHARLES: Or, God forbid, a Tampax! Just my luck (laughs).

CAMILLA: You are a complete idiot! (laughs) Oh, what a wonderful idea!

CHARLES: My luck to be chucked down the lavatory and go on
   and on, forever swirling round on the top, never going down.
CAMILLA: (laughing) Oh, Darling!
CHARLES: Until the next one comes through.
CAMILLA: Oh, perhaps you could come back as a box.
CHARLES: What sort of box?
CAMILLA: A box of Tampax.

Charles was clearly trying, in his own unique way. But most British men remain unperturbed by their reputation for being the least romantically attuned people on the planet. "Re sexual intercourse," the poet Philip Larkin wrote, "Always disappointing and often repulsive, like asking someone else to blow your own nose for you." I once accused Robert of being emotionally autistic, after he had been working so hard on his latest book that he seemed unable to string his words together into sentences when he condescended to come down and commune with the rest of us. "Darling, I know," he said affectionately. "I *am* artistic."

"There's a feeling men have that women are going to ruin their fun and their lives and chain them indoors, and make them do things they don't want to do, and not let them do the things they do want to do," my friend Cindy, an American who has had two English husbands, told me. "The idea of being alone with a woman is too scary, because then they might have to deal—or to talk about themselves."

The men can be so difficult that the women don't know how they are supposed to handle it. Feminism, such as it was, seems to bring Britons out in hives, raising the media-clichéd specter of the sort of bra-burning, man-bashing, non-leg-shaving harridans who apparently so terrorized British men back in the 1970s. Now feminism is practically considered a dirty word. When she was minister for women in the Blair government, Margaret Jay announced that she was not a feminist, because "in politics, feminism is seen as negative, complaining about things." In Britain, postal workers are still postmen and firefighters are still firemen, and women working in London's financial district are subject to the kind of casual sexism that would end careers and cause banks to be slapped with class-action suits back in New York. But the women don't help themselves, is my feeling. For one thing, everyone still seems to call them "girls."

Most British women reject the honorific "Ms." (it is pronounced "Muhz," not "Mizz," in Britain) as too militant and stroppy. The woman who delivered my children, one of London's most experienced obstetricians and the only Miss in a sea of Mr.'s in her elegant Harley Street office building, told me that it had "connotations of aggressive feminist undertones."

The novelist Kathy Lette, an Australian expatriate who has a fine fictional eye for the challenges a typical British husband brings to a marriage, said that when she tries to get people to call her Ms. Lette, rather than her married name, Mrs. Robertson, "they look at you like you've turned into Lorena Bobbitt"—Lorena Bobbitt being the Virginia housewife who chopped off her husband's penis and threw it out the car window in 1993.

"Women here have been lulled into a false sense of security," she said. "When I moved here, I thought I'd come to New Man planet. The men talked about gardening and opera and quoted huge whacks of poetry. They knew Shakespeare's sonnets by heart. I thought, Oh, they're so sensitive. But it's a big scam—they're just as sexist as Australian men, but it's much more hidden." For a while, she and a group of women got together once a month for dinner, giving an award at the end of the meal to the one whose husband had exhibited the worst behavior. One woman regularly won. Her husband once put the kettle on—which, in this context, was like setting an egg timer for forty-five seconds—and then grabbed her for sex. "We'll be done in no time," he said.

In Edith Wharton's *The Buccaneers*, the young heiresses shipped over to England in the late nineteenth century find their new husbands are either sexually inept, involved with other women, or as chilly as the cavernous picture galleries in their stately homes. Wharton took as one of her models the American heiress Consuelo Vanderbilt, sold off in marriage at eighteen by her socially ambitious mother to the young Duke of Marlborough.

Although he had a great title and an estate full of ponds, fields, sheep, cows, and indentured servants, the duke also had a girlfriend and no intention of giving her up (he also had no money: that was Consuelo's job). He expected his new wife to produce a "link in the chain," a son, but made little effort to get her in any kind of mood for it. He spent their wedding ceremony staring into space and their honeymoon reading stacks of congratulatory telegrams from his titled friends. At meals, seated at one end of a long table, he played with his silverware and dishes, fiddled with his chair, and twirled his pinkie ring. "After a quarter of an hour, he would suddenly return to earth, or perhaps I should say to food, and begin to eat very slowly, usually complaining that the food was cold!" Consuelo wrote later.

Because her husband never spoke to her, the duchess began knitting during dinner; the butler stood in attendance outside the dining room, reading detective novels.

Things are different now. Dining room tables are smaller, for one thing. I have not met anyone as extreme as the duke, although I have sat next to my fair share of taciturn misanthropes at dinner parties, some of whom have actually chatted with one another behind my back about masculine topics like politics, leaving me with no one to talk to. Once, someone asked me what kind of work I did before I got married.

As far as British seduction techniques, I have had limited personal experience. But in my unmarried twenties, I visited London for a long weekend and met a charming, handsome Englishman at a fancy party. Taken in by his smooth manners and verbal dexterity, I went back to his house for a nightcap. Out went Mr. Darcy; in came Austin Powers. The man kissed like someone kissing for the first time, stabbing into my throat with his tongue, and then reverberating it back and forth as if he were a Boy Scout trying to start a fire. He groped and grabbed at elements of my person like a climber who, locating a secure handhold on the rockface, clamps down and will not let go.

His tie off and his linen shirt askew, he lay down on the sofa and

announced that he felt sick. Although he still wanted me to stay over. Although it was unclear whether he remembered my name. I said I was going, and, as we stood at the door, he drew my attention to his pelvic region, where, in the words of Elaine on *Seinfeld*, he had taken it out.*
I hastily took myself out to the nearest taxi. Clearly it hadn't worked out with us, so the next day, he telephoned another American he had met at the party, and invited him—it was a him—out for a dinner date.

To be fair, British men do not always think American women are so great, either. They regard us as noisy, forward, unsubtle, unironic, neurotic, and far too much work. They recoil at our efforts to get them to talk about their feelings. I once terrorized an elderly English gentleman by asking him over drinks whether he'd ever said "I love you" to his adult son. Of course he loved his son, he spluttered; it was the idea of having to *say* it that was so appalling.

Another time, a man confided to me at a dinner party that he had been abandoned by his father as a child and had not seen him for twenty years. Such conversations are par for the course in New York, a sign that you are getting somewhere, the appetizer before friendship's main course. But when I tried to ask follow-up questions, the man looked at his watch and sighed deeply. He was actively bored by his own traumatic experiences.

In 2002, several foreign women publicly complained about the hopelessness of British men. "The modern British male knows nothing about courtship, and what he does know might frighten him," Leah McLaren, a comely Canadian journalist, wrote in the *Spectator*, describing dates with a dozen or so truly horrific specimens. But then the men struck back, saying it was the fault of the pushy, needy, demanding Americans.

"They're out there, they're loud, they're bitter and they're kooky," said James Brown, then the editor of *Jack* magazine, a journal for men who wish to be boys.

---

* Note to male readers: this is a poor seduction technique.

"Sorry [. . .] but you nasal, gum-chewing U.S. girls are frighteningly sexless and just plain dull," the *Daily Mirror* said in an editorial.

"They believe in the supremacy of their feelings (which come straight from the greeting-card industry) [and] then have the gall to say we lack emotional intelligence," Oliver Bennett, an Islington bachelor, said. "Buy them dinner, and you may be accused of 'oppressing' her. Don't, and she'll cast you as a 'loser.'" As Bennett fumbled with the check at the end of one meal, he related, his date snarled: "'What exactly is the status of this meal?'

"It was like being with a nasty bank manager, rather than someone with whom you wish to sleep," he said.

Robert Kelsey, an Englishman who worked as a banker in New York in the late 1990s and who wrote a book about his dating mishaps, told me that the American women he went out with were forever psycho-analyzing him, harping on about emotional issues, and accusing him of being "in denial" when he deployed his customary British feints: diversion, obfuscation, and stupid drunken banter.

One woman appeared to be unhealthily obsessed with Kelsey's relationship with his parents, even though it was their first date and she had never met the parents in question.

He tried to laugh off her questions, saying: "Families are so dull, aren't they? Let's talk about something else," Kelsey told me. But that only piqued her interest.

"She thought, Oh, this guy's got issues with his family, like I had some kind of dysfunctional relationship with them and this would be the key to understanding me."

He also found that New York women's relative abstemiousness made them less likely to jump into bed. In Britain, the idea is to get so drunk you barely know who you are sleeping with. "A relationship in Britain emerges through a series of accidental drunken shags," he said. "You get off together and you wake up together, and then maybe you get off together the next night." When an English couple vaguely say they met "through friends," it usually means they met while trashed at a pub, slept together, and only then got to the next step—having a conversation.

If anyone can combine the best of both worlds—English mystery with American sensitivity, a great accent with a great love of women—it seems to me, it is Daniel Craig in his role as Agent 007 in *Casino Royale*, the James Bond film released in 2007. He looks good in a dinner jacket, affects humorous insouciance in the face of peril, and knows the proper technique for injecting oneself in the heart when going into cardiac arrest. But he also understands that when a woman is slumped, weeping, in the shower, her evening gown covered in blood, what she really wants is a man with well-defined pectoral muscles to get in there beside her and slowly kiss her fingers, one by one.

But, alas, this Bond suffers for his sweet soul; his heart is broken after the love of his life betrays him (and then dies a watery death in his arms). Does he sign up for extra sessions with his shrink? Does he call his friends and drone on about his problems? He does not. He puts his hurt behind him, picks up his gun, and retreats to the kind of emotional isolationism that Englishmen are so good at, the kind that makes you want them even more.

TWO

HONORABLE MEMBERS

*Some of the comments that were made . . . were very, very
personal, about a woman's shape, or her hair, or her face, or
her clothes, and that's not normal.*
                                        —Beverley Hughes, Labour MP

I f there was ever a bastion of unreconstructed maleness, it was the
House of Commons, the lower and more powerful of the two houses
in Britain's legislature. It looked perfectly normal, but it operated
like an old-fashioned men's club or a university debating society. The
bathrooms said "Members" on the door, but they really meant "men."
You could buy whiskey in the Commons shop, but not fax paper. There
was a shooting gallery where legislators could play with their guns, but
no day-care center where they could look after their children.

It had always been that way; the men who ran the country preferred
it like that. But after the 1997 election, their comfortable masculine
equilibrium was disturbed by the infiltration of 120 women legislators, more than had ever been elected to the Commons before.* If the
women seemed alien to their 530 or so male colleagues, the institution seemed bizarre to the women. It seemed fusty and out to lunch, a

---

* One hundred and one were from the Labour Party; most were first-time MPs.

club whose rules no one would explain. It also appeared to lack many modern amenities, like e-mail and a decent telephone system.

But the freshwomen were sure their presence was just what the old institution needed. Blair had just become Prime Minister, promising to sweep away the musty traditions of the past; the idealistic women MPs thought they could help sweep them away, too. Also, they were pleased at what already appeared to be signs of change. Claire Curtis-Thomas, a professional engineer and the new MP from Crosby in the northwest, was happy, for instance, to see a modern red ribbon tied to her hanger in the legislative coat room.

She was less happy several months later, when the subject unexpectedly came up. "In the tearoom, there was this sort of conversation," she said, "and it went, 'This place is absolutely crap, it's stuck in the Dark Ages,' and I went, 'Of course it's not stuck in the Dark Ages . . . take, for example, our AIDS ribbon on the coat hangers in the Members' cloakroom.' And there was this absolute thunderous silence, and then somebody turned to me and said, 'Claire, that's for your sword.'"

The culture shock reverberated everywhere. "Blair's Babes," as the papers called the Labour women, were in their thirties and forties and had made it to Parliament by way of local politics and labor unions, where modern workplace standards applied. They simply couldn't believe what they found.

It was not only the ribbons, whose existence suggested that the MPs were still meant to operate as dandyish dueler-lawmakers, swashbuckling their way through the chamber. It was all of it: the absurdly late nights, the raucousness of the debates, the rudeness, the personal attacks, the puzzling old-fashioned conventions. When a new legislator tried to breast-feed her baby at a committee hearing, the Commons Speaker ruled that she could not, on the grounds that drinking and eating are forbidden in committee rooms.

The new MPs were used to regular working hours, maybe not nine to five, but at least something vaguely reasonable. But because Parliament generally started after lunch and ended toward midnight, often going on through the night, members sometimes had to sleep in their offices. They went out to dinner, repaired to the bar—there are seven-

teen places to buy alcohol in Parliament, not including the gift shops—
and then returned noisily to the chamber. The rule of the late-night
sessions, set down by the party whips, was: It didn't matter if you were
drunk, as long as you were there.

"I've seen them jabbing people in the shoulder, shouting in people's
face, getting drunk," Tess Kingham, the Labour MP for Gloucester, told
me. "It would not be tolerated in any other workplace. It would be called
institutional bullying, and people would be off consulting the union."

The men behaved like teenagers whose exclusive treehouse stocked
with porno magazines had been invaded by the girls from the progressive
school down the road. Like the guys who sat together at my high school,
rating the passing girls from 1 to 10, the legislators audibly critiqued the
women's bodies and general appearance. They ridiculed their high voices,
which could sound shrill and reedy amid the macho bellowing. They made
obscene gestures and accused the women of irrational behavior.

The women suggested that an absence of early boundary-setting
might be impeding their colleagues' ability to progress through life's
standard stages of maturation. "I don't even think they're consciously
being sexist," Jane Griffiths, one of the new legislators, told me. "I think
they behave like schoolboys because nobody's ever told them not to."

"Schoolboys" was a good way to describe it. To understand what the
women were up against, it helps to understand what Parliament was
like anyway. It was not like an ordinary legislature in the sense that people came in, passed some laws in conditions of relative gravity, and then
went home. Instead, it was more an extension of its members' early education. Many legislators, particularly during the long Tory era that preceded Blair's Labour government, were graduates of public schools that
were run like mini city-states, with arcane vocabularies in use nowhere
else, elaborate rules of conduct, and ancient customs that included the
promotion of a high sense of entitlement and the acceptance of regular
bullying and casual cruelty. Some were old beating acquaintances from
school.* Some were veterans of the debating societies at Oxford, Cam-

* A member of Thatcher's cabinet was such an avid flogger at Eton that he was known,
apparently, as "Hitler," while an official in Blair's government was said to have once told

bridge, and other universities, where formal debates featured verbal pyrotechnics; point scoring; ad-hominem attacks; childish jokes, and much boisterous participation from the peanut gallery.

The way Parliament is configured encourages discord in itself. The setup is uncomfortable and infantilizing: the legislators don't have their own seats or their own desks, but rather jostle elbow to elbow and bottom to bottom for space on uncomfortable leather benches, like members of a church choir or people waiting at a bus stop (when the chamber is full, some people have to stand). Instead of sitting collegially in a consensus-building semicircular or horseshoe-shaped chamber like, say, that of the European Parliament—which most British legislators deride as hopelessly worthy and dreary—the two parties perch on either side of the chamber, glaring at their opponents across a space the distance of two sword lengths. This means they are close enough to barrack, or heckle, the enemy, but not close enough for hand-to-hand combat.

Although MPs can say a lot of unpleasant things, they have to do it while calling one another "the honourable gentleman" or "the honourable lady," and they are barred from accusing one another of cheating, lying, or being drunk. Nor can they use whatever the Speaker of the House considers "unparliamentary language," an idiosyncratically applied rule that over the years has eliminated the terms "blowhard," "coward," "git," "guttersnipe," "hooligan," "political skunk," "rat," "swine," "stool pigeon," "traitor," and "Pecksniffian cant"—Pecksniff being the opportunistic hypocrite in Dickens's *Martin Chuzzlewit*—from the menu of available insults.

It gives some sense of the tenor of debates to know that as prime minister, John Major had to withdraw his description of Tony Blair, then the leader of the Labour opposition, as a "dimwit." The former Labour MP Martin O'Neill had to rescind his suggestion that Angela Browning, a Tory legislator, was "a second-rate Miss Marple," a reference to Agatha Christie's twittery, elderly, crime-fighting spinster. The late MP Willie Hamilton had to take back his characterization of Prince

---

a beatee: "What you need, boy, is a dose of pain. Yes, a dose of pain. And it will recur whenever you don't do what's required of you."

Charles as "that young twerp." And Tam Dalyell, a peppery Labour MP from Scotland, was ejected from the chamber when he accused Prime Minister Thatcher of being "a sustained brazen deceiver . . . a bounder, a liar . . . a cheat and a crook." (Crafty members know how to circumvent the rule against calling other legislators liars: Churchill once accused an opponent of "terminological inexactitude.")

The Speaker, who wears a kind of Pilgrim's bib and jacket and, as the warden of standards, often tells the honorable members to shut up and sit down, is supposed to keep everything under control, mostly by glaring disapprovingly, bellowing, "Order! Order!" and threatening to kick them out if they don't behave. But parliamentary debates can be shockingly rude, not so much *Masterpiece Theater* as *World Wide Wrestling*. One person's boorishness is another's "traditional vigor and forthrightness," as the Commons Web site describes the permitted conduct in the chamber, or, to put it another way: "The House of Commons has never thrived on excessive politeness and restraint."

It is in this spirit that the Labour MP Tony Banks once got away with telling Margaret Thatcher she was behaving "with the sensitivity of a sex-starved boa constrictor," and with saying that Terry Dicks, another MP, was "living proof that a pig's bladder on the end of a stick can be elected to Parliament." Michael Foot, another Labourite, was allowed to call the Tory MP Norman Tebbit "a semi-housetrained polecat." In 1978 Denis Healey, the Labour chancellor of the exchequer, compared being criticized by his Conservative counterpart, Geoffrey Howe, to being "savaged by a dead sheep."

Some of the humor is a little broad. In the Blair government, John Prescott, the deputy prime minister, was not reprimanded when, angry that a Tory had criticized his grammar, he yelled, "You twit!" across the aisle. And it was considered perfectly acceptable for a grown-up elected legislator to shout, "Giovanni, a gin and tonic, please!" as Nicholas Soames, a former Tory minister, shouted at Prescott, an old-style working-class Labour member who had once been a bartender on an ocean liner. ("It was meant to be a jolly joke," Soames explained later.)

"Taxi! Taxi!" the Labour backbenchers would call out when Patrick Nicholls, a Tory whose driver's license was suspended after he was caught drunk driving, got up and tried to speak. "Moo!" they would shout at Douglas Hogg, in recognition of his service as agriculture minister during the worst of the 1990s mad-cow crisis, when British cows that had eaten contaminated feed contracted a disease that made them go insane and drop dead. "Baa!" they yelled at Quentin Davies, after a flock of sheep starved to death on his estate and he was charged with and convicted of cruelty to animals.

The MPs also enjoyed participating in the traditional schoolboy sport of drawing unflattering attention to the physical deficiencies of others. Baldness, fatness, poor grooming, weird hair, dismaying clothes—all popular topics. Once, Desmond Swayne, a blustery Tory known for his garish ties and old-fashioned views, forgot to brush his hair before coming to work, only to be greeted by a bunch of Labour MPs "barking like werewolves," as he put it, an allusion to his lupine coiffure and to the fact that he was the MP for New Forest West, where werewolves are said to come from. "Someone—I don't know who it was, I think he was sitting behind Dennis Skinner—said, 'Eh, it must be a full moon,'" Swayne told me.

The individual insults were only part of it. Seeing the brawling debates, I sometimes found it hard to believe that these were elected officials carrying out the grave business of governing a viable country. It was fun to watch, but there was no getting away from it: they were acting like the boys in *Lord of the Flies*. During a debate on how the BBC covered the government's use of intelligence before the Iraq war, both front benches erupted in primitive noises of unhappiness, derision, and incredulity. It was hard to hear what they were saying.

"I will not tolerate anyone shouting, not even ministers!" the Speaker bellowed, glaring pointedly down at the Labour chief whip, his little collar vibrating with fury. "If I see an honourable gentleman or lady shouting, I will ask that person to leave the chamber!"

In another debate, on the government's record on asylum seekers, Blair was mocked, barracked, and hissed at repeatedly (if you read the official account, in *Hansard*, Britain's equivalent of the *Congressional Record*, you see that the prime minister's statements are regularly punctuated by the notation "interruption": sadly, *Hansard* does not provide details). Unable to identify the worst offenders, the Speaker threatened the parliamentary equivalent of canceling playtime and sending the whole lot to the "naughty stair."

"Order! I tell you this: when people hiss, I cannot find out who is hissing, so the next move is that I suspend the House, and we do not have Prime Minister's Question Time!" he screeched, barely intelligible above the din. No supper, either.

This is all highly amusing to watch, of course, and keeps the legislature on its toes while providing a steady source of entertainment to visitors and people following along on TV. And Britons, understandably, feel that if they had to choose between the punchy near-anarchy of their own debates and the dull high-mindedness of the ones in the U.S. Congress—with its legislators who think so well of themselves and who tend to drone on far too much about patriotism and the American people—they would choose their system every time.

"It was so boring—completely appalling," said a friend who works for a British paper and who once had to cover Congress. "It was like they were taking huge doses of sleeping pills."

Another big difference between the two systems is that the prime minister is not immune to the jeering; there is no respect in parliament for high office. Tony Blair outlasted four Conservative leaders in a decade, in part because he performed so nimbly at Prime Minister's Questions, the weekly gladiatorial contest in which the premier defends his record against a barrage of rude opposition attacks. No matter how bad things got and how sarcastic his opponents were, Blair remained unbeaten, Teflon Tony, a gleam in his eye, a hint of a grin on his face suggesting a little secret known only to himself.

His bounce, resilience, and ability to perform on cue were important in helping him to hang on to power and knock out one opponent after the next. First came the outgoing prime minister, John Major, the weary, gray, thin-lipped embodiment of the dwindled Conservative past, a man of whom it was said that he tucked his shirt into his underpants and who spent his post–prime ministerial years writing an exhaustive book on the early history of cricket.

William Hague, his successor, was a dazzling debater and quick wit who knew just how to annoy Blair. But Blair managed to turn Hague's youth and humor against him by portraying them as lightweight callowness, and Hague was also hampered by a round face, strangely infantile expression, and gap in his teeth that, taken together, made him look like a bald Alfred E. Neuman.

The next one, Iain Duncan Smith, developed some kind of psychosomatic frog in his throat—*Private Eye* magazine called him "Iain Duncan Cough"—and sounded chronically full of phlegm, despite liberal applications of throat lozenges. "Do not underestimate the determination of a quiet man," he intoned portentously, but his attempt at gravitas backfired. From then on, the Labour backbenchers chorused, "Shush" and put their fingers across their mouths whenever he tried to say anything.

After Duncan Smith came Michael Howard, older and undeniably distinguished, but unable to recover from a fellow Tory's judgment that there was "something of the night" about him, which made everyone think of Dracula (his father was from Romania). He was replaced in 2005 by David Cameron, thirty-nine years old and oozing the self-confident entitlement common to Old Etonians (he was one). Cameron was a cool, agile debater. Once, when Blair argued that current troubles in the asylum system were the legacy of failed Tory policies, Cameron said with a smirk: "The Prime Minister will be blaming Sir Robert Peel next"—Peel being the Conservative prime minister who, as home secretary, introduced the modern police force to Britain in the nineteenth century.

PMQs may look like pure theater. When CNN first began televising the contest in the Thatcher era, the network advertised it as the spectacle of "a sensual blonde ritually humiliating balding, middle-aged white males in public." But it is also an important tool in British political life, reflecting a leader's relative power and grip on his government at any given time. Prime ministers use it to assert supremacy and prove they are up to the job; newspapers use it to keep score, as if it were a prizefight; the opposition uses it to torture the government and expose its weaknesses.

"May I urge the Prime Minister to find time in his busy day to rethink his holiday plans?" John Maples, a Tory MP, once inquired of Blair during PMQs, smooth and sincere as a snake. The prime minister was under attack at the time for accepting free vacations in exotic foreign locations from his rich friends, rather than doing the decent thing and taking his holidays in uncomfortable B&Bs along the rainy, windswept British coast.

John Prescott, Blair's short-tempered deputy, who slumped like a great big Humpty Dumpty on the Labour front bench, his face screwed in a permanent scowl, was often involved in some scandal or another. Once a tabloid newspaper printed an article about his sex romps with a busty blond secretary who was not his wife. The account was illustrated with a photograph of Prescott at an office Christmas party, the mistress's legs all but wrapped around his neck, an image that tended to detract from his dignity when he subsequently appeared in Parliament.

Prescott was a bare-knuckles debater, a pugilist who had once turned around and punched an egg-throwing protester in the face at a campaign rally, a master of the art of the calculated flamboyant insult. When Labour was in opposition, he once called the Conservative Party "the most desperate, despicable, seedy, grubby, hopeless, lying, hideously incompetent bunch of third-rate, double-dealing disasters this great nation has ever seen." But he was prone to malapropism when flustered, and this time he was not on top form.

Presenting a piece of legislation, he attempted to say "a fair and affordable pensions scheme," but instead said "an affair and affordable scheme," which the Conservatives found hilarious. They also found it hilarious—as you would if you were about twelve—when a Labour colleague, trying vainly to help, asked if Prescott intended to take a "hands-on role" in the plan.

Prescott was later accused by the newspapers of improperly accepting a Stetson hat and other Western-themed gifts while enjoying the hospitality of a rich American Labour contributor at his ranch in Colorado. He got up to speak in a debate, but didn't get very far. Suddenly, the chamber was awash in lame Western references. "Howdy!" the Tories cried.

Blair was on his way out by then, and the Tories were wasting no opportunity to call him a washed-out, superfluous has-been. He was the "David Brent of Downing Street—utterly redundant, just hanging around the office," Cameron said, referring to the embarrassing boss on *The Office* television series. "It's high time he and his deputy saddled up and rode off into the sunset."

That was the kind of place the women found when they walked into Parliament en masse for the first time in 1997. They tended to be less tickled by the cleverness of the atmosphere than the men were. Barbara Follett, a feminist Labour MP and the wife of the novelist Ken Follett, said, alliteratively, that the Commons was "competitive, confrontational, conservative, conformist and ceremonial—and at least two centuries out of step." Prime Minister's Question Time, she said, was "a cross between a kindergarten and a zoo." Sarah Teather, another MP, said it wasn't right to call it an old boys' club. "It feels rather more like a teenage public school—you know, a public school full of teenage boys."

The new ones, particularly those from traditions in which more attention was paid to the nuances of behavior, were shocked when the rough-and-tumble insults common to legislative debates were turned against them. They were even more shocked when they realized that their male colleagues at times seemed unable to discuss in a mature fashion issues like defense and education with members of the opposite sex.

Not to mention wildlife. "It was appalling," said Candy Atherton, the MP for Falmouth and Camborne, describing what happened when a woman colleague, in a debate about agriculture legislation, brought up its potential effect on wild birds. ("Bird" in British slang means roughly the same thing as "chick" does in America.) "I suddenly became aware that there was a load of noise and the Tory benches were falling about," she told me. "Quite clearly, they thought it was hilarious that a woman was asking about birds. They were like juvenile schoolboys on a day out."

Joan Ruddock, the former Labour minister for women, ran into trouble when she spoke during a debate about the strip-searching of women by the army in Northern Ireland. "Oh, I'd like to strip-search you any day," she heard a Tory MP say.

Body parts were a particular problem. Some men snickered when the issue of cervical cancer came up during a debate on cancer funding, due to that daring racy concept, perhaps unfamiliar to them (and perhaps even worse than the vagina): the cervix. "Breasts, of course, just finish them off completely," Clare Short, who went on to become the international development secretary, told me. Breasts: their very existence. The women began noticing that when they got up to speak, some men cupped their hands in front of their chests and wriggled their fingers around—the universal gesture for, "Look at me groping my imaginary breasts!"—while muttering the word "Melons."

All this was strange to watch from the outside, too. I still remember the huge uproar in the New York State Legislature in the early 1990s when Assemblywoman Earlene Hill related how a fellow legislator had mistakenly said "sex" instead of "six" in a speech and then, looking at her, ad-libbed: "When I think of Earlene, I think of sex." It set off a huge debate on Sexism in Government as the men in Albany rushed to denounce the hideousness of their colleague's behavior. (The political ethos was so different there that the mortified guilty party, a big assemblyman named Harvey Weisenberg, felt compelled to state publicly that he had been "totally insensitive" and that "there is no place for a comment such as I made in our society.")

So what? would have been the response in Parliament, if something so minor had even come up at all. But if the sexism was casual and unchecked, it seemed also to run along party and generational lines: most of it came from older men, and most of it came from Tories, who were more likely to fit the stereotype of the legislator as a rich, public-school-educated, foxhunting, 1950s-era buffoon. Few people ever officially objected, although Desmond Swayne, the MP with the mussed-up hair, caused a bit of a stir once during a defense debate when he obnoxiously quoted the twelfth century monk Saint Bernard of Clairvaux as saying, "To be always with a woman and not to have intercourse with her is more difficult than to raise the dead." ("As one is not capable of the latter," he added, trying to be funny, "one is certainly not capable of the former.")

That was too much for Harry Cohen, a Labour MP, who said that the remarks were "patently nonsense." A petition went around denouncing not the sexism per se but "the utterly shameful use of a quotation of St. Bernard of Clairvaux." Only about two dozen MPs, out of a total of 650, signed it, and Swayne dismissed them as "fanatical zealots" who had failed to understand his "light-hearted allusion." In the *Guardian*, the columnist Simon Hoggart chastised "the feminist sisterhood" for having a sense-of-humor failure.

In 2005, Boni Sones, along with Margaret Moran and Joni Lovenduski, published *Women in Parliament: The New Suffragettes*, based on interviews with eighty-three women elected to Parliament since 1997. The book, and a companion documentary, sounded like the evidence in a sexual-harassment lawsuit, except that no one was suing anybody.

"The level of occupational abuse is—if you really take it seriously—well, you'd never get out of bed," Tessa Jowell, who went on to hold several cabinet positions, was quoted as saying.

Patricia Hewitt was quoted as saying that it got worse after the MPs had "had a good dinner." Phyllis Starkey said: "It was shocking, literally shocking to me, to have such remarks made by people I perceived to be professional persons." Beverley Hughes said the men would openly talk about "a woman's shape, or her hair, or her face, or her clothes . . . the size of [her] breasts and things like that." Glenda Jackson, the two-time Academy Award winner who quit acting for the unglamorous life of a Labour MP in 1992, said that during a defense debate, a Tory called out: "Stick to what you know, Glenda."

Angela Eagle said that "they're nasty to every woman who's ever said anything in the chamber." Gisela Stuart recalled that once when she wore red shoes, a colleague said, "Remind me, is it red shoes no knickers, or red hat no knickers?" Dari Taylor said that when she resigned from the defense committee, leaving one other woman serving on it, the chairman stood up and said: "One down, one to go."

But to women who served in the bad old days—defined as anything up until the mid-1990s—this was child's play. In a previous generation, the former MP Barbara Castle said in her memoirs, she once had to repel a drunken male colleague who *attempted to remove her blouse* during a late-night debate on, of all things, transportation.

Teresa Gorman said when she was first elected, in 1987, she was regularly propositioned by lascivious coworkers. "They're sex-starved by 10 or 11," she said. "It's a case of any port in a storm." Jean Carson recalled how she overheard one legislator say disgustedly to another, "Look at this; the place was filling up with women," when in fact there were about 50 women and 600 men (this was 1992, not really so long ago). "I just thought, 'This is bizarre; I didn't think people like this still existed.'"

Gillian Shepherd, first elected in 1987, was irked when the Tory MP Ivor Stanbrook, a former cabinet minister, repeatedly called her "Betty."

"Look, you know, my name isn't Betty," she said, to which he replied: "Ah, but you're all the same, so I call you all Betty."

There were too many of them; they were all alike; they were unattractive.

"They lack fragrance, on the whole," the late MP Sir Nicholas Fairbairn* said of his female colleagues.† "They all look as though they are from the 5th Kiev Stalinist machine-gun parade."

Unlike poor Harvey Weisenberg, the poster boy for sexism in the New York State Legislature, the men caught in these situations were not inclined to apologize. On the contrary, one former MP, Gyles Brandreth, *boasted* that he and his friends whiled away the 1990s by rating the relative fanciability of the women MPs. "Harriet looked quite deli-

---

* Fairbairn was hardly one to talk. He enjoyed coming to Parliament in a variety of flamboyant Scottish costumes, and always wore a miniature pistol attached to his belt. Once, during a debate on the sexual age of consent, he gave an alarmingly graphic description of sodomy—what body part would typically go where—and had to be suppressed. "We can well do without talk like that," the Speaker interjected sharply.

† "Fragrance" is an odd word to use in this context, but it is a favorite of stuffy establishment men. When the novelist and politician Jeffrey Archer sued the *Daily Star* tabloid for libel after the paper claimed that he had slept with a prostitute, Archer's wife, Mary, testified in a rather dignified fashion on his behalf. Summing up the case, the judge, Mr. Justice Caulfield, wondered why anyone would sleep with a prostitute when he could sleep with Lady Archer. "Has she elegance? Has she fragrance?" he asked rhetorically. "Would she have, without the strain of this trial, radiance?" Caulfield got a little carried away by enthusiastic fantasies. Speaking of Archer, he continued: "Is he in need of cold, unloving, rubber-insulated sex in a seedy hotel?" Archer won the case, but was later convicted of perjury and sent to prison.

cious, tousle-haired and bleary-eyed," he wrote in the *Daily Telegraph*, recalling his favorite erotic-fantasy moment, which took place after he, the Labour MP Harriet Harman, and others had fallen asleep in a committee room during an all-night session on the finance bill. (They woke just in time to vote to abolish the Business Expansion Scheme.)

Swayne told me that he had never seen his colleagues making rude gestures in reference to breasts or any other body parts—lewd behavior, he said, that would have caused him to "thrash" his students when he was a schoolteacher.

If you believe what these women say, it seems that all we do is sit there and cat-call each other. But look at the debates we've had in the last few months—they've all been perfectly reasonable. . . . The fact that every now and then they're punctuated by a joke and a few ribald comments—well, that's part of our tradition.

And Anne Widdecombe, a redoubtable Tory MP, called the complainers "wet" and said that she didn't mind being mocked for being fat, since two of her male colleagues were also regularly mocked: William Hague for being bald and Kenneth Clarke for wearing Hush Puppies to work. "They moan that men are rude to them, but the men are just as rude to each other," she said.

The Labour women singled out a particularly noisy Conservative, Nicholas Soames, as a source of much of the objectionable behavior. Soames, a grandson of Winston Churchill and a close friend of Prince Charles, was a caricature of an Old World Tory: florid, fat, heavy drinking, a master of the indolent, articulate put-down. When he served as minister for food in the early 1990s, *Private Eye* called him the "minister for overeating" (his schoolboy nickname, still in use, was "Fatty.") He once showed up for Parliament dressed in a tweed hunting suit.

"Going ratting, Soames?" said a fellow MP, Tim Sainsbury, whose family founded one of Britain's largest supermarket chains.

"I say," Soames replied. "Fancy being lectured about your gear by your grocer!"

He was an equal-opportunity insulter. What sort of things did he say, when it came to women? "Sexist remarks—maybe about someone's legs or someone being a lesbian," said one MP, Jackie Ballard. Another MP said that she'd once overheard him talking about giving a nearby woman a "good rogering."

Soames said that the allegations were offensive and untrue, that some of his best friends were Labour women and that he had never insulted the MP Lorna Fitzsimons's legs, since she was always wearing pants and "is thoroughly unsuitably dressed."

"These girls have got to take the rough with the smooth," he said. "This isn't a parish council. This sort of blubbing and whining just shows that a lot of these women are absolute drips. Their complaints are ridiculous; if they can't take it, they should get out."

He had his sympathizers. The *Spectator* printed an article titled, "If You Are a Tory Politician, Why Not Be Fat and Sexist?" A letter writer in the *Telegraph* called one of the complainers "a miserable old stick." In the *Liverpool Daily Post*, Chris Moncrieff spoke admiringly of the late Joan Lestor, a former Labour MP, who, when asked what she missed about being in Parliament, replied "the sexual harassment."

"It is a pity that some of our current grim-faced women MPs don't have that kind of sense of humour any more," he wrote.

A group of women went to the Commons Speaker, Betty Boothroyd, to complain. "They were saying, 'This isn't Parliamentary, this is silly stuff, and it's actually very undermining,' " Dari Taylor told me. "And she said, 'Look, I'm going to give you one piece of advice. You either cope with the heat, or you get out.' "

The women had more complaints. They felt it was a bad idea, for one thing, for legislators to vote while drunk.

Everyone did it a lot, drinking. From April to November 2005, a time when Parliament sat for only ninety-three days, the bars in Parliament sold 23,886 liters of alcohol. A further 17,959 liters were consumed at receptions and other functions. The legislators would then come back to the chamber and have debates that consisted of, according to Tess Kingham, "talking nonsense for hours, throwing out months of work on . . . important private bills by simply shouting out

'Object!' and spending inordinate time debating how long we should be debating."

Kingham quit Parliament after one term, saying she wanted a real job, not "a cultural experience in a gentleman's club."

A lot of the men agreed, at least, that the working conditions were insane. Peter Bradley, a Labour MP, called the House of Commons "a ridiculous parody of a Parliament." Another MP said: "It is not macho, or clever, to work such ridiculous hours." Doug Henderson, another Labour MP, said that Parliament "is not about this nonsense of staying up all night, very inefficiently making silly points, often drunken points, after 10 p.m."

But others told the women to suck it up and get on with things. Margaret Thatcher—the ideal female colleague for old-fashioned male legislators, in that she functioned virtually as a man, with that flirtatious edge—had done just fine in the Commons, thank you very much, they said; and she hadn't whined and harped on about breast-feeding and child care and how tired and sensitive and offended she was.

"Keeping ministers up late into the night, listening to silly, drunken speeches, is an extremely important part of the point of the Parliament," Tom Utley declared in the *Daily Telegraph*. Julie Kirkbride, a Tory MP who became a heroine to her side because she had a new baby yet still managed to come to work without fussing, said the complaints came from a minority of people, whom she called "the militant mothers."

"It's our democratic duty to scrutinize legislation, rather than say, 'Oh, deary me, I don't want to stay up all night,'" Kirkbride said.

"When you join a business, do you immediately start complaining that you have to work inconvenient hours?" Eric Forth, a right-wing Tory known for his colorful attire, asked me. He sounded like Henry Higgins singing "A Hymn to Him" in *My Fair Lady*. Professor Higgins, of course, had Colonel Pickering nearby to bluster "Of course not!" in response. I just let Forth hold forth.

"And then do you say, 'And by the way, can I breast-feed in the office as well?,'" he said. "And what's with this family-friendly thing? Suppose you're a typical member of Parliament and your family lives 200 miles away. What's the difference between your getting home at 5 or 7 or 10? Would you rather the M.P.'s are in the government, or on the town?"

Forth, who died in 2006, said at the time that he relished the late nights as an opportunity to consider legislation from every angle, debate its finer points, slow it down and generally inflict maximum "irritation and annoyance and discomfort" on the government. He said he did not want to see any "poor delicate creatures" feeding their babies at work, as some Labour women had demanded the right to do. "Only the very bravest can stand up and say, 'I don't want to see breasts in the House of Commons, thank you,'" he told me. "We've all got to do breasts these days, apparently."

They couldn't keep this up forever; not in the new millennium, not with all this unfavorable attention. In 2002, Parliament voted to start earlier and finish earlier each day, so MPs could go home at a decent time. The barbershop was replaced with a unisex hair salon, offering perms and blow-dries. The men's bathrooms no longer said just "Members." The place did not smell so much of cigar smoke. Although breast-feeding remained forbidden in the chamber and in committee rooms, breast-feeding areas were set aside and clean white nursing chairs installed ("But what about clean white chairs for incontinent old men?" the Liberal Democrat MP Sandra Gidley asked).

But there was still a shooting gallery, and still no day-care center. And, in 2005, Parliament voted to reverse its earlier decision and resurrect some of the old hours—too many members complained that they could not get enough work done in the allotted time and that it made them sad, seeing the Commons so deserted and forlorn in the evenings, its bars so empty. The legislators worked through the night less frequently, but returned to the old system of working eighty hours a week or more.

Had the sexism eased by the time Blair left office? "Most of the changes have been fairly cosmetic," Gidley told me. "It takes a while to change attitudes, and sexism in some ways is a fact of life—it's just as prevalent in Parliament as anywhere else. You just learn to deal with it. The worst thing you can do is get all girly about it."

She said the best defense was a good offense. "It's bizarre that you have these aging, overweight, balding men who seem to think they can comment on the dress sense and style of any woman," she said. "I've been sat there when men have been making comments about a woman's appearance, and I just think 'Look at yourself.' Sometimes I turn around and say, 'Well, what do you think they think of *you*?' "

Some of the women who stuck it out said that it was as much a matter of their adjusting to Parliament as of Parliament's adjusting to them. This seemed a shame to me, to have to lower your standards to fit in to your piggish workplace, but they said it wasn't as bad as all that.

"We're no longer target practice," Dari Taylor, the MP who had been humiliated when she resigned from the defense committee, told me. "We've changed, but the House has changed. I don't think any of the women are harangued the way we were in the early days. I think we've learned to use humor the way that others use humor."

The objectionable Nicholas Soames was a case in the point, the women said. He had cleaned up his act—whether because he had been exposed in the newspapers or because he had finally embraced his inner feminist, they had no idea. But maybe it was because they had fought back.

Soames was a man of obvious rotundity. A former girlfriend had once compared making love with him to having a large wardrobe fall on top of you, with the key sticking out of its lock.

The Labour women seized on the remark as the solution to their troubles. For a time, whenever Soames got up to speak, they would turn imaginary keys in imaginary locks with their hands.

"Click!" they would shout.

THREE

A FACT TOO GOOD TO CHECK

Donald Cameron had no qualifications for any profession except the ability to drive a moderately crooked furrow and to direct the fire of a six-gun battery of eighteen-pounder guns, and so he resolved to try his fortune as a journalist.
— *England, Their England,* by A. G. Macdonell

Journalism is not a respectable activity in Britain; it has certainly never been considered a profession, for which qualifications and decent conduct are required.
— *Economist,* August 25, 2007

Just as the U.S. Congress is duller but somehow more respectable than the British Parliament, so American newspapers are generally less amusing but more trustworthy than British ones. (The obvious exceptions include supermarket tabloids like the sadly defunct *Weekly World News,* although I was always partial to its half-human, half-bat creation, Bat Boy, who once took time out from his vampiric duties to run for governor of California.)

But even the mainstream British papers belong to an exotic species. It can take some time to get a measure of them, and sudden exposure can be disorienting, if not alarming.

My old boss Warren Hoge, then the *New York Times* bureau chief in London, once went out to lunch with a friend who had just arrived from America. She looked shaken and said she'd had a bad episode with her taxi driver who, passing himself off as a benign and helpful figure on the way in from the airport, offered her his newspaper to read when they became stuck in traffic. "Warren," she said, "he gave me . . . pornography!"

Well, not really. It was just the *Sun*, the Rupert Murdoch–owned tabloid that is Britain's most popular newspaper, with a daily circulation, in 2007, of some 3.1 million copies a day. (By comparison, *USA Today*, the best-selling daily, averages about 2.25 million every weekday—in a country whose population is about five times the size of Britain's.) Although the paper looks as if it hardly expects to be taken seriously, what with all the pictures of celebrities and articles about drunken antics on its front page, it prides itself on being both a reflection and an arbiter of the national mood. Knowing that the *Sun* can turn against them as quickly as it can support them, British governments openly court and flatter Murdoch to get his approval of their plans and his endorsement in national elections.

The *Sun* likes a short, snappy headline and a cheeky cause, particularly one involving its readers' favorite obsessions: celebrities; sex; celebrities having sex; and the inferiority of residents of other European countries. It likes obvious puns and unsubtle jokes. When Jacques Delors, a Frenchman who was then head of the European Commission, said he supported increased European economic integration, hardly the crime of the century, the paper's front-page headline was, "Up Yours, Delors!" When the French banned British cows as possibly still harboring mad cow disease, even though Britain said they weren't, the *Sun* distributed anti-French "Froggie" buttons for its readers to wear. "Gotcha" was its headline when the British Navy torpedoed and sank the *General Belgrano*, an Argentine cruiser, during the Falklands War, killing 323 people.

The *Sun* specializes in short items unlikely to tax the mental capacities of its target audience: one-paragraph news articles, one-sentence paragraphs, one-word sentences. Sentences without verbs. Its masthead editorials, called "*The Sun* Says," are often just two sentences long.* The paper is stuffed with gossip, human-interest stories, sports

---

* **Also, each of the two sentences tends to be printed in a different format, like this footnote.** *If the first is in boldface and the second is in italics, they are easier to tell apart and easier to understand.* If you have to have a third sentence, you can put it in normal type.

stories, stories about TV stars, and plugs for other Murdoch properties, like programs appearing on Sky TV or films produced by Fox. In the summer of 2007, for instance, the *Sun's* critics, reporters, and entertainment writers were extremely excited, nearly every day, about *The Simpsons: The Movie*, a Fox film which was coming out imminently and which Murdoch had high hopes for.

Most of all, the *Sun* is known for what Warren's unnerved friend noticed that day in the taxi: its Page Three Girls, the topless young women wearing dirty looks and skimpy underpants who appear daily and prominently on the third page. The girls wore clothes until 1970, when the editor had an idea: take off their shirts. Within a year daily circulation had soared by 40 percent, from 1.5 million to 2.1 million.

Personally, I don't know what to make of all those big bare breasts. It is annoying to pick up a paper that the prime minister courts and flatters, and that is read by non-sex-offending commuters on the subway, only to be assaulted by an enormous pair of boobs, as the *Sun* persistently calls them, waving in your face. Every now and then someone tries to start an anti–Page Three Girl movement, on feminist, journalistic, and humanitarian grounds. But the girls are not going anywhere. The biggest reform in my time was the paper's pledge to stop featuring models with breast implants, on the grounds that readers preferred perky real boobs to extraperky fake ones.

In 2004, the MP Clare Short mentioned in passing that she thought the government should "take pornography out of the press." The *Sun* immediately initiatied a "Hands off Page Three!" campaign that including sending a double-decker bus over to Short's house, filled with semi-naked Page Three Girls wielding glossy photographs of themselves.*

---

* The Page Three Girls on-a-bus ploy has also been used on other occasions, most notably when the *Sun* launched "Operation Vakey Vakey" (a Germanization of the expression "wakey wakey," meaning "get out of bed") during the 2001 soccer World Cup. A fake oompah band consisting of Page Three Girls in abbreviated Bavarian costumes was deployed to Munich to play outside the German team's hotel at dawn on the day of its match against England, in retaliation for the English team's being assigned a hotel next to a noisy beer hall. (Headline: "The Oompah Strikes Back.")

England won the match, 5 to 1. The girls were arrested, but the charges were later dropped, inspiring an even better headline: "Stick It Up Your Oompah."

It got one of the models to change her name to Clare Short so that it could run pictures of "Clare Short, topless" on page 3.

"It's not porn, like she's saying it is," said a *Sun* model identified as "Lashana Nottingham." "It's only like going topless on the beach. It's not like it's the bottom half."

After seeing this for long enough, you start forgetting how offended you were. You lose your bearings. The girls and their boobs become as much part of the background reality as other jarring aspects of the British press: the opinion pieces masquerading as straight news; the obsession with stars, sex, diets, and gossip; the way the papers' biases show so nakedly that one event can be covered from five completely different angles in five different places; the prevalence of errors and the reluctance by many papers to correct them; the vicious, undisguised mutual loathing between reporters and the politicians they cover.

London is a newspaper town and Britain a newspaper-loving nation. Although circulations are declining, as they are everywhere, Britons still bought more than twelve million national papers every weekday in 2006, among the highest rate per person in the world; the papers as a whole reach between 60 and 70 percent of the population. Readers have eleven daily national papers to choose from. On one extreme there is the cleavage-stuffed *Daily Sport* tabloid (2007 circulation just over 108,000), which at some point abandoned any pretense of covering the news per se so as to devote more attention to young women in and out of their underwear. On the other extreme is the *Financial Times* (circulation 426,000), with its sober market analyses and articles about European interest rates. Its front pages tend to be illustrated with fetching photographs of overweight, fully dressed business leaders.

For someone like me who adores newspapers, a London newsstand is as good as a candy store, the papers laid out like treats on a shelf, full of crisp promise. That so many are actually quite bad detracts only slightly from the joy that they exist at all. But you learn quickly to tell which ones are worth reading, which ones you cannot trust, and which ones are useful only in the sense that they would come in handy should you need to start a quick fire.

The strange thing is that although Britons devour the papers, they also hate them. They even hate the good ones, respectable broadsheets like the *Guardian*, the *Daily Telegraph*, the *Independent* and *The Times* of London. Sometimes they seem to hate the fact that the papers exist at all. Reporters in Britain are reviled more than politicians, which is saying a lot. As battered as we are, American reporters still believe we are regarded as an essential component in a working democracy. It says so right there in the U.S. Constitution. But Britain has no First Amendment (and no written constitution), no belief in the right to know, no equivalent of Woodward and Bernstein or Watergate, and no real conviction that the press has a consistently valuable role in checking the excesses of the government. (It does, however, have the Official Secrets Act.)*

The British papers are unquestionably funnier, more playful, and more opinionated than ours. They're often more stylish, more sophisticated, and more interesting to read; the writing is often demonstrably better. British journalists believe that newspapers are by nature biased, and that it is better to say so up front than to disingenuously affect neutrality, which is what they think American papers do. "If you have five different arguments from five different papers, you get to come to your own truth," one columnist told me.

Also, it is unfair to lump all the papers together. Given the constraints of British culture and the secretiveness and paternalism of the political system, some newspapers are admirably thorough, courageous, and even serious-minded. But the good ones suffer by association with the tabloids and their low standards. British papers have such a woefully poor collective reputation that no one seems to expect them even to be accurate.

Of course, as the shadowy Mr. Baldwin argues in Evelyn Waugh's classic journalistic satire, *Scoop*, it is a mistake to assume they're com-

---

* The Official Secrets Act makes it very hard for newspapers to print articles about national security, however true, that cast the government in a bad light. If they do, then they risk prosecution and injunctions that forbid them from publishing. By the same token, government officials can be prosecuted for leaking sensitive materials to the media.

pletely inaccurate, either: "That is the popular belief," he says, "but those who are in the know can usually discern an embryo truth, a little grit of fact, like the core of a pearl, round which have been deposited the delicate layers of ornament."

The dubious-accuracy issue makes for an awkward environment in which to be a newspaper reporter in Britain. When I worked in America, I was used to people's being impressed by my job, or at least returning my calls. In Britain, I have often been thwarted in the pursuit of a story by the unvarnished contempt of potential interviewees, including official spokesmen for government agencies like the Home Office, who seem to regard even simple questions—when, who, how much—as insulting impositions on their time.

Once I called a lawyer involved in a legal case I was trying to write about.

ME: I'm a reporter for the *New York Times*, working on an article about X. Could I talk to you about the court case?

LAWYER: No.

ME: Well, I'm just trying to get it right so that I don't make a mistake in print.

LAWYER: I never talk to reporters, because they always get everything wrong. (hangs up)

Another time, I phoned the lawyer for Michael Carroll, the so-called Lotto Lout (a chronic petty criminal, he had gained tabloid notoriety by blowing the £9.7 million he won in the lottery on cars, drugs, alcohol, and legal fees for all his court appearances). I wanted some guidance on which of the reporting about his client's heinous behavior was accurate and which had been made up by the papers. "Unless you pay me, I really don't have time to talk to you," said the lawyer, Neil Meacham. Was it true that Carroll was about to have his own reality television show? I asked. "The only thing that is certain in life is uncertainty," Meacham proclaimed cryptically. Then he hung up, too.

There is not enough news to go around for all those newspapers, and the competition is brutal. The papers are always looking for ways to set themselves apart. Tabloid reporters in New York are pretty aggressive—the *News* and *Post* guys used to eat me alive when I covered the New York City Police Department—but at least they don't routinely pay their sources for interviews. Another former *Times* bureau chief here, John Darnton, told me about a British tabloid reporter he'd met who bragged about his skill in getting grieving relatives to talk about how they felt immediately after unspeakable tragedies involving the death of their loved ones.

Most reporters, even the ones who think nothing of standing in a pack and shouting, "Why'd you kill her?" at recently arrested murder suspects, recoil from this particular assignment. But not this reporter. He had a signature trick: after securing the heartfelt interview from the weeping relative, he'd deliberately behave like a jerk—ostentatiously snatching photographs from the mantelpiece, asking intrusive, obnoxious questions, breaking the china. The idea was to be so reprehensible that the disgusted family would kick him out and never talk to the press again—leaving him with a lifelong exclusive.

Reporters are relentlessly pressured by their bosses to create splashes where none exist, to break stories before their competitors do, and to embellish the facts—to turn in articles that are " 'improved,' buffed up, spun out of spindly strands of everyday dullness"—for shock or entertainment, as the BBC reporter and television host Andrew Marr writes in *My Trade*, his book about his profession. If they have to kind of make it up, so what? That's why they have a handy little tool called "the fact too good to check."

"When I published those stories, they were not lies," declared Kelvin Mackenzie, who edited the *Sun* in the 1980s. "They were great stories that later turned out to be untrue." He once had to pay Elton John £1 million in damages after printing a pair of stories claiming that John was visiting underage male prostitutes and also that, annoyed by his rottweilers' incessant barking, he had had their voice boxes surgically removed.

Or, as Jessica Callan, a former gossip reporter for the *Daily Mirror*, put it: "The conversations celebrities had with us often bore no relation to the words that were printed in the column." ("Amazingly," she added, "we were never sued for having imaginary conversations.")

My *Times* colleague Mark Landler once went to Heathrow to report on how the latest terrorist-driven security crackdown was affecting the passengers. It wasn't. Nothing was happening.

"Nothing is happening," observed a reporter from *The Times* of London, who had already been at Heathrow most of the day, unsuccessfully scouring the terminals for stranded, or even mildly inconvenienced, passengers.

Mark wondered why he was still there, in that case.

"My editor said I'm not allowed back until I have a traffic chaos story," the reporter said.

Sometimes the papers get things so spectacularly wrong that they end up printing hilariously groveling retractions written, essentially, by their legal teams. This is generally because they have been sued and lost, or to keep from being sued in a legal system that is often openly hostile to the press. I once heard a judge say disdainfully in a libel trial that the *International Herald Tribune* was "the sort of newspaper you get for free on an airplane," a description that did not put it in the best light for the jury in the case. They found the paper guilty and fined it £75,000, plus the plaintiff's substantial legal costs. (The trial—in which the plaintiff was allowed to testify that he had dyslexia and not written, or even read, his own published autobiography and was therefore not responsible for what was in it, an assertion that ruined the *Tribune*'s entire case—was ludicrous; in the United States it would never have made it to court. But then, neither would the judge have been wearing a moth-eaten wig and a Spanish Inquisition–style robe.)

The alternative to that sort of humiliation is this sort of humiliation: "We are happy to make clear that Mr. Auchi is not linked to Saddam Hussein," the *Mail on Sunday* wrote in a little correction box in 2006, referring to an article it had published earlier on the subject of Mr. Auchi's links to Saddam Hussein.

Or: "We now accept that there was no factual basis for the statements or implications contained within the article," the same paper said, two years after reporting that the frumpy, home-loving head of a Scottish canned-soup company had turned into a ruthless, gym-obsessed, Lycra-wearing, sports-car-driving lesbian, much to the dismay of her husband.

The *Channel 4 News* anchor Jon Snow was surprised one Sunday when he opened that day's *Mail* and found a photograph of a young woman next to a racy account of their pot-fueled, three-year affair. Oops! Snow had not had an affair with the woman, nor had he smoked pot with her: he had never seen her before in his life. He consulted his lawyers. The following week, the paper had an update on the story. "There is no truth in these allegations," it reported.

As far as factual errors—figures, names, dates, spellings, and the like—British papers generally try not to correct them, unless they have to. I once asked a friend at *The Times* of London why that was, and he said it was "boring" to read that a man identified as "Mr. S. Biggles" was really named "Mr. Y. Biggles" (never mind what Mr. Biggles thought). When they are forced to print corrections, usually because someone complained with particular vehemence, the papers tend to park them in obscure little crannies where readers can't find them.

The *Guardian* is the noble exception. Since 1997, it has run a daily "Corrections and Clarifications" column on its editorial page, and delightful reading it is. Except to its competitors. "It is a cynical ploy to cover up the paper's major mistakes," a reporter at a competing paper told me. But I have a soft spot for the column. With the dry humor that infuses good British papers—boring writing is useless writing, is their thinking—the column pokes gentle fun at the paper's errors, even when the errors take place in the actual corrections column (once the column printed a correction admitting that it had misspelled "misspelled" twice in a single week).

Here are some examples:

The great crested newt shown on the front of the Society section . . . was, as sober inspection confirms, upside down.

We prematurely knighted John Scarlett (for the 13th time).

Yesterday, subscribers to Fiver, an e-mail bulletin service from the Guardian's football website, received . . . a message sent by a reader . . . [ending] with the words "Just fuck off." This would

normally have been seen by just a handful of people . . . but regret-
tably it was automatically sent to all subscribers.

Griff Rhys Jones was bizarrely—and mistakenly—identified as
The Dobsons of Duncraig.

A caption in Guardian Weekend . . . read "Binch of crappy travel
mags." That should, of course, have been "bunch." But more to the
point it should not have been there at all. It was a dummy which
we failed to replace with the real caption. It was not meant to be
a comment on perfectly good travel brochures.

Yesterday was Wednesday, despite an assertion that it was once
again Tuesday.

The same spirit infuses one of my favorite features in the British papers: the annual fake April Fool's Day stories. This reflects the essential paradox about the British newspapers, that one of the worst things about them—their inability to take themselves seriously—is also one of the best things.

I love the April Fool hoaxes, which are often plausible enough that you have to think twice when you read them. One year, the *Daily Mail* reported the discovery of a new breed of herring, the red herring, off the coast of Cornwall. Although the fish had previously been confined to the pages of Agatha Christie novels, the *Mail* found some nice photographs of herrings swimming in a fish tank, some of them painted red. Another year, it said that the male pigeons in Trafalgar Square were being fitted with knitted cardigans to lower their sperm counts and make it harder for them to impregnate female pigeons.

Other April Fool stories are more esoteric. The *Guardian* once produced a fake glossy magazine entitled *Ciao!*, featuring the French philosopher Jacques Derrida posing graciously, *Hello!* magazine–style, in his lovely home. Another time, it devoted an invented travel section to the joys of San Serriffe, a semicolon-shaped country that it said was usually found in the Indian Ocean, comprising the islands of Upper

Caisse and Lower Caisse (head of government: General Pica. Capital: Bodoni). Many readers, missing the printers' terminology and failing to ask the obvious question: Where was San Serriffe when it wasn't in the Indian Ocean?, telephoned the *Guardian* to see how to book tickets.

The best hoax took place not in the newspapers, but on television. In 1957, eight million viewers watched a BBC *Panorama* documentary about the annual pasta harvest in Switzerland. After plucking the (already cooked) spaghetti strands from the trees, a group of cheery peasantlike Swiss folk were seen laying them carefully to dry in the sun. Their crop was bountiful that year, the BBC said, on account of the success of the country's "spaghetti-weevil" eradication program.

No one doubted the accuracy of the BBC back then. Also, pasta was so exotic that many Britons had not eaten it yet and didn't know that it doesn't traditionally come from Switzerland.* But they learned a handy household hint: If you wanted to grow it at home, all you had to do was stick a strand of spaghetti in an open can of spaghetti sauce, and wait for it to take root.

Accuracy is one thing; no one expects the press to be fair, either. If you're a public figure—a category that encompasses everyone from the Pope to any blond seen within a five-mile radius of Prince William—you are never safe from the fickle fluctuations of the papers' judgments. They love you; they hate you. Yesterday, you were the best thing that ever happened to British politics, Gladstone, Pitt, and Churchill rolled into one; today, you're a corrupt, contemptible charlatan. No one likes a winner for long. If you came from nowhere and achieved fame, they especially don't like you.

The broadsheets make their agendas clear by the way they report the stories in their news pages. The tabloids are just blatantly mean-spirited. Cherie Booth, Tony Blair's wife, came in for sustained journalistic abuse while he was prime minister. She was a distinguished human-rights lawyer and feminist who upset the press by refusing

---

* Or trees.

to give up her job, her last name, or her fondness for fashion that did not always work for her—little white booties, for instance. She thought that reporters were vermin, or worse. "Are you a journalist?" she hissed at me when I tried to introduce myself once, after she gave a speech in New York. I felt like a war criminal, or a pedophile. "Because I *don't talk to journalists.*"

But it is a poor idea to scorn the vicious, grudge-bearing British tabloids; if you treat them with contempt, they will bite you back. They cast Booth as a moneygrubbing, wacky-therapy-practicing, freeloading termagant. They ran articles, and who knew how true they were, describing what they said were her bizarre health practices: wearing inflatable Flowtron pants to reduce leg bloat, using "acupressure earrings" to reduce stress, and employing a "bioelectric shield" to ward off harmful radiation from household appliances, like coffeemakers. They said she took part in a "rebirthing" ceremony in Mexico in which she and the prime minister shouted and smeared mud and ripe fruit on each other.*

The papers also went out of their way to print the most grotesquely unflattering photographs of Booth that they could find—unwise haircuts, unwise clothes, visible cellulite, the works—many of which caught her unusually wide mouth curled in a Cruella de Vil–style rictus, so she looked vaguely insane. After Blair resigned and he and Cherie left Downing Street for the last time, taking the ritual walk from the front door to their waiting car, Booth waved merrily at the assembled reporters. "Bye," she trilled. "I don't think we'll miss you."

In one of Blair's last speeches in office, he called the media a "feral beast." But much of the fault lay in his own government, particularly with

---

* While Booth often complained, her complaints rarely generated official corrections. But an article in the *Independent* mentioning a woman named Carole Caplin, who for a time was one of Booth's closest friends and her unofficial style adviser, resulted in the following correction in 2007: "Following the portrait of Tony and Cherie Blair published 21 April in the *Independent* Saturday magazine, Ms Blair's representatives have told us that she was friendly with but never had a relationship with Carole Caplin of the type suggested in the article. They want to make it clear, which we are happy to do, that Ms Blair 'has never shared a shower with Ms Caplin, was not introduced to spirit guides or primal wrestling by Ms Caplin (or anyone else), and did not have her diary masterminded by Ms Caplin.'"

his chief spokesman and consigliere, Alastair Campbell. Campbell was a former tabloid editor whose greatest talent was that he had the mind of a current tabloid reporter, an ability to go even deeper into the gutter than even the papers themselves. Press conferences when he was in charge were like scenes from *Who's Afraid of Virginia Woolf?* minus the alcohol— filled with swearing, shouting, and bullying sarcasm on both sides.

Campbell's diaries, published after Blair left office, show that the press's hunch that Campbell found them contemptible and/or imbe- cilic was correct. He calls the political editor of Sky News a "cunt." A political correspondent for the *Mail on Sunday* is also a "cunt." The former politician-turned-writer Roy Hattersley is a "fat, pompous bas- tard," the columnist Simon Jenkins is a "total wanker," the *Mail's* Paul Eastham is a "silly fucker," and Matthew Parris of *The Times* of Lon- don is a "little shit."

Although not everyone would use quite that language, those seem to be fairly common views: that journalists are, at best, pompous bastards. The sleazy journalist is a familiar figure in literature, even in the Harry Potter books. The mosquitoey Rita Skeeter, a reporter for the scurrilous *Daily Prophet*, is always hanging around Harry and trying to catch him off guard; her Quick Quotes Quill hovers in the air, misquoting in mid- interview. Even novels whose subject is the press and that are written by current or former journalists tend to perpetuate the view that newspa- pers are cesspools of inaccuracy, that newspaper proprietors are grasping megalomaniacs, and that reporters are lazy, amoral drunks.

The hero of Waugh's *Scoop*, William Boot, isn't really a reporter at all, but an animal lover who writes a head-in-the-clouds nature column for a London paper called *The Beast*. Boot's prose tends to the fanciful: "Feather-footed through the plashy fens passes the questing vole," is his most famous line, and when we meet him he is upset because his sister mischievously replaced the word "badger" with the words "great crested grebe" in his recent column about badgers, although nobody noticed.

Summoned to meet the editors, he thinks he is being fired. But he isn't: they've mistaken him for a different, foreign-correspondent Boot and want him to cover a war between two feuding factions in faraway Ishmaelia, a country no one has ever heard of.

"I think it's the Patriots and the Traitors," says the foreign editor, who, when Boot arrives in his office, is poring over his atlas, trying to locate Reykjavík.

The editor tells Boot how to cheat on his expense account and ships him off to cover the war outfitted with, among other things, a collapsible canoe, six tropical linen suits, a portable humidor, a set of surgical instruments, an astrolabe, a cane for whacking snakes, and a Christmas hamper containing mistletoe and a Santa Claus costume.* When he finally arrives, a friendly wire-service reporter tells the story of a legendary reporter named Jakes and his great journalistic coup: successfully covering a revolution despite oversleeping and missing his stop on the train.

Undeterred by the minor inconvenience of not having witnessed the event he was meant to be writing about, the story goes, Jakes then checks into his hotel and immediately cables off "a thousand-word story about barricades in the streets, flaming churches, machine-guns answering the rattle of his typewriter as he wrote, a dead child, like a broken doll, spreadeagled in the deserted roadway below his window—*you* know."

Jakes isn't as far from real-life journalism as you might think. In December 2006, Toby Harnden, a correspondent for the *Daily Telegraph*, attempted the difficult maneuver of writing a vividly detailed article about the execution of Saddam Hussein *before it actually happened*. He got some of the particulars wrong—"At the appointed time, a black, cone-shaped hood will be placed over his head," Harnden wrote, though it wasn't—but blamed it later on what he called "that 'old media'

---

* Boot was based on the legendary journalist William Deedes, who, twenty-two and with little idea of what he was doing, was sent by the *Morning Post* to cover the war in Abyssinia, as the British then called Ethiopia. Observed by Waugh, who was on assignment for the *Daily Mail*, Deedes took seven pieces of luggage that weighed a quarter of a ton all told and were transported to the train station in two London taxis (Waugh traveled with a single suitcase). Deedes's equipment included a pith helmet, two riding costumes (one for winter, the other for summer), white tie and tails, special mosquito-repelling boots, and a large, zinc-lined cedar trunk meant to keep the ants out. "Most of the office thought they'd probably never see me again," Deedes, who died in 2007, said.

difficulty of the fixed newspaper deadline and the complications of writing across time zones."

"Writing about Saddam's hanging before it happened was not my finest hour," Harnden explained later on, in a blog. "It was one of those tricky journalistic challenges when no matter how much you hedge and speculate, the reality will always mischievously diverge from the finely-tuned piece one filed."*

Complicating the notion that journalists are a shady bunch is the way they talk about themselves. They are just hacks, they say. They have a morbid British fear of appearing to work too hard or seeming to take themselves too seriously—even the very good ones. Expert practitioners of the national sport of self-deprecation, they like to brag about how little work they do and how incompetent they are.† They believe, mostly, that American newspapers are dull and worthy and that American reporters are humorless, workaholic apparatchiks. When Howell Raines, the executive editor of the *New York Times*, had to resign after a scandal in which a reporter had fabricated numerous stories, the British reporters' overriding emotion was schadenfreude at a disgrace following what they considered our nauseating smugness and self-righteousness.

At the *New York Times*, the front-page meetings are models of earnest collegiality; there is a lot more kidding at the British ones.

---

* Harnden's unusually candid remarks caused much mirth on the Web, and his alarmed editors removed his blog from the *Telegraph* Web site and sent out a stiff memo to the staff: "Please avoid blogging about your relationship with your employer, whether the Telegraph Media Group as an entity, 'the desk' or 'my boss,' even in jest," the memo said. "Think carefully before blogging about journalistic 'tricks of the trade.'. . . Such comments are frequently misconstrued and can easily backfire."

† "Much of the job of the foreign correspondent—or this one, anyway—is to copy out the papers of the country he is reporting from," Harry Mount, a former *Telegraph* correspondent in New York, wrote in the *Spectator*. He was describing an incident in which a researcher from Fox News complained that Mount had plagiarized an article from the Fox Web site by copying the first seven paragraphs, nearly verbatim, in a piece in the *Telegraph*. "He was quite right," Mount observed. "That's pretty much what I'd done, changing the word order here and there. This is completely standard practice, by the way. As long as you credit the sources, which I'd failed to do." Mount, a witty stylist who was clearly exaggerating for effect, went on to write *Carpe Diem: Put a Little Latin in Your Life*, a best-selling book about Latin.

They laugh at each other; they laugh at the news; they assign every-one jokey public-school-style nicknames, from editors in the room to world leaders on other continents—"Bin Liner" (garbage bag, in British) for Osama Bin Laden; "Dinner Jacket," for Ahmadinejad, the president of Iran. The editors might make mordant jokes about unfortunate incidents. When Piers Morgan, then editor of the *Daily Mirror*, heard that the majestic Concorde had crashed and gone up in flames in Paris, his initial glee at the big story turned to disap-pointment when he heard the details: instead of celebrities and well-known politicians, the Concorde had been carrying a large group of (now dead) vacationing Germans.

"'What?' I shouted," he writes in *The Insider: The Private Diaries of a Scandalous Decade*, his account of his journalistic career so far. " 'Is this just a load of bloody Germans?'. . . I sat back in my chair and groaned. 'Oh, for fuck's sake, a hundred old Germans. It's not a story.' " (Morgan would later be fired and escorted from the building after the *Mirror* printed apparently fake photographs of British sol-diers torturing Iraqi prisoners in 2004. He has since written two best-selling memoirs, become a columnist for *GQ* magazine, and achived fame as a judge on the popular American television show *America's Got Talent*.)

The staff meetings at the *Daily Mail* are so famously vulgar that they are known, apparently, as "the Vagina Monologues," "cunt" being a favorite word of one of the editors.* According to *Private Eye*, which tends to exaggerate but in which grains of truth generally lurk: "A typi-cal greeting of one *Daily Mail* hack by another might go as follows: 'I say, have you been double-cunted yet?' ('Double-cunted' means 'to be called a cunt by the editor twice in one sentence.')" It goes on to relate

---

* "Cunt" is nowhere near as offensive in Britain, where they swear more than we do anyway, as it is in the United States. It's a common insult, sometimes used as a term of affectionate abuse between men who are taking the piss out of, or teasing, each other. I can barely type it, let alone say it. My friend Sebastian once told me what happened when he went to a matinee of the British play *The History of Boys* on Broadway, in a the-ater full of elderly ladies bused in from the suburbs. "Cunt," one of the characters said, and there were audible gasps from the audience. Several ladies walked out in protest.

an incident in which a midranked editor is being bawled out for "some footling blunder":

HIGH-RANKED EDITOR: "What are you?"
MIDRANKED EDITOR: "I'm a cunt, sir."
HIGH-RANKED EDITOR: "No, you're not. You're a fucking cunt."

As it happened, the word "cunt" was uttered directly from the podium at the 2005 British Press Awards, popularly known as the "Hackademy Awards" (they are like the Pulitzers, without the back-patting self-importance). About nine hundred British journalists gathered in the swanky Hilton Hotel on Park Lane, where they would be given dinner, all the wine they could drink, and the opportunity to hear whether they, or any of their friends, had won anything and thus made it worthwhile to have attended the bloody ceremony in the first place. The first person to address the crowd was Bob Geldof, the scruffy former Boomtown Rats singer who irritates many Britons because of his constant haranguing about things they should care about but don't, such as Africa.

Here in Europe, though, Geldof was in a weird mood. He bragged about the size of his penis. "I've just been down at the bog," he announced to the guests, "bog" being "bathroom," "and it's true that rock stars do have bigger knobs than journalists." He then went on an impromptu rant praising the *Sun* and denouncing the *Daily Mail* and the *Independent*, managing in one fell swoop to annoy everyone who worked for the *Mail*, the *Independent*, or any paper other than the *Sun*—the vast majority of his audience.

Geldof tried to turn their attention to the forthcoming G-8 summit meeting, but the journalists were growing restless and would have preferred to drink in peace, particularly since they had just been insulted. Someone heckled Geldof, whereupon Geldof called him a "twat."

"You'll have a Clarkson moment in a fucking minute," he said.

Students of the press awards knew he was alluding to a previous occasion when Jeremy Clarkson, a ubiquitous personality whose main job is to write and talk about cars on TV, had confronted Piers Morgan, still hanging on to his job at the *Mirror*, in the middle of the ceremony (the *Mirror* had published a variety of photographs of Clarkson apparently kissing and groping a woman who was not his wife). Clarkson, already unhappy at losing the Motoring Correspondent of the Year prize to someone else—he "took it well, though, repeatedly shouting 'cunt!' at the top of his voice," Morgan wrote later—set upon Morgan. He punched him several times and called him, for lack of a more imaginative expression, a "fucking cunt."

I had been hearing stories about the dinner for some time: the drunkenness, the denunciations, the intrigue, the food fights, the class warfare between the tabloid people and the broadsheet people, who tended to look different, dress differently, and speak in different accents from one another. My friend Allison, who was once named Interviewer of the Year, said that if you won, you should collect your award and deliver your acceptance speech while continually moving across the stage, like a car running the red lights in a dangerous neighborhood in downtown Pretoria. The key was never to stand still, because standing still would make you too easy a target for your enemies and detractors to shout and throw things at.

In addition to the Clarkson incident, another high point of the ceremony in years past had been the time, in 1999, when the *Guardian* won the award for Newspaper of the Year. This is a mysterious category: Several nebulous press organizations give out Newspaper of the Year prizes every year, so several papers at once can claim the title. For a year.* Anyway, it is a fiercely fought designation, and on that occasion, the *Guardian* won it, and its editor went up to collect the award. But the editor of the *Sunday People*, another content-free Murdoch rag, could not contain his disapproval at what he considered the injustice of the tabloids' failure to win. Rising from his chair and storming onto the

---

* The *Daily Express*—sometimes known as the *Diana Express* for its devotion to the theory that Princess Diana was possibly murdered by a vast establishment conspiracy led by Prince Philip, the queen's octogenarian husband—doesn't need awards to feel good about itself. It has awarded itself its own prize, proclaiming daily on the front page that it is "The World's Greatest Newspaper."

stage, he seized the microphone and proceeded to share his thoughts on the broadsheet/tabloid dichotomy with the startled crowd.

I was writing some articles about the British press, and thought the dinner would be a good opportunity to talk to people there about the differences between journalism in the United States and in the UK. But it was hard to do any reporting. The journalists from the tabloids seemed to mistrust the reportorial convention of taking notes. No one wanted to say anything serious about the press (How dull! was the general feeling). Conversation was also hampered by the din, the tropical sweatiness of the atmosphere, and the hatred vibrating through a room many of whose inhabitants actively despised one another (and possibly me). They were also packed too closely together, increasing their fractiousness and bad temper.

"Are you enjoying yourself?" I asked a tabloid editor who was sitting alone, his employees having abandoned him in search of better gossip at a different table. Sweat blossoming across his face, his table strewn with empty wine bottles, he was not at his best.

"Not fantastically," he said, "because we never win." He said that "never," in his particular case, meant something like fifteen years. "No," he said in response to my next three questions, according to my notebook, before coming up with: "I don't really want to say anything."

The nominees represented every paper from the most boobs-obsessed tabloid to the straightest broadsheet. The format made no sense. It was like holding an awards ceremony for the entire animal kingdom, pitting carnivores against herbivores, birds against amoebas. Twenty-eight awards were presented, in such categories as Scoop of the Year and Food and Drink Writer of the Year. Many were sponsored by corporations representing the industries the reporters were writing about.

It was not a mutually respectful celebration of the British newspaper industry, and it did not take place in an atmosphere of camaraderie and bonhomie. For one thing, the losers were not happy for the winners. "What's he ever fucking reported, except what fucking Alastair Campbell told him?" a man sitting near me groused when

Trevor Kavanagh of the *Sun* was named Reporter of the Year.* The rule seemed to be that journalists cheered only for winners from (a) their own papers, or (b) other papers owned by their proprietors. Should their nominee fail to win, the losing tables would respond by denouncing the corrupt nature of the judging, speaking loudly so as to drown out the winner's remarks, or actively heckling.

The evening ground on. The mood became increasingly feral. The tabloids, inexplicably, won a lot of prizes. Employees of the Murdoch-owned *Sun* and *News of the World*—a tabloid that *Private Eye* calls *News of the Screws* because its main purpose in life seems to be writing stories about who is bonking whom—established their own cheering-and-catcalling bloc. Whenever someone from either paper was announced as a nominee, everyone from the Murdoch tabloid tables would rise to their feet and cheer; if the name of a reporter from a competing paper was announced, they would jeer and catcall.

The acceptance speeches were either short and funny, or short and bitter. The winner of the Political Journalist of the Year award, a reporter from the *Daily Mail*, used his speech to rehearse an old grievance against an old enemy, the political editor of the BBC.

Jeremy Clarkson, who succeeded this time in his quest to win the Motoring Correspondent of the Year prize, gave a speech that was five words long: "Piers Morgan is an arsehole."

The tabloids had a great year, winning fifteen awards. Newspaper of the Year went to *News of the World*. It was hard to know what to make of this. By its standards, the paper had had a bumper season, with scoop after scoop about the extramarital affairs of famous people. It reported, for instance, that David Beckham had cheated on his wife with his good-looking personal assistant—reportedly after paying the personal assistant something like £300,000 pounds for her story, which to my mind made it less compelling as a piece of legitimate news.

Why that meant that the *News of the World*'s performance was

---

* This was not a far-fetched conclusion. In *The Blair Years: Extracts from the Alastair Campbell Diaries*, Campbell—in between ranting about how much he hates the media—brags about how easy it is to plant stories in supine newspapers.

superior to that of, say, the *Independent*, which focused on unpopular but essential topics like the war in Iraq and government incompetence, was hard to understand.*

The weird thing was, they really seemed to care about the awards. Or at least the winners did.

"It's all shite," a woman at my table explained, "until you win something, and then it's just a well-deserved recognition of talent."

POSTSCRIPT

The 2005 ceremony was generally regarded as an embarrassing debacle, and the next year the sponsors of the awards instituted a series of reforms. For instance, they held the event earlier in the evening, so that people would have less time to get drunk. Although there was some minor jealous grumbling, it was a much soberer affair.

"Press Awards Shocker," the *Independent on Sunday* reported. "No Punches Thrown."

---

* Several years later, the *News of the World*'s editor, Andy Coulson, would resign in disgrace when the paper's royal correspondent was convicted of illegally wiretapping the private cell phones of members of the royal family. Coulson was subsequently hired as the chief spokesman for the Conservative Party.

FOUR

DISTRESSED BRITISH NATIONALS

IAGO: Your Dane, your German, and your swag-bellied
Hollander—drink, ho!—are nothing to your English.
—*Othello*, 2.3

When I thought about the press awards later, it was clear what had happened: if I had drunk more alcohol, I would have enjoyed myself more; if the British journalists had drunk less, they would have behaved better. But the equation is not necessarily straightforward, and the line between not enough and too much is hard to establish.

Most Octobers, I cover the Man Booker Prize, an occasion where members of the literati converge in a fancy medieval banquet hall in east London to hear who has won the country's most important fiction award so they can proceed to attack, sneer at, and feel jealous and insecure about the decision. The dinner beforehand tends to drag, and when you are seated next to someone who has nothing to say and seems weary of his (and your) very existence, you feel strongly that you should have spent the evening at home, watching *CSI: Miami* reruns in your pajamas. I felt this particularly keenly one year, when the man assigned to sit on my left, a moderately successful publishing executive, turned out to be a twitching parody of a tongue-tied Englishman spooked by normal social interaction. He answered in monosyllables. He failed to initiate topics of conversation. He stared at his bread roll, shuffled in his chair, fidgeted shiftily with his napkin. Aside from the occasional phlegm-displacing sound, he was a silent dinner partner.

I tried the man on my right, who worked for the fisheries arm of the Booker conglomerate.* After we had exhausted the topic of Salmon Farms: Cruel or Crucial? he got up and wandered away, and I never saw him again. But when the main course arrived, a strange transformation had taken place back to the left. Mr. Silent had become Mr. Forthcoming, even Mr. Amusing. He listened to what I said, told complex anecdotes with memorable punch lines, spoke expansively about literature, filled the water glasses of others without being asked, leaned in close for a tête-à-tête. A tribute to my charm and Pamela Harriman-esque conversational skills! I had drawn him out, I thought; I was getting the hang of this place.

But it wasn't me. It was the wine.

This became clear after several more hours crept by. The biggest drawback of the Booker dinner is its interminability. Drinks (and no snacks) in a cavernous anteroom are followed by a period of bovine shuffling as people are herded toward their seats by officials in comical livery; an insubstantial dinner that is slow to come and slow to go; and dead air between the courses. It is hard to sustain the chat through this long march toward midnight, and it is for occasions like this that alcohol was invented. The waiters kept it coming. But unfortunately, by the time we got our coffee, my man had had too much, and his conversation flowed down the pathway to nowhere. He started and abandoned subjects. He spoke in non sequiturs, repeated himself, grew sweaty and red faced. Finally, he went quiet again, clutching his glass in contemplative desperation.

I felt slightly alarmed, given that he was now in an obvious drunken haze. Was he an alcoholic, or just having a bad night?

---

* The prize, for the best novel published by a British or Commonwealth author each year, used to be sponsored by Booker Plc., an international food wholesaler whose diverse holdings included salmon farms. In 2002, the Man Group, an investment company, took over the sponsorship, and the official name is now the Man Booker Prize. The winner gets £50,000 and the promise of huge international sales.

I tried to divest myself of my usual ethnocentrism and embrace cultural relativism, the way they taught us in Anthropology 101 freshman year in college. By British standards, this man was not a hopeless drunk, not even close. And besides presenting me with a useful piece of information—you should take advantage of a man's lucid middle period as a conversational golden age in the history of your meal, because you won't get much before or after—his performance helped illustrate the benefits and drawbacks of alcohol as a tool and a prop and a backdrop to British society. In a nation of the chronically ill at ease, alcohol is the lubricant that eases the pain of frightening social encounters, an essential prelude to relaxation, joie de vivre, and even, at times, rudimentary conversation. But because Britain is an example of what is known as an "ambivalent alcohol culture"—which means they haven't worked it out completely—they can take it too far, too fast, with corrosive consequences to general health, happiness, and productivity.

I have many British friends who in America would be considered functioning alcoholics, the equivalent of 1950s Cheever-esque businessmen from suburban Connecticut who greeted the end of the workday with a couple of predinner martinis before moving on to the wine and the whiskey. It is normal for them, part of the fabric of their lives, perfectly acceptable, and it would be considered rude and strange to comment on it.

But I had come from current-day New York, where drinking heavily is reserved for the weekend, and drinking to the point of insensibility is an activity for the very young or the very-likely-to-be-headed-for-AA. By contrast, Britons seemed to drink all the time. It was a shock. It was a shock to see how enthusiastically they knocked back the booze at Sunday lunches in the country, and how high their tolerance was.* It was a shock

---

* Once I took the train to Gloucestershire for a Sunday lunch party that, typically, included lots of really good red wine. I got a ride home with another guest, a respectable GP from London. She seemed perfectly fine, although I did find it slightly odd that—even after I mentioned that the gas needle in the car was pointing to "empty" when we set off— she failed to stop at a gas station. We ran out of fuel and broke down on one of the busiest highways leading to London. First, she called 999, the British equivalent of 911. And then, and this is what I found alarming, given that we were going to be talking to the police, she opened her handbag and whipped out a roll of strong breath mints and a Thermos of black

to see, after we had our first weekday dinner party (and everyone stayed until 1 a.m., never mind their jobs) that the dinner table was covered in twice as many empty bottles of wine as there had been guests.

Our sobriety is just as mystifying to British people, of course, another example of America's wearisome puritanism. After a casual lunch with our friend Sara one summer at her house in East Hampton, my husband and I were talking about the other guest, a blameless magazine writer. "It's a shame that he's an alcoholic," Robert said. He had leaped to this bizarre conclusion, it turned out, on account of the hostess's failure to offer wine with lunch. In Britain, we would have been plied with drinks as soon as we pulled into the driveway.

Britons love to drink and love to boast about drinking. Like hungover frat boys who wake up sick on sticky, beer-soaked floors with someone else's underpants on their heads, but who then brag about their awesome night of partying, they have an amused tolerance for drunken high jinks, even when practiced by flat-out drunks. One of the reasons that the late queen mother was so beloved was because she spent the last decades of her life wafting around in a benign alcoholic haze.* The comic play *Jeffrey Bernard Is Unwell*, about the real-life columnist who wrote about his boozy misadventures in the *Spectator* (one journalist described it as a suicide note in installments), has been a perennially revived West End hit since its opening in 1989, with Peter O'Toole in the title role. The title refers to the explanation the *Spectator* printed in place of Bernard's column when he was too drunk to write it. (He died of renal failure in 1997, at the age of sixty-five.)

Farther back, Shakespeare's plays teem with merry, sozzled characters who are at their funniest, punniest, and bawdiest when drunk.

---

coffee—the same emergency remedies that would later be used by Charles Kennedy, the Liberal Democrat leader who was trying to hide his alcoholism from his parliamentary colleagues—and began ingesting them as fast as she could.

* Many of her most-quoted lines have to do with drinking. Once, after touring a garden in London, she stayed on for tea. "I hear you like gin?" her hostess blurted out nervously. "I hadn't realized I enjoyed that reputation," the queen mother replied. "But as I do, perhaps you could make it a large one."

Falstaff is one of the most famous literary appreciaters of booze, believing that a nice sack of sherry allows Englishmen to lose their repression and become what they usually aren't: forthright, fiery, and emotional.

> Hereof comes it, that Prince Harry is valiant;
> for the cold blood he did naturally inherit of
> his father, he hath, like lean, sterile, and bare
> land, manured, husbanded and till'd with
> excellent endeavour of drinking good and
> good store of fertile sherris, that he is become
> very hot and valiant. If I had a thousand sons,
> the first humane principle I would teach them
> should be, to forswear thin potations, and to
> addict themselves to sack.
>
> (*Henry IV, Part 2*, 4.3)

For the British, alcohol is a relaxant, an emollient, a crutch, a relief, an excuse. If they go overboard it is the get-out-of-jail-free card that allows them to throw up their hands, palms out, and disavow responsibility. The tale still goes around of the chronically drunken writer who, carried away by booze-buoyed passion, rashly suggested to his mistress that they leave their spouses and run off to Paris together on the cross-Channel ferry. Leaving a note on the mantelpiece for her husband announcing that the marriage was over, the mistress duly packed her bag and traveled to Dover—only to find that the plan had not been a real plan at all, just a scheme dreamed up by a man too intoxicated to take himself seriously. I don't know what happened next, but I would like to think that she got back home in time to dispose of the letter.

British fiction is full of people who get drunk and, after fleeting moments of overpuffed confidence, come crashing down. Nervous about giving the prize-day speech at the Market Snodsbury Grammar School, the buffoonish Gussie Fink-Nottle in P. G. Wodehouse's *Right Ho, Jeeves* steels himself with the better part of a bottle of whiskey, supplemented by a pitcher of orange juice spiked with gin. The drink transforms him from quivering nervous wreck "picking feverishly at the

lapels of his coat in an ecstasy of craven fear," Wodehouse writes, into a
walking argument for the notion that a little inhibition is a good thing.
Suddenly expansive, he ridicules the students, calls the headmaster a
"silly ass," and tells mean jokes about his friend Bertie Wooster, who
is in the audience. The debacle causes his fiancée to break off their
engagement and sends Bertie—who'd suggested a bracing drink for her
friend in the first place—reaching for the bottle himself.

In British politics, actual drunkenness is considered perfectly fine
as long as it doesn't descend into public sloppiness or cross the divide
between amusing and alarming. An example of alarming: when Lord
Watson of Invergowrie, a Scottish MP and Labour peer, got monumen-
tally drunk at a hotel in Edinburgh after the Scottish Politician of the
Year awards in 2004 (he had not won) and set fire to the curtains, using
matches concealed in his sporran, sporrans being those little ceremonial
purses Scots wear over their kilts.* (He said at his subsequent trial that
he was upset because his wife had suffered a miscarriage.) He was sentenced to sixteen months in prison, served half of them, and was ejected
from the Scottish Parliament, though he retained his seat in the House
of Lords.

The late Alan Clark, an employment minister and the resident
upper-class bon vivant in Mrs. Thatcher's government, got away
with drunkenness because his was the supercilious, sharp-tongued,
Churchillian kind. Clark once went to a friend's house for dinner
before an important late-night speech in Parliament. They split three
bottles of top-of-the-line cabernet sauvignon. Having glanced at the
speech, which had been written by some bureaucrat in his office, Clark
noted only that it "seemed frightfully long" before returning merrily to
the Commons, puffing on a cigar. But the chamber was crowded with
women from the Labour Party, who by nature did not approve of Clark.

Clark felt alienated from his words, even as he uttered them. Struck
by the obfuscation, leaden language, clichés, flabby constructions, and

---

* A classic question to ask a kilt-wearing Scotsman, along with "What do you have on
under there?" is, "What do you keep in your sporran?" Now we know: matches.

double negatives he saw before him, he mocked his own remarks. He began rushing: "I gabbled. Helter-skelter I galloped through the text. Sometimes I turned over two pages at once, sometimes three. What did it matter? There was no shape to it. No linkage from one proposition to another. The very antithesis of an Aristotelian pattern."

Some legislators thought his performance was funny; others did not. Unable under parliamentary rules to call him drunk, Clare Short declared Clark "incapable." Some Tories demanded that she withdraw her remarks. Another MP asked if members of Parliament were in fact allowed to address the House while in that sort of condition. The night rattled on in this unpleasant vein, until Clark found himself being driven away after midnight in his government car, his assistant, Joan, next to him. "What was that row about, Minister?" she asked him.

"They were saying I was drunk," Clark replied. "But I wasn't, was I?"

"No, Minister, of course you weren't. I've never seen you drunk."

The Palace of Westminster has supported the excesses of many politicians over the years. Herbert Asquith, who served as prime minister from 1908 to 1916 and was often unsteady on his feet in Parliament, was known as "Squiffy," which means "tipsy." A music hall ditty at the time went: "Mr Asquith says in a manner sweet and calm / Another little drink won't do us any harm." William Pitt the Younger was an old-fashioned alcoholic who drank three bottles of port a day, having taken it up on the advice of his doctor. He died in 1806, still young at forty-six, of liver disease. Churchill started with an after-breakfast drink and took it from there, wafting through the business of governing in a state of virtual pickledom. "I drink Champagne at all meals and buckets of claret and soda in between," he wrote, leaving out the port, the whiskey, the wine, and the brandy that also formed part of his daily diet.

Although occasionally his drunkenness interfered with his job—participants at a meeting of the defense committee in 1944, which dragged from 10 p.m. to 2 a.m., noted that he was barely making any sense—Churchill's drinking could also sharpen his wits. According to one version of the classic story, he once told a fellow legislator who accused him of being drunk: "Yes, madam, I am drunk. But in the morning I will be sober and you will still be ugly."

"Always remember," he said once, "that I have taken more out of alcohol than alcohol has taken out of me." Franklin Roosevelt himself told his cabinet that he "supposed Churchill was the best man that England had, even if he was drunk half his time."

George Brown, the gifted Labour politician who served as foreign secretary in the 1960s, was such a notorious alcoholic that anyone wanting to get anything coherent out of him had to see him before lunch. *Private Eye* invented the phrase "tired and emotional," meaning drunk off one's tree, just for him. Once, at a dinner for the Turkish president, Brown sprang to his feet and declared: "You don't want to listen to this bullshit—let's go and have a drink." Brown is also the star of the all-time-best alcohol-related anecdote in British politics. It may count as a fact too good to check, but so what. The story goes that as the music struck up at a fancy reception for visiting Peruvian dignitaries, Brown lurched up to a guest who was prettily attired in flowing purple robes and asked for a dance.

"First, you are drunk," the guest replied. "Second, this is not a waltz; it is the Peruvian national anthem. And third, I am not a woman; I am the Cardinal Archbishop of Lima."

Drink wrecked Brown's career, but he is still remembered with affection. "In Russia, political drunkenness is merely funny; in Europe, it is disgraceful; in Britain we applaud the conviviality of the sociable drinker, but condemn the weakness of the drunk," Ben Macintyre wrote in *The Times* of London. So it was that in 2006, the Liberal Democrat MP Charles Kennedy, whose love of the bottle was an open secret, had to resign as party leader not because he was an alcoholic, but because his alcoholism had gotten out of hand. Kennedy, a chatty man who resembles the talk-show host Conan O'Brien, was a popular figure, and no one wanted to have to tell him how bad it was.

It had been a long time coming. Years earlier, his drunkenness had led to the breakup of his relationship with his girlfriend, a literary agent who caught him urinating on a client's unpublished manuscript. He could be so out of it in Parliament that aides regularly had to take him aside and ply him with coffee and mints. He missed important debates, sweated and stumbled his way through speeches, and on the campaign trail in 2005 replied with stunning incoherence to a journalist's question about his party's economic program.

Although people had raised the issue—Jeremy Paxman, the host of the BBC program *Newsnight*, once asked him on the air, "At home alone, do you finish off a bottle of Scotch?"*—they always had to apologize and retract their remarks. He denied it to the end, when he finally admitted publicly that he had a "drink problem." No, he didn't need treatment, he added: he was cured, having not had a drink for a month.

Still, there was a faction that believed Kennedy had been merely a victim of unwarranted puritanism. The *Guardian* columnist Simon Hoggart wondered if Kennedy really qualified as an alcoholic. He described two people who, in his opinion, did. One was a political cartoonist who once passed out into his avocado at a literary lunch and who, on another occasion, sat in a wordless stupor during a radio program in which Hoggart was also a guest.

"I'm afraid I hadn't had a drink," he said later.

"But it was 8:30 in the morning," Hoggart responded.

"Ah, well, you see," said the cartoonist, "I probably start drinking earlier than most people."

Hoggart's second alcoholic example was an old college friend who had twenty-four bottles of Carlsberg and a bottle of Crawford's whiskey delivered to his dorm each night, and who would go on to choke to death on his own vomit.

---

* Television journalists are much ruder and much less reverential and folksy in Britain than in the United States, and television news programs are much less dumbed-down. When people mention Paxman, they mention that he is credited with saying that his approach to politicians is to ask himself, Why is this lying bastard lying to me? (he says he never said it). He is known for his sharp skepticism and relentlessness. He once asked a politician the same question a dozen times on *Newsnight* in an effort to get a straight answer. The drawback to this approach is that many politicians flat-out refuse to appear on the show, and *Newsnight* and other programs are vulnerable to the criticism that they do more bullying and point scoring than listening.

"Charles Kennedy, it strikes me, was nowhere near that situation," Hoggart concluded.

Alcohol lies at the bottom of many unfortunate public situations in modern Britain. In 2005, an evening barbecue for officials of ASLEF, the "macho, booze-swilling" train drivers' union, in the words of one official, erupted into a violent melee. The general secretary was observed insulting and attacking the other guests in a particularly offensive manner. ("I think he had been in the pub all day," one witness said, called later to speak to investigators.) A union report describing the party later said that the group's top two officials—the president and the general secretary—"engaged in what could be described as a 'brawl,' a 'fight,' or 'wrestling.'"

Seven people lost their jobs.

In other drink-related news, standby psychologists, the production crew, and, eventually, the police had to enter the *Big Brother* television show house in 2004 when the cast—dosed with alcohol to get them to open up and say provocative things—erupted into a drunken fight on the air. The following year, a top official of the British Transport Police, was overheard at a pub announcing: "I am going out to get drunk. That's a way to relax." Gesturing happily to a large back bag he was carrying, he said: "I know I am going to lose this bag in this pub or the next one." (The official in question later denied having said it.) Meanwhile, the eighteenth birthday party for Coleen McLoughlin, the girlfriend of the gifted but potato-faced soccer star Wayne Rooney, descended into chaotic farce when their two families got drunk and began brawling on the dance floor. The families were particularly upset when the free bar closed at 2 a.m. "Eugene was covered in blood," one guest told the *Daily Mail*, referring to Rooney's uncle. "Wayne's dad was being held down by Coleen's dad and . . . her younger brother Anthony came close to being bottled."

Louise Casey, the "coordinator for respect" in the Blair government (her unenviable task was to "tackle disrespect" in society), referred to her boss, Home Secretary Charles Clarke, as "Charlie Boy" in a speech to law-enforcement officials in 2005. She then advised the audience to "binge drink whenever you want" and to "turn up in the morning pissed" as a way to handle stress.

And in 2006, after leaving a reception at the Irish Embassy in a particularly bubbly state, the Bishop of Southwark was witnessed climbing into the backseat of a parked Mercedes that belonged to someone else.

The owner of the Mercedes was surprised to find him there, creating a disturbance. "This guy was hanging out the back of my car, chucking toys about," he recounted later. "He was out of his head."

Witnesses recalled that the bishop had been going around announcing, "I'm the Bishop of Southwark." But the bishop claimed to remember nothing, and was at a loss to explain the disappearance of his cell phone, crucifix, and briefcase.

"It would be entirely out of character if I was drunk," he said indignantly.

Britons may forgive themselves their drunkenness and treat it as a bit of a joke. But alcohol abuse is a serious problem. Tony Blair, whose teenage son was once found vomiting and insensible on a London street after a night of carousing, said that binge drinking was in danger of becoming "the new British disease." Per capita drinking across most of Europe has decreased in the last forty years. But in Britain, it has increased. People start younger, drink more, and are increasingly likely to binge drink. Government figures released in 2007 show that British adults on average drink the equivalent of 11.4 liters of pure alcohol a year each, translating into more than 180 bottles of wine, or 1,137 pints of beer.

The government once estimated that the total cost to society, in medical bills, missed work, cleanup charges, and increased policing, is about £20 billion a year. A study released in 2007 found that the number of hospital admissions for alcohol-related liver disease in Britain had more than doubled in the previous decade, to 39,725 from 16,252. The Welsh Assembly reported that from 2006 to 2007, the number of people being treated for alcohol misuse in Wales—many of them in hospital emergency rooms—increased by some 40 percent. "There's no social group that's immune to binge drinking, except the elderly—although we recently had a 90-year-old who drank five pints and fell down as he tried to leave his local pub," Dr. Paul Atkinson, a consultant in the emergency department at Addenbrooke's Hospital in Cambridge, told me. Each year, according to one survey, some 125,000 young people suffer serious facial injury or disfigurement after heavy drinking, usually because of falling down, having a car accident, or being maimed in a fight.

"It's very common to have head injuries," Atkinson said. "I've had people who've inhaled their teeth into their lungs."

Newspaper articles advertised by headlines like "Mass Drunkenness Has Turned Us into a Nation of Barbarians" are now staples of daily news reports. In one of its endless studies on the subject, the Home Office concluded that binge drinking had become "so routine that young people find it difficult to explain why they do it." The centers of many cities and towns have become centers for drunken violence on weekend nights. George Street in stately Oxford is now known locally as "Vomit Alley." New rules relaxing pub closing hours, so that not all pubs are required to close at 11 p.m., were meant to ease the situation somewhat by staggering the times when drinkers were decanted into the street, but it just meant that drink-related crime was spread out across the night. In 2007, the Liberal Democrat Party said that there had been 1,087,000 incidents of alcohol-related violence in the previous year—constituting nearly half of all violent crime.

The effects of binge drinking are all too obvious to anyone brave enough to take certain trains late at night, or to stand outside pubs or clubs at closing time, or to venture into the centers of towns and cities across the country late on Friday and Saturday nights. Older people call these places no-go areas, and are afraid to go there lest they be "the victim of a drunken yob beating them up, kicking them or headbutting them," as Ian McCartney, then chairman of the Labour Party, said in a speech ("yob" means "hooligan").

The behavior can be beyond gross. Here is a conductor's description of the Saturday overnight train from London to Aberdeen, a service that was eventually canceled because no one wanted to work on it.

"It was like an alcoholic bullet flying through the night," the conductor said. "The buffet car was a cesspool. They were climbing into the berths with Christ knows who. It was madness. They'd pull the emergency cord. They'd vomit. Break guitars over each other's heads. You can't be having that on a nice train."

Why are Britons worse than other people? One reason is that they are repressed and drinking helps them open up. Or at least that is their excuse. In *Watching the English*, the social anthropologist Kate Fox writes that "by blaming the booze, we sidestep the uncomfortable question of why the English, so widely admired for their courtesy, reserve and restraint, should also be renowned for their oafishness, crudeness and violence."

Fox told me that Brits purposely act like idiots, knowing they can disavow responsibility.

"One thing that is common to ambivalent drinking cultures is the belief that alcohol is a disinhibitor and makes us violent," she said. "It certainly interferes with your motor functions and your ability to speak rationally, but it doesn't cause you to go up to people, say, 'Oy, what are you looking at?' and start punching them."

Also, Britain has no equivalent of Continental-style café society. "You'll never find Sartre in an English café for two reasons," the writer and critic George Steiner once said. "A) No Sartre. B) No café." Also, while a slightly tipsy Englishman can be a joy to talk to, a seriously drunken one is likely to have moved far beyond literature and philosophy— Sartre's or anyone else's—as possible conversational topics.

The traditional British pub used to be a dank, dark, masculine, and rather joyless place where serious drinking (followed by fighting) took place. Many city pubs have been reinvented as family-friendly affairs with goat's cheese and foccacia-laden menus instead of skuzzy bags of potato chips, but the old-style heavy-drinking pub still plays an important part in British social life. Countless marriages have been lost—or maybe, held together—by the husband's desire to escape to the pub, the British equivalent of Fred Flintstone's all-male lodge. There they can talk about sports, or, if they are particularly sensitive, talk about their wives, whom they refer to as "the wife."

Or they can talk about nothing, anesthetized by the alcohol. There is a joke about two men who drink pint after pint together in the pub, companionably silent. A few hours pass. On his tenth pint, the first man raises his glass and says, "Cheers!" The second man glares at him. "Look," he says, "did you come here to talk, or to drink?"

Drunken Brits are one of the country's most visible exports. The expansion of the EU has brought with it the rise of low-budget airlines that fly to cities you can't pronounce in countries you can't find on the map, all for less than the cost of dinner and a movie in London. Other Europeans sometimes feel as if Britain treats their continent as one huge pub, followed by one huge bathroom. More than anyone else, Britons are notorious around Europe for their drunken behavior, characterized by violence, throwing up, outdoor urination, brawling, and breaking things.

This is especially bad in resort communities like Ibiza and the Canary Islands, well-known partying locations where Britons go on cheap package vacations. Here they spend their days lying in stupors on the beach, frying their pasty northern skin into something resembling flayed bacon, and their nights partying, rampaging, having sex in public places, and getting arrested.

Stag parties, and their female equivalents, hen parties, have evolved from drunken nights on the town to weekends of solid drinking in exotic foreign cities. I once flew to Prague on EasyJet (price of round-trip last-minute ticket: £50) to do a story on Britons who hold their stag parties there. There are two main reasons: (1) Czech beer is cheaper than British beer; (2) Nobody knows you, so it doesn't matter if you behave really badly. Suffice it to say, you do not go in order to see the sights.

The plane left at 6:15 a.m., which meant getting up at 4:00 a.m. so as to get to the airport by 5:00. Beer—that is the word that best summarizes my flying experience that day. Most of the passengers— groups of young men wearing matching shirts with amusing stag-party slogans on them—seemed to have been up all night at the pub. I tried to talk to some of them. They did not want to talk to me. They were like high school students, embarrassed to be singled out, staring glassy-eyed out the window, hoping no one would see them answering any questions.

Why did they choose Prague?

"We looked on the Internet and these were the flights that were available," said one guy, maybe thirty-five, whose breakfast, three cans of Kronenbourg, was lined up in front of him. He snickered. "I thought we were going to Barcelona."

His even-more-unfriendly friend, unshaven and paunchy, finished his first round. "Bring the trolley to me with a big straw!" he shouted to the flight attendant, who seemed unperturbed by the Hooters-like scene on the plane. What did the straw man plan to do in Prague? "Get drunk, I suppose; have some drinks and have a good time." He said they had chosen Prague as their destination because, "Why do you go to different restaurants and eat? Same difference."

"Could I get your name?" I asked, thinking of quotes for my article.

"I wouldn't have thought so," he said.

But if the atmosphere on the plane was unpleasant, the atmosphere in Prague was poisonous. It is a beautiful gem of a city, and I was looking forward to taking it in. I checked in to a brand-new hotel near Wenceslas Square, the haunting spot where Václav Havel addressed a sea of anticommunist protesters in the 1989 Velvet Revolution.

My hotel was opulent with postcommunist decadence, an Art Deco crossroads for the new Europe. It was a world away from Rocky O'Reilly's, a transplanted Irish pub just down the street, which was filled with British men in large groups, drinking for drinking's sake. Except for the cheap prices and Czech staff, they might as well have been in downtown Dublin or central London. The bar served Guinness and British food; used English on its menus and signs; and had its many televisions permanently tuned to major British sports events on satellite.

One group, whose members included an insurance underwriter and a police officer ("The first thing the gaffer warned me is not to get arrested," he said, the "gaffer" being the boss), had gathered in celebration of the forthcoming nuptials of their friend Andy, thirty-one years old and fetchingly dressed up in a pink wristband, rouge, and lipstick.

"We've had something to drink," one announced, redundantly.

"It's cheaper here than in Blackpool," said another, as if that explained it.

They were all but one sheet to the wind, still coherent; another group at a different table was a little further along, attempting to flick sugar cubes into their water glasses and playing a complex drinking game whose rules included No Using Your Left Hand, No Pointing, and No Saying the Word "Point." One wore a headpiece in the shape of a plastic turd. He had visibly expressed annoyance, or "gotten a turd on," and would have to wear the hat until someone else got annoyed at something else, whereupon he could then pass it on. I found it pretty annoying, actually, just looking at the hat.

These were men in their early thirties whose touristic research had consisted of finding and printing out lists of Prague drinking establishments and strip clubs on the Web. They said that British society no longer allows for male-only activities, except possibly for football matches (but even those are becoming more feminized, with ghastly, anodyne family sections that ban even swearing), so that the stag weekends are important bonding opportunities.

"It's the extreme end of men's behavior," said one guy, who had left a wife and one-year-old son at home. "The other half is washing up, cooking, looking after the baby." He said he was too insecure and uptight to have a real conversation with his male friends without a drink in his hand.

Rocky O'Reilly's owner, Robbie Norton, told some stories of previous British visitors. A party of twenty-three, fresh off the plane, consumed 180 vodkas and sixty cans of Red Bull in a single Friday afternoon. "I know that sounds totally insane," he said, "but they came back and did the same thing on Saturday and the same thing on Sunday."

You can spot the Brits a mile away, he said, because they are the ones most likely to be dressed in Batman or Superman outfits and because they are the noisiest people in Europe. "There'll be a table of four guys and they'll be shouting at each other and I'll say, 'For Christ's sake, he's sitting right there!'"

Ivo Lorenc, a Czech café owner whom I met through Ian Fisher, a colleague who was then based in Warsaw, rents out apartments in a glorious sixteenth-century building near Prague Castle.

"The British treat every day as if it were New Year's," he said. These are the guys who ask him where to get the best beer—there are more than one hundred different kinds in the Czech Republic—who mix lager with absinthe, and who leave his apartments in a shambles. One group of four stayed for just two nights but left behind one hundred empties. He and his restaurant-owning friends regularly share British-tourist horror stories, like the one about two dozen Britons who, enraged at being served warm beer (although you would think they would be used to it), simultaneously upended their glasses and left without paying; or the one about the Britons who drove everyone out of the café when, after too much absinthe and vodka, they began vomiting on the floor; or the one about the group who stripped en masse and ran around in their underpants; or the one about the three stag groups from Manchester, Leeds, and Birmingham who hated each other on account of rooting for different soccer teams, and who ended up having a free-for-all.

Sometimes the behavior is of the "you just have to laugh" kind, such as when a group of fifty-three women arrived from Cardiff—each dressed up as the Welsh singer Tom Jones.

It got worse. I will spare you most of the details except to say that hours later, when I happened upon Andy's stag party again by chance, they had been transformed into a walking manifestation of a hysterical *Telegraph* headline about "Binge Britain." They were out of control, and unhappy. The encounter ended with my running down the street while they ran after me, trying to rip my notebook from my hands.

I'm sure they forgot all about it when they finally woke up from their hangovers; half the Brits you see in places like that seem to have lost all reason over or memory of their own behavior. The problem of drunken Britons abroad is so bad that Parliament at one point considered a measure that would impose an £84.50 "call-out charge" for any drunken person who ran into trouble and had to be rescued by a British embassy late at night.

The Foreign Office has a name for such people, the ones who get "drunk, incoherent and lost" and need emergency assistance: Distressed British Nationals. So far, Prague had the most, and sometimes the embassy was taking sixty drunken calls a night from Brits who lost their wallet or couldn't remember the name of their hotel or other pertinent information, like what city they were in.

In written evidence to Parliament, one British diplomat in Prague described a Distressed British National who got separated from his party and then passed out in a taxi.

"The driver drove him to the airport, stole all his money, and kicked him out," the diplomat said. "Because he was so drunk, he thought he was going home, and tried to get on any plane leaving the airport." Found roaming around a nearby hangar, the distressed person was then escorted to the police station. "Nobody knows how he got into the hangar," the diplomat said.

I hate to sound like a spoilsport, but it's hard not to feel that there is a large problem here that many people simply refuse to confront in any serious way, no matter how much doctors warn about liver cirrhosis or the newspapers inveigh against the perils of Booze Britain or the government enacts new antisocial-behavior laws. It's hard to expect the public to change its attitude, when many of the people it most admires—sports stars, younger members of the royal family, politicians—spend so much of their time getting publicly trashed. Consider what happened in the fall of 2005, after the English cricket team somehow managed to defeat Australia in the never-ending cricket match known as the Ashes. For cricket lovers, 2005 was a glorious time. England and Australia were archrivals, and England had not won the match since 1987. For a small happy period, cricket supplanted soccer in the national consciousness. The team, made up of clean-cut family men, virile and handsome in their crisp white trousers and V-neck sweaters, became bona fide heroes, as English teams always do when they actually manage to win something.

What did they do when they beat the Australians? They went down to the pub. They went to many pubs. They went to the bars of their hotels. They went, carrying bottles of beer, to Trafalgar Square for an official celebration. They went, already drunk, to No. 10 Downing Street, where the prime minister held a reception in their honor. They went on a thirty-six-hour orgy of drunken carousing.

Andrew Flintoff, star of the series, was also star of the afterparty. He appeared on television with muddied speech, bloodshot eyes, and an unsteady gait. He was seen drinking first thing in the morning and last thing at night, outside and indoors, alone and in groups. He was overheard boasting that he might now become an honorary freeman of his town and that the post included a useful perk: free police rides home when you're too drunk to make it on your own.

He walked around for a while with the word "twat" drawn in pen on his forehead, courtesy of his teammate Steve Harmison, who pounced while Flintoff was unconscious on the team bus. ("Anyone who falls asleep on the team bus knows the dangers," Harmison noted. He also said: "You can't work as hard as we did and not deserve a drink.") Later, Flintoff would be named Sportsman of the Year, and would deny that he had urinated in the prime minister's garden during the postmatch party.

The team's antics threw the country's media commentators into a quandary.

Yes, binge drinking is bad, they said: it leads to antisocial behavior, wrinkles, liver disease, cancer, the breakdown of society, and so on. But on the other hand, these national champions who had given England back its sports pride were also lads who deserved a bit of fun.

Faced with the choice between puritanism and libertinism, most raised a metaphorical pint and joined in.

The team's aftermatch partying, wrote the tabloid columnist Michael Booker, had validated the behavior of millions of Britons who "enjoy one too many sherbets every now and again." He added: "Now and then the only thing that will really do—and I won't be popular with Mrs. Booker by saying this—is a pant-wetting, day-night blowout."

Not surprisingly, the England team went on another spree after that—a losing spree (the next time the Ashes came around, England would lose that, too, by the humiliating score of five games to zero). But the players drank as much in defeat as in victory. In 2007, after his team lost a disastrous opening match in a tournament in St. Lucia, Flintoff went to a bar and reportedly drank for eight hours with members of the "Barmy Army" of traveling cricket fans.

At 4 a.m., Flintoff decided to go for a ride in a pedalo, a small pleasure craft powered by pedaling (thereafter, his pedalo would be known as a "fredalo"). He commandeered one from the hotel and rode it out to sea. But he got into trouble, rocking it from side to side and then capsizing it, and had to be rescued by staff members from the hotel. He was too drunk to get back by himself.

FIVE

MORE THAN A GAME

Of course it's frightfully dull! That's the whole point!
—line from the film *The Final Test,* by Terence Rattigan

I feel greatly hampered by my ignorance of cricket because I am aware that it is a metaphor everywhere in English life. I know I'm missing something. I just don't know what it is.
—Paul Theroux (1983)

I once had the pleasure of seeing Freddie Flintoff, a tall, broad fellow with a mop of unruly blond hair and a devilish glint in his eye, in the flesh. At the time, he wasn't noticeably drunk: he was playing an important international cricket match, although it looked to me as if he was mostly standing around the field, waiting for the afternoon to end. I was at the Oval cricket ground in south London, where England was playing the West Indies. Some British friends had invited me and were attempting to explain what was going on.

"In India," said my friend Nick, leaning in close as if about to impart some top-secret item of inside information, "In India, it can get so tense the crowds *riot.*"

I looked for signs of incipient rioting. Not far from Freddie,* a

---

* His name isn't really Freddie; it's Andrew. He got his nickname because his last name, Flintoff, sounds like Flintstone. This is a common British nicknaming technique, the lazy

security guard lolled back in his chair, fanning the stale air with a piece of paper. Some spectators were reading novels. Others read the news-papers—all eight or so sections, this being Saturday. They were dozing and having little personal reveries. They chatted, ate sandwiches, and drank wine in plastic wineglasses they had brought from home in elabo-rate wine-cooling hampers.

Sports was clearly being played, and occasionally a wave of gen-tle applause rippled through the stands, like long grass blowing in the breeze. The spectators would bestir themselves enough to examine the scorecard for dramatic signs of change. But on the whole, the match seemed like a distant backdrop, a tableau vivant, and the crowd seemed about as unengaged as it is possible to be when you are physically pres-ent and sitting in seats you have paid for with your own money.

Flintoff and his teammates, fielding, stood there hoping for the ball to come their way. They had been doing a lot of standing and hoping. The game had been going on for four days. The West Indies team was losing by epic proportions. I don't mean a couple of runs, or even, say, ten points: The score was 470 to 147, which is pretty bad, however you look at it. I felt sorry for the poor West Indians—it seemed so embarrassing—but this sort of thing is apparently routine.

The scoring was only one of many bewildering aspects of the game. Learning about cricket in middle age is, like studying Mandarin, an effort best left to scholars, optimists, and members of the Foreign Ser-vice. I had had a hard time since I got into a taxi to go to the Oval and my cabbie, a monosyllabic specimen of lugubrious disposition whose main nontaxi passion turned out, serendipitously, to be cricket, tuned in to the game live on BBC radio.

It sounded like one of those Monty Python skits featuring upper-class twits and their puzzling pursuits. The phrases that escaped the plummy exaggerated drawl of the announcer, the famous cricket com-mentator Henry Blofeld (his nickname was "Blowers"; his father went

---

reference to a deceased famous person (or, in this case, cartoon character). My husband's colleague the distinguished journalist Peter Beaumont, for instance, is known as Binky, after Binky Beaumont, the legendary West End producer.

to school with Ian Fleming and is believed to be the inspiration behind the Persian-cat-stroking archvillain Ernst Blofeld in the James Bond novels), were so alien as to be virtually meaningless.

"One forty-two for three," he announced in tones of high excitement. It was some sort of score, but it was unclear how he had arrived at it, and what "for three" meant. Was it related to "oh-for-three" in baseball? Unlikely. I began to feel the way Bill Murray feels in *Lost in Translation*, dizzy with incomprehension.

I leaned back and thought of England and tried to give myself over to Blowers's soothing cadences, the richness of his vowels, the rarefied pronunciation—the spoken equivalent of calligraphy. This was gentleman's commentary for a gentleman's game. When a West Indies player punched the air in excitement after his one-hundredth consecutive run, known as a century,* Blofeld described the gesture as "a lovely sign of West Indian joy" in "a splendid innings" (innings-with-an-*s* is singular in cricket). The player had hit the ball "marvelously hard" and had used "magnificent strokes."

Blofeld was a character of deep eccentricity, known for lapsing into impromptu monologues about, say, the trouble with pigeons' waddling across the cricket pitch, or field, and the tendency of local buses to emit distracting noises as they passed by. Today, he praised the fans for their top-drawer comportment. "The Oval crowd has behaved itself impeccably," he said, "with no unnecessary or unwarranted incursions on the ground."

If Britain had a national sport, it would probably be soccer—it has more fans, more money, more excitement, more action. But professional soccer is the world's game, adored everywhere (except America), while cricket is peculiar to England and its former possessions (except America). It is a game of empire and a game of nostalgia. It is a game that, when played a certain way, has a peculiarly English feel to it. In 1990, the right-wing politician Norman Tebbit devised the notorious "cricket test" to gauge the patriotism of Britons from ethnic minorities. If your family was originally from Pakistan and you lived in Britain, he

---

* It doesn't take one hundred years, obviously, but it can feel that way.

asked, which team would you root for—England, or Pakistan—when the two countries played each other in cricket?

While most international test matches of the kind I was watching are much the way they always were, cricket as a whole, especially county cricket—very roughly, the equivalent of major league baseball, with a lot less money—has had to adjust to a world where spectators have less time and less patience. In the last decade, it has been revolutionized by efforts to make it quicker, faster, and more user-friendly. Games are shorter; plays are flashier; the pace is quicker. Relatively speaking.

This was not one of those kinds of matches.

I harbored a deep innate skepticism, or, as you might say, a bad attitude. On a purely practical level, the game seemed preposterous. Never mind the joke names, like "silly mid-off" and "deep fine leg," awarded to respectable positions in the outfield, not to mention the existence of a "third man," but no first or second man. Or the "not out" that follows renderings of runs scored, *but only sometimes*. Or the way that bowls (what Americans call "pitches") can be referred to as "leg-breaks," "off-spinners," and "googlys"; and the way that "wicket" refers both to the little stumps where the batsmen stand, and also to the ground between the two stumps where they run, while the "pitch" is the actual field.

Or the players' habit of yelling, "Howzat?!" a word that the spell-check on my computer instantly changes to "cowpat," when they want to protest a play to the umpire.

Other conventions appear baffling, if not perverse. The offense always has two batsmen on the pitch at once, and they run back and forth, switching places (one can get out while the other stays in). The outfit worn sometimes by the umpire—a funny hat and a white coat—makes him look like someone who, after the match, intends to report to his real job, in the butcher shop. The players wear elegant white trousers and shirts, sometimes accessorized with white cable-knit sweater vests, as if they were Edwardian gentlemen of the sort who leap about the lawn and wave parasols over the heads of nearby maidens. This meant that in our game, all the players wore essentially the same uniform: a sea of white.

"How do you tell them apart?" I asked.

"There are no black players on the English team," Nick said. (That was indeed true, although, historically, a number of gifted players for England have been of Pakistani or Afro-Caribbean descent.)

Cricket games usually last all day. That is distressing enough. But in international test matches, one game can last for five days. A test series, made up of numerous five-day games, can go on for the better part of a summer. Meanwhile, a single batsman can score hundreds of runs in one turn at bat, a turn that might last *for days* (I am serious about that). He can also bat indefinitely but purposely score no runs at all—the equivalent of a baseball player's hitting foul balls until the cows come home—in a complicated strategic maneuver designed to ensure that the match ends in a draw.

Watching players try not to hit is not inherently enthralling.

"Occasionally, you'll get an entire day's play without a single wicket falling," Hugh Chevallier, deputy editor of *Wisden Cricketers' Almanack*, the annual cricket bible, told me cheerfully, when I telephoned him for a story I was working on. (A wicket falls when a player goes out.) His voice took on a nostalgic tone. "It happened a couple of years ago when India beat Australia."

"A draw can be exciting," concurred my friend Tim.

There's a strange *Through the Looking-Glass* element to many sports in Britain, when compared with American ones: the superficial materials are the same (a small ball and a bat; a large ball and a hoop) but the games are topsy-turvy and inside out.

My daughters, for instance, play netball, a classic schoolgirl sport. Although it involves two teams' competing to throw a ball through two baskets, it would be wrong to assume that it's just basketball with a refined accent. The players, who wear little pinafore-style garments over their clothes announcing what position they are playing (because they might forget otherwise?), are forbidden to bounce the ball; they are forbidden to run, walk, or move with the ball; they can only pass it from stationary person to stationary person, which is tiresome in the extreme, especially when you think too hard about the fact that it is a game that rewards players for *not moving*. In elementary school matches, the ones with which I am most familiar, the whistle blows about every two seconds, because that's how frequently the possessor of the ball makes an illegal move. At our school, an exciting game would be defined as one in which the score is 4 to 3.

As far as baseballesque sports go, the Brits have another one: rounders, in which you run around four bases—home is something else entirely—in an effort to score. It's what British girls play instead of cricket. My daughters play it, too, and their school likes it when the parents come in and participate. I once took part in a mother-daughter rounders match in Kensington Gardens, near our house, assuming that I would just pick it up as I went along.

Lesson one: You are supposed to swing the bat with one arm out to the side, as you would hit a forehand in tennis.

I swung and missed.

Lesson two: You are meant to advance to first base, *regardless of whether or not you have successfully hit the ball.*

"Run!" the nine-year-olds yelled.

Lesson three: Do not fling your bat to the ground as if you were Sammy Sosa; keep it in your hand while running to first (there is no reason for this, unless it is to club the opposing players).

It was very confusing, sometimes like baseball, and other times not. I made it to fourth base about six times during the game, but that did not count as six runs for our side. Once I got to fourth and scored half a point; another time I got there but scored no points.

I spent most of 1978 watching the World Series–winning Yankees on television, and I know how dense and cryptic baseball is, how hard to justify to the uninitiated. But—and I'm sorry to say this—cricket is worse. Its quirks are quirkier; its rules more complicated and convoluted; its conventions contradicted by more exceptions and oddities. To take one example: in international matches, they don't use artificial lights. When the light is bad, either because of dusk or regular bad weather, always a possibility, an official trots out with a special light-measuring gauge to stick into the air. If the light reading falls below a certain level, he can declare the day over. Just like that. No matter who is ahead.

As my old boss Paul Fishleder used to say, running his hands through his hair when struggling to explain the offbeat stories he was assigning us at the *New York Times* Metro Desk, "it's just so . . . weird!" But for me, the hardest thing about cricket is its inflationary nature. Baseball scores are low and miserly; cricket scores are high and extravagant. In the hundreds, which tends to my mind to detract from the excitement and craftsmanship of each particular run. Let's just say that cricket provokes less demand for instant replays on television. Which is why, I suppose, the fans read the newspaper during the games.*

As I sat in the Oval that day, I became anxious about the offense-defense disparity. If in baseball the rule is that good pitching beats good batting any day, or vice versa, then in cricket the rule seems to be: Everyone scores a lot. Doesn't that imply an underlying structural weakness?

No, no, on the contrary, Nick said. The skills in cricket are exactly the same skills as in baseball; it's just that "the accounting mechanism is different."

Cricket fans love a high score. The great Trinidadian player Brian Lara, believed by many to be the finest batsman of his generation, set the world record—400 runs, or a quadruple century—for the most runs scored *in a single innings*† at a cricket test match against England in 2004.‡

When he reached 375, surpassing his previous personal best, Lara

---

* That is the opposite of soccer, incidentally, where the game can end with no one scoring, and there is no shame in it. Although soccer fans long for a "result," meaning that someone has actually won, they have taught themselves to expect nothing. Sometimes I will come home and find Robert riveted to a soccer match on television.

"It was a great game!" he'll say afterward.

"What was the score?"

"Nil–nil!"

† An innings lasts until all eleven players on a side have had a turn to bat, or until their side's allotted fifty overs—an over being six bowled balls—are up, whichever comes first.

‡ It took Lara 773 minutes, or nearly thirteen hours, spread out over two days. That means he was at bat for, say, six hours one day, and seven hours the next day, including breaks. They do take a lot of breaks. Breaks for lunch. Breaks for tea. Breaks for weather. Breaks for gloom—you name it, they are taking a break.

paused, dramatically removed his batting helmet, and kissed the ground. Baldwin Spencer, the prime minister of Antigua and Barbuda, trotted out from the stands, and everyone took a moment to stop and admire Lara's achievement. Then Lara resumed play, retiring only after he had scored his 400—or, as the announcer noted "400 not out" (meaning, roughly, that even though he was out, he wasn't). The game paused again so the England players could come forward, one by one, and shake his hand.

Afterward, Lara described the congratulatory telephone call he got from the previous world record holder, with 380 runs, the Australian cricketer Matthew Hayden. It was a fine display of English self-deprecatory modesty all around. "He enjoyed the period he had the record, and I am sure he is capable of doing it again, as are a lot of very good batsmen around the world," Lara said. "I really appreciated that he took the time out to make the call."

But what I thought as I sat there watching the English and West Indians swing and run, swing and run (there is no such thing as a "strike" in cricket) was, it must been excruciating. You could have left the stadium, done all your Christmas shopping, educated your children—and when you came back, Lara would have been doing the same thing he had been doing before. Swing, hit, run.

I am not the only one to have noticed.

In 1897, a man named Douglas Moffett wrote a poetic lament about the tedium of a game in which the batsmen, hoping to pull off a draw, blocked the ball and never ran anywhere. Bowl, block; bowl, block. By the time it was over, he and the other spectators were nodding off, bored out of their mind. "Wearily I yawned while I sat and watched the play," his poem began.

"Watching Tavare bat," the *Observer* reported nearly one hundred years later, about a player known for wandering aimlessly around the field for minutes at a time before he felt mentally prepared to address the ball, "was a bit like waiting to die."

"A lot of people who don't play cricket think it's boring," Nick told me, in what was the recurring theme of our long afternoon together. "But if you understand the game, it's very very tense."

But that is the secret, right there. Tedium is both the burden and the gift of cricket. Part of the tension *is* the tedium. Cricket is to other sports what the slow-food movement is to lunch at McDonald's. Its fans take the long view. They become Patience on a monument. They embrace the joys of delayed gratification. Like bad weather, Latin verbs, and the threat of succumbing to malaria while claiming parts of Africa for yourself, cricket requires the stiff-spine fortitude of the old-school Englishman.

"I don't think I can be expected to take seriously any game which takes less than three days to reach its conclusion," Tom Stoppard once said, explaining his opposition to baseball. Or, as my friend Anthony said, "The occasional dullness and boredom is what makes it true to experience." It is a game, said a fan I once met named Richard Peart, for people who "like to endure things."

Cricket dates back to the twelfth century and provides a link between England and its former international possessions. In its way, it is as important to England's view of itself as baseball is to America's. Like baseball, it inspires a wealth of philosophizing and is "full of theorists who can ruin your game in no time," as the England player Ian Botham put it. It also generates an unhealthy obsession with statistics and an inexhaustible supply of literature. Any cricket anthology is sure to include essays about the sport as a metaphor for country, empire, the English character, life itself; autobiographical accounts of seasons played and lessons learned; paeans to former players and lamentations on why no one today is as good; pointillistic reproductions of famous past games; affectionate tributes to players whose memorable quirks—taking forever to bat; bowling with a strange chickenlike motion of the elbow—endeared them to the fans; and, worse, an unusually high output of doggerel, epic poems, humorous verse, and sentimental ballads.

We have some great baseball novels, but we also have "Casey at the Bat." The English have the cricket poems of Lord Byron, John Betjeman, William Blake, Alfred, Lord Tennyson, and Harold Pinter, who in addition to being a playwright, provocateur, and Nobel Prize winner, was the chairman of the Gaieties Cricket Club. Famous literary cricket enthusiasts from the past include Siegfried Sassoon, who once boasted of his "creditable record for a poet," and James Joyce, who in a tour-de-force passage from his novel *Finnegans Wake* secreted the slightly altered names of thirty-one cricketing stars inside the text, like little disguised Easter eggs hidden in the woods.

Although cricket is played in all the most exclusive schools, it's also a democratic sport, played just as enthusiastically in cricket clubs and in village greens across the country. When you drive around in the summer, cricket players are always part of the backdrop, like sheep, suggesting "a tranquil and unchanging order in an age of bewildering flux," the historian Geoffrey Moorhouse wrote.

In the tiny village in Cambridgeshire where my husband, Robert, and I have a cottage (this cottage, which Robert bought in a celebratory spending spree years before I met him, has been cause of much domestic discord, but I am pleased to report that we recently installed heat) twenty-two men materialize as if by magic on most summer weekends and spend the day playing out there in the field across the street. Their wives organize elaborate teas and lie around with their children in the grass; this gives them something to do during the languor.

Who knows if the men are good players, or what the score is, or even which player belongs to which team? But it is very relaxing, knowing they are there. They evoke simpler, happier days when England was green and pleasant and people had all the time in the world.

The quintessential village cricket match comes in A. G. Macdonell's 1933 novel *England, their England*. A team of overeducated Londoners—a publisher, a poet, a professor of ballistics, a former Cambridge rower dressed in his Varsity blues—travels to bucolic Fordenden to play a team that includes the village blacksmith, the village tax collector, the village baker, and the proprietor of the village pub. Some old codgers, "victims simultaneously of excitement and senility," turn out to watch; there is also "an ancient leaning on his scythe" and a mob of urchins yelling, "Take him orf!" in reference to the blacksmith, who is having a bad bowling day.

Batting for the London team is the famous novelist Southcott, elegant in a pale pink silk shirt and perfectly creased flannel trousers. While the blacksmith is warming up, the novelist uses the time to take in the view:

> At last, after a long stillness, the ground shook, the grasses waved
> violently, small birds arose with shrill clamours, a loud puffing

sound alarmed the butterflies, and the blacksmith, looking more
like Venus Anadyomene than ever, came thundering over the crest.
The world held its breath. . . .

But the blacksmith overbalances, falls down, and sprains his ankle;
his ball hits a teammate; the teammate is propelled headfirst into a bed
of stinging nettles, and the ball is declared invalid. It is that sort of day.
Members of the London team keep sneaking off to get drunk. One falls
asleep in the outfield. Another fluffs a catch, explaining that he has been
"admiring a particularly fine specimen of oak." The game ends in a tie.
Everyone goes to the pub. Mr. Harcourt, the poet, makes a speech, in
Italian, "about the glories of England" before passing out in the corner.

There is less time for that sort of thing now, a development that distresses the old-timers. But the history of cricket is the history of the struggle between the old ways and the new, between purists and the populists.

Some traditionalists fix the beginning of the end at 1935, when
a notorious change to the leg-before-wicket rule—it has to do with
whether or not a bowled ball smacks a batsman in the leg before it
reaches his bat—took effect. Although it perhaps seems like a small
point, the LBW rule inspires as much passion and debate as the desig-
nated-hitter rule in baseball, or the penalty kick in soccer. Looking back
on a lifetime of cricket, in 1976, G. O. Allen, treasurer of the Maryle-
bone Cricket Club, said he had a "great and deep-rooted regret" about
his failure to campaign effectively against the "the evils of the LBW
law"—"the most disastrous piece of cricket legislation in my lifetime."

After LBW, there were more destabilizing changes. There was the
elimination, in 1963, of the traditional distinction between "gentlemen" and "players"—the gentlemen being the amateurs, the players the
professionals.* There was the horror of one-day international cricket,
introduced in the early 1970s as an acknowledgment that five-day

---

* The idea had been that amateurs, somehow, were more respectable than professionals
and so would be considered as belonging to a different class altogether. The two groups
rode to matches in separate train compartments; used separate doors to enter the playing
fields; and had their names rendered differently on match scorecards.

matches, while still the platonic ideal, were not always practical (or even, strictly speaking, enjoyable) for fans with jobs or other extraneous commitments. There was the dismay caused by the installation of electric lights in some county cricket grounds, allowing the scandalously unnatural playing of games at night.

At some point, too, players began discarding their Australian-style bush hats in favor of safety-conscious batting helmets, which made them seem less relaxed. They worried about whether their beer bellies made them look fat out on the field, and took to power dieting, doing abdominal exercises, and getting expensive haircuts. They started wearing colored uniforms, sometimes branded with sponsors' logos, for some games, a radical development that cricket conservatives derided as "pajama cricket." County teams gave themselves zippy, competitive names, such as "the Wolverines." Fans even indulged in "the wave."*

Some fans wore costumes to matches, to liven up their own enjoyment. When I was at the Oval, for instance, I was seated in front of a party of men in pirate outfits—eye patches, bandannas, wigs, hats, fake hooks—who were having a very nice time making pirate noises, even if the people around them were not sharing fully in the fun. "Americans!" hissed a man at the end of my row (for the record, they were not).

But there was still the issue of the game itself, and it had long been clear to cricket officials that something would have to be done—a speeding up, a clearing away of some of the impenetrability—to attract new fans.

The number of people who are physically willing to actually sit through live games has been falling steadily for decades. From 1997 to 2001, total attendance at county cricket matches declined by 17 percent, to 1.03 million in 2001. A survey by the England and Wales Cricket Board found that the game had only five hundred thousand regular attendees. Most of the disaffection came because the games

---

* This practice is still shunned as prohibitively vulgar by the posh people in the expensive pavilion seats, who rise only to applaud fine plays or to help themselves to drinks from the bar.

took too long—the shortest county cricket match in 2002 lasted *six hours and ten minutes*—and were played at times inconvenient to the average productive citizen, like 11 a.m. on Tuesday.

The game was also suffering from an image crisis.

"Cricket has had a slightly unfair reputation of being populated by sufferers of Asperger's syndrome," Hugh Chevallier of *Wisden* told me.

In 2003, the England and Wales Cricket Board rolled out a new monthlong tournament for its eighteen county teams, called Twenty20 cricket* with games designed to take three hours, tops. People waiting to bat had to sit in baseball-style dugouts in view of the crowd, instead of lazing around the pavilion, watching television. They had to jog briskly into position, instead of ambling along (if it took longer than ninety seconds, they were declared out, which shows you what it must have been like before). Teams began luring spectators with pajama parties, in which fans wore their real pajamas. They sponsored "girls' nights" and fancy-dress days, hired clowns and pop singers, set up face-painting booths, and brought in Jacuzzis.

If it seemed reasonable enough—who wants to do anything for six hours, really?—the innovation provoked a certain amount of bitterness among the older generations. David Frith, who edited the now-defunct *Wisden Cricket Monthly* between 1979 and 1996, spoke to me so vehemently on the subject that sparks of annoyance seemed to shoot through the telephone into my ear. If he had been dead, he would have been rolling over in his grave.

"Some batsmen have been known to bat for ten years"—he meant ten hours—"without stopping, and we marvel at the grit and stamina of people who can do that. You can just get out there and say, 'I'm not bothered about too many runs, but I'm just going to stay there.'"

Frith appeared not yet to have recovered from the introduction of one-day matches some thirty years earlier. He called them "crash-bang-wallop" cricket.

"It's people who have got no attention span that seem to be the

---

* Motto: "Twice the action, half the time!"

problem," he said. "I'm damn glad that I don't have a short attention span."

Perhaps, he acknowledged, he is not representative of the public at large.

"You're talking to someone who was branded a dinosaur because I wrote a piece for *The Times* condemning *Wisden* when its editor decided to throw away 140 years of tradition," Frith said. He was referring to the decision of *Wisden Cricketers' Almanack* to put an action photograph of the cricket star Michael Vaughan on its cover in 2003.*

Frith was not the only one who failed to appreciate the photo. The *Guardian* writer Frank Keating said that *Wisden* had a "misguided mania for modernity." Ian Wooldridge of the *Daily Mail* said that putting a real person on the cover of the magazine was like "slapping a picture of Judas Iscariot on future editions of the Holy Bible."

"It's sad to contemplate what's happening," Frith told me. "It's driven people who consider themselves 'normal' into a corner."

I attended a Twenty20 match that first summer, right after the new format was unveiled. The game was between the Middlesex Crusaders and the Kent Spitfires, and it was played at the Richmond County cricket ground. Many of the spectators were unfamiliar with the revised format; many were unfamiliar with cricket at all. As the organizers had hoped, the game had attracted a nontraditional crowd, with a healthy complement of families, younger people, and curious cricket-virgin locals. There were more women than usual, perhaps emboldened by the notion that if it took only three hours, there would be time to go out to dinner afterward.

Although black clouds rolled ominously along and drizzle fell intermittently, there were moments of late-afternoon sun. Beer and curry were plentiful. People sat on fold-out chairs or wandered around. The players stepped lively. They walloped the ball without pausing for con-

---

* This was the first time in the *Almanack*'s history that the cover illustration was of something other than an abbreviated table of contents.

templation or for other reasons. Failed batsmen exited the field to the pitiless Queen anthem "Another One Bites the Dust."

In the audience, a debate raged as to whether this was a good thing.

I met Fiona Boddy, a young and lively representative of a public relations firm, who was still emotionally scarred from an international cricket match several years earlier in which she spent a day watching a batsman deliberately try to hit into a draw. (She was spending this match, by contrast, in the line for beers.) Time had compressed and expanded until the clock actually seemed to be moving backwards, she recalled; the only respite was the rain that fell occasionally, like a gift from God. "It was the most excruciating thing ever," she said.

But Roger Jay, a cricket fan for seventy-five of his eighty-three years, had the opposite view. He sat in the stands, binoculars in his hands and a permascowl on his face. "This is a children's game; this is cricket for the masses," he snorted. "This is just smash-crash-bang cricket." One of the things that upset him most was all the "slogging" going on—slogging being when a batsman whacks at the ball in order to score quickly and often.

Trying to score a lot quickly does not seem like an ignoble purpose, in a game whose object is, you might think, to score, but that is how Jay saw it.

"They're so anxious to make runs that they lose their wicket before they've established themselves," he complained. "One or two of these players are beautiful batsmen, but they need a couple of overs"—an over being the bowling of six balls by one of the bowlers—"to be able to see the ball properly."

But Jay is not the target audience for Twenty20 cricket. Members of this demographic could be found nearby, with their potato chips. I met Dave Burgess, a retired retail manager whose enjoyment of the game had been heretofore confined to watching highlights programs on television. I met his son Karl, a social worker whose favored cricket-following method was to "flick the radio on and off every now and then and check the score."

They had been pleasantly surprised by the pace of the match. "It's fast, quick, entertaining, and you know you're going to get a result," Dave said.

"I seriously think this could be the revival of cricket," Karl said. Indeed, receipts at the front gate that day were £20,000, ten times the average take for a county cricket match.

The thrill continued to elude me, although I appreciated the wholesome good looks of the newly aerobicized players, shown to fine advantage in manly trousers that were far superior to baseball pants. Burgess gestured to the field, where the batsmen ran back and forth between the wickets, as similar batsmen had been doing in similar circumstances for centuries, and said it was best not to take on too much too quickly.

"You have to talk in degrees of excitement," he said. "In cricket terms, this is exciting."

It was a lovely afternoon, and it included some beer, something pleasant to watch, and a great deal of relaxed chatting. At the end, there was plenty of time left to go out to dinner. I never figured out who won, or indeed exactly how they kept score, but somehow, that seemed beside the point.

SIX

TOILETGATE

*Class is fun, or it should be; it is also fascinating with its infi-
nite nuances and gradations. It is every Englishman's parlour
game. A snob, in the derogatory sense, is someone who takes
the whole ridiculous business seriously.*
— Julian Critchley, Conservative MP

In 1998, a year after Princess Diana died, her brother, Earl Spencer,
announced that he had unilaterally decided to change the correct
pronunciation of their family's ancestral home, a not-quite-castle
called Althorp in rural Northamptonshire. It had been *AWL-trupp*, for
some perverse aristocratic reason; now it would be *AWL-thorp*, "a version that everyone can pronounce and understand." He broke the news
in a press release, which I thought was sweet of him. I had never gotten
a press release, particularly about pronunciation, from an earl before.
The British newspapers, who had it in for Spencer because he had publicly accused them of hounding his sister to death, took a more cynical
view. "A staggeringly important world announcement by Earl Spencer,"
reported the *Daily Mirror*.

It might indeed have seemed like a small useless point, as irrelevant
as the finer gradations of the leg-before-wicket rule. Who cares how
to pronounce the name of some fancy country house in the middle of
nowhere that you are never likely to visit? But in its modest way, it was

a blow for practicality in the class war still bubbling along confusedly, and confusingly, beneath the surface of British life. "I'm glad he's finally bowed to public opinion," Christine Whiley, who runs the tiny post office in nearby Great Brington—a classic feudal village in the sense that much of it is owned by Spencer and populated by citizens who would once have been known as "serfs"—told me. "Visitors were always embarrassed when I told them they were mispronouncing it."

Spencer had not metamorphosed overnight into a backslapping, bonhomie-radiating, pub-going person of the people. It was an advertising ploy: he wanted to attract visitors to the Diana memorial exhibit at Althorp and knew that the hoi polloi might be confused by the house name. Not to mention his name in general. Like a lot of lords, he has several ancillary titles—in addition to being an earl, he is also a baron and a viscount. Before he inherited the earldom from his father, Spencer had different titles from those he has now, and his last name was not Spencer, but Althorp (the same as the house, if that helps). Nonnobles have always had a hard time getting their mind around the whole confusing concept. Spencer once arrived at a new job in New York and found his name listed as "Al Thorp." After Diana died, one foreign television station reported that her body was heading to its "final resting place, at Antwerp."

Class in Britain is a slippery, bewildering proposition, particularly because it's not supposed to matter anymore. Everyone keeps saying so. John Major was talking about a "classless society" back in 1990. Tony Blair declared soon after becoming prime minister that "we are all middle class now." By the end of the Blair era, with Britain newly rich, many had come to believe, as the columnist Alice Thomson said in the *Daily Telegraph*, that "it doesn't matter any more where you come from, but how much you are worth."

But it's still there, even if no one can articulate exactly why and how. Class in Britain is like what hard-core porn was to Supreme Court Justice Potter Stewart: impossible to define, but you know it when you see it. Or, conversely, if you have to ask, you'll never understand. Actively thinking about class distinctions—or even worse, letting on that you care—is in itself fatally déclassé.

But people still do care. Or at least they notice. Or at least they notice that other people notice and care. They just do it sneakily, burying their conflicted feelings beneath centuries of accrued denial, evasion, self-consciousness, unease, embarrassment, double-bluffing humor, and fake insouciance. If class is no longer the obsession it was when George Bernard Shaw wrote that no Englishman could open his mouth "without making some other Englishman hate or despise him," it is always there in the background, like a constant low-grade toothache.

The subject is a minefield for foreigners, especially on account of all the denying and evading. On the other hand, we benefit from being perceived as essentially class-free—or classless, really: too ignorant to know any better. When I do the wrong thing—use the wrong word, even hold my fork in the wrong hand,* ask questions that British people would consider obnoxiously intrusive, not to mention asinine—I have a good excuse. She's not rude, *she's just American*, is what I hope they are thinking.

But even the gauche and ignorant can't help observing that the British upper classes have linguistic conventions that set them apart from everyone else and seem, when you think about it, preposterous. Althorp-the-old-way was just one of many pronunciation sand traps, a velvet rope dividing Us from Them. A lot of aristocratic names defy rationality. One of Spencer's middle names is Maurice, which comes out in conversation as *MORE-is*, as, incidentally, does the name of the title character in E. M. Forster's *Maurice*. Other names are so long-winded that they sound as if the parents must have been kidding. How else would you explain Prince Charles's full name, Charles Philip Arthur George Mountbatten-Windsor, or the existence of a nonfiction character named Isabella Amaryllis Charlotte Anstruther-Gough-Calthorpe (the last bit of which is pronounced *CAW-thorp*)?

Upper-class pronunciations are all over the place. The Cholmondeleys are pronounced the *CHUM-leys*. The Earl of Harewood is the Earl

---

* It's not that silverware is a huge issue. But their cutlery customs are the opposite of ours. They're taught to hold the fork in the left hand, the knife in the right, and never to switch the two. The fork spears; the knife cuts. They would never mention it, but they register it quietly. Sometimes in restaurants, waving your fork around in your right hand, you feel as if you come across as some kind of clueless swamp creature.

of *HAR-wood*. The Beaulieus are the *BEW-leys*, in accordance with
the convention that French words should be pronounced as far away
from the actual French style as humanly possible, just to show those
French people who's boss. Beauchamp Place, a street in Knightsbridge:
BEACH-um Place. Jacques, in Shakespeare: *JAKE-weeze*. Your valet is
your *VAL-let*. (Madame Tussauds wax museum? To some Brits it's "*MA-
dum TOO-sod's.*")*

You might think people whose names contain built-in pronunciation land mines would tire of having to explain, and spell, and respell,
and endure the cries of mirth from reservation clerks. Wondering about
CHUM-ley, I called Cholmondeley Castle, the family seat, and asked
the lady who answered the phone how we civilians were supposed to
know about all those unwieldy silent syllables. Natural selection, she
said, basically: "I think it's one of those things that either you know or
you don't know." I tried Hatfield House, home to the ancient, noble,
unpronounceable Cecil (rhymes with "thistle") family. "It's one of those
class-distinction indicators that people like to hang onto to show that
they're upper class," the librarian explained.

If the snobby upper classes feel secure with their eccentric conventions,
the nervous lower classes try frantically to upgrade. The social-climbing
character Hyacinth Bucket in the classic television comedy *Keeping Up
Appearances* insists on being called *boo-KAY*. (My husband works with
someone whose last name really is Bouquet; his coworkers tease him
by calling him Bucket.) In the same way, the humorous Sidebottoms at
some stage fancified themselves into the *sid-AY-beau-TOMS*, the Deaths
inserted a strategic apostrophe to become the De'aths (pronounced *DEE-*

---

* Nor do regular pronunciations necessarily reflect the order of the letters in words.
Worcestershire, as in the county or the sauce, is a perfect example: visiting Americans
display their ignorance by calling it *War-CHEST-er-shire*, but it's actually *WUSS-ter-
sheer*. I live near Gloucester (pronounced *GLOSS-ter*) Road. Oxford has a Magdalen,
and Cambridge a Magdalene, College; both are pronounced *MAUD-lin*. It goes both
ways. My husband thinks that the city in Connecticut is called *NEW Haven*. And,
sweetly, many Britons seem to believe that Maryland is actually *MERRY-land*.

ath), and the B'Stards just hope that no one mentions the obvious: that, courtesy of some far-off illegitimate ancestor, they are really Bástards.

Some families are riven by pronunciation warfare, even in the same generation. Jonathan Powell, who was Tony Blair's chief of staff, pronounces his last name to rhyme with "towel." But his older brother, Sir Charles Powell, a Conservative who was private secretary to Prime Minister Margaret Thatcher and has higher aspirations, rhymes his name with "roll" (the novelist Anthony Powell preferred the fancier way, too). Former prime minister John Major, always sneered at as the son of a man who worked in show business and then sold garden gnomes, had an older brother named Terry Major-Ball. When John was born, his mother insisted that his last name be Major, drop the Ball—which might help explain why he became prime minister and Terry did not.

Any historical discussion of class in Britain is bound to return to the 1950s, when the socially astute author Nancy Mitford divided the population into two groups in her famous essay "The English Aristocracy": U, for upper class; and non-U, for everyone else. But while Mitford got the credit for the conceit, she was just responding to a paper published in an obscure Finnish academic journal by Alan S. C. Ross, a professor of linguistics at the University of Birmingham in England. In his paper, "U and Non-U: An Essay in Sociological Linguistics," Ross argued that people's vocabulary and word choice were instant class indicators.

He gave examples. Such as: U speakers said "house," "ill," and "rich"; non-U speakers said "home," "sick," and "wealthy." U's used table napkins and lavatory paper; non-U's used serviettes and toilet paper; At lunchtime U's ate lunch but non-U's ate dinner.*

Finnish linguistics journals not being widely disseminated abroad, Ross's paper went largely unnoticed until Mitford got hold of it and published her response a year later, with expanded lists of U and non-U

---

* The professor also took the opportunity to share his random observations of the upper classes, such as: "When drunk, gentlemen often become amorous or maudlin or vomit in public, but they never become truculent."

words. She framed her observations as light amusement, and they may well have been, but they also weren't: they accurately described contemporary upper-class usage and behavior. U-speakers really did say "sofa," "rich," and "jam," as Mitford wrote, and not "settee," "wealthy," and "preserves." U: "Pudding," "false teeth," "spectacles," "telegram," "England." Non-U: "Sweet," "dentures," "glasses," "wire," "Britain."

Mitford's piece, with her naked discussion of an issue that most people preferred to leave shrouded in the mists of the unexamined, caused a sensation. Leftists denounced her as an anachronistic snob; aristocrats pretended it had never happened; others drew up their own lists. Her friend Evelyn Waugh wrote a not-altogether-serious essay in response, arguing that class was in some ways all in the head. "Everyone has always regarded any usage but his own as either barbarous or pedantic," he said.

One of Waugh's friends, for instance, used the expression "MIF"—meaning "milk in first," a reference to the supposedly déclassé habit of putting the milk in a cup before the tea—to denote social inferiors. Another followed an ironclad but idiosyncratic sartorial rule: "No gentleman ever wears a brown suit."

"Almost everyone I know has some personal antipathy which they condemn as middle-class quite irrationally," Waugh wrote. "My mother-in-law believes it is middle-class to decant claret. Lord Beauchamp thought it m.c. not to decant champagne (into jugs). . . . There are very illiterate people like Percy Brownlow who regard all correct grammar as a middle-class affectation. Ronnie Knox blanches if one says, 'docile' with a long 'o.' I correct my children if they say 'bike' for 'bicycle.' "

A half century later, it sounds absurd. Surely none of this matters any more? But U and non-U, the lavatories and the toilets, what you can and cannot say—the whole thing was revisited in 2007, when Prince William split up for a time with his college sweetheart, Kate Middleton. They got back together several months later, but at the time, the end of their affair made perfect sense. They were both in their early twenties. He was enrolled in officers' training school, and we know what that is like; we saw *An Officer and a Gentleman*. Their relationship seemed to lack a certain erotic spark. As one newspaper pointed out, while Prince Harry and his voluptuous good-time girlfriend, Chelsy Davy, always appeared to be coming up for air in the midst of a drunken marathon shagfest, William and Kate looked as if sex had not necessarily occurred to them yet.

But the newspapers had another explanation: class. Kate's family was said to belong to the "aspirational middle class," a snippy way of saying they hoped for more and were not embarrassed to say so. Mr. and Mrs. Middleton had done well for themselves by setting up Party Pieces, a successful mail-order business (when my daughters were small, I ordered things like mermaid-themed plastic cups and Barbie plates for their birthday parties from Kate's parents' company). But that wasn't all. Mrs. Middleton also chewed gum in public, used the dread word "toilet," and had, in her youth, *worked as a flight attendant*. That was the worst. It was reported that whenever they saw Kate, William's friends muttered, "Doors to manual"—a point that, whether true or not, played right into the anxieties of the class-conscious public.

The papers had a field day with Toiletgate, as they were soon happily calling it. But they wanted to have it all ways at once. They broached the issue of class, debated and obsessed over it, but then tried to laugh it off. Perhaps *other* people cared, they said; but they didn't, although why not take their quiz to find out what class you are? "What Class Are You?" asked the *Daily Mail*, devising questions like, What kind of rug do you have? (Shag: lower class. Natural oak floor: middle class. Thread-bare: upper class.) The *Daily Telegraph's* quiz suggested that while the lower classes use "Say again?" when they can't hear, the middle classes say, "Pardon?" and the upper classes bray, "What?" A reader wrote in to suggest that class could be determined by the seating arrangements of two couples out for a drive. "Working class, men in the front," he wrote. "Middle class, man with his own partner in the front. Upper class, man with the other partner in the front."

I called Mary Killen, who discusses subtle points of etiquette in the "Your Problems Solved" column in the *Spectator* magazine, and asked if all those things were true. She instantly reeled off a further list of shib-boleths—the upper classes don't put tomatoes in the refrigerator, for instance, she claimed, which I thought was odd—and said you could tell by what sort of marmalade weekend guests brought along as house presents.

Huh? Gelatinous commercial marmalade reflects the tastes of social group C, the government designation for the lowest class, Killen explained. Store-bought thick marmalade with chunks of fruit in it, like Frank Cooper's (that is the brand we have in our cupboard): social group B, the middle class. Chunky but runny: group A, because "that shows that you have access to stockpiles from a country house."*

Also: "There is a fashion for Quality Streets," among the upper classes, Killen said, referring to a cheap assortment of chocolates available in every gas station in Britain. If you buy an expensive collection from Fortnum & Mason, or bespoke chocolates from the Chocolate Society, or enroll your hosts in the Handmade Luxury Upper-Class Chocolate of the Month Club—that is trying too hard. You look anxious and nouveau.†

There was an ancillary, but no less important, issue when it came to Kate Middleton's unfortunate mother: She was said to be too candidly enthusiastic about the potential social benefits of being the possible mother-in-law of the future king of England. All that thrusting ambition was a terrible PR misstep, although who could blame her?

---

* The government flat-out divides the population into "social grades," based on occupation. Doctors and lawyers belong to group A; nurses and police officers belong to group B. Group C1 includes clerical workers and students. Group C2 includes factory foremen, plumbers, and bricklayers. D: shopworkers, manual laborers, apprentices. E: casual laborers, pensioners, and the unemployed.

† Just as rich Americans from old-money families in New England frown on ostentation —they might invest in land, furniture, and boats, for instance, but drive run-down old cars and wear ancient khakis and holey sweaters—so do many old-money Britons recoil from lavish displays. One titled woman I heard about, with a seriously big estate on tens of thousands of acres, had a horror of offering her guests chocolates from boxes that were obviously newly purchased, for fear of "appearing rich." She preferred to bring out half-empty boxes that she had had for some time. I once interviewed an aristocrat in the graciously furnished library of his manor house in Somerset, the centerpiece of which was a large bucket into which dripped water from a leak overhead. He took me on a tour of the house. "Oops," he said, as we passed a particularly cold bathroom. "This window unfortunately fell out onto the lawn."

Status by association has a proud tradition in Britain. Double-barreled names (Spencer-Churchill, for example) are just a way to show that you have two illustrious sets of forebears (and, in the old days, a way to inherit money and land you might not have gotten otherwise). In *Pride and Prejudice*, the unctuous Mr. Collins boasts at every turn about the exquisite condescension of his insufferable patroness, Lady Catherine de Bourgh. Buildings across the country are decorated with plaques announcing which important person or—even better—which member of the royal family presided over their public openings.

I never thought those really mattered until my husband and I were touring a school we were considering for our daughters. Up on the wall was a plaque announcing that the new wing had been opened by an important Conservative politician. Our guide looked pleased about the status of this man—presumably the biggest celebrity they could manage to get—and his association with the school. "The girls went here, you know," she murmured, "the girls" being his children.

Another school we'd seen several years earlier, when our daughters were younger, had an even better string in its bow in the form of an illustrious alumnus. It was a labyrinthine school, with warrenlike corridors and students taking classes in rooms as small as closets (many London schools are strapped for space). The walls were covered with pictures of students in groups—sports teams and clubs and classes.

"Did you see all those photographs of Prince Charles?" Robert asked as we left.

I hadn't, but I didn't yet have the eye for those sorts of things.

Another time, as I shopped at Rigby & Peller, an expensive lingerie boutique in Knightsbridge, I was startled to see a photograph of the queen on the wall near the changing rooms. This is where she buys her underwear, a salesclerk told me proudly. An undignified image flashed through my mind. (It wasn't as if they had a wall of celebrity customers, either, as in a barbershop or Italian bistro. They just had the queen, balefully watching you try on bras.)

The royal family is more present in consumer affairs than you might think, lending its regal imprimatur to products in a strange kind of commercial endorsement. Weetabix, for example. Prince Charles uses it, or at least it says so on the box in our kitchen. "By appointment to HRH The Prince of Wales," the Weetabix box reads, underneath a nifty little reproduction of Prince Charles's coat of arms, "Manufacturers of Breakfast Cereal." James Baxter & Son Ltd., "Purveyors of Potted Shrimp," gets a similar endorsement from the queen.

There are some eight hundred companies with such royal warrants, as they are known, although it would be a mistake to imagine that the royals shop for the products themselves. "It means that a particular company has a trading relationship with Buckingham Palace," a palace spokesman told me. "There may be a florist which holds the queen's warrant, but that doesn't mean the queen goes in to the florist herself."

In contrast to aristocrats like my picnicking earl and his cruddy cars and packaged ham, people who are not so secure in their social position try really hard to make it look as if they do and use the right things. A taxi driver once told me about a passenger he'd picked up from the supermarket, who proceeded—during the cab ride—to transfer her groceries from their low-rent supermarket bags into classic green Harrods shopping bags that she just happened to be carrying around in her purse. Presumably she wanted to impress any neighbors who might espy her as she made the journey from the taxi to the front door.*

Is it that straightforward, that nakedly obvious? Can products, vocabulary, clothes, and pronunciation instantly mark you as one thing or another? Beats me. But everyone seems completely aware of where he or she stands in the hierarchy. "What class are you? I'm working class!" the mother of the bride chirped to the mother of the groom at a wedding I went to, neatly illustrating her own point: A middle- or upper-class person would never put it so baldly. She would pretend

---

* Harrods, once the local shop of the rich upper classes, along with Fortnum & Mason, stirs complicated emotions now. Some people feel it has become too expensive, glitzy, and celebrity-fied. Others object to its in-your-face owner, Mohammed al Fayed, who constantly feuds with the British establishment, has continually lost his long campaign to obtain a British passport, and is Egyptian. Harrods's royal warrant was summarily withdrawn after al Fayed charged that the car crash that killed his son, Dodi, and Princess Diana was an establishment plot orchestrated by Prince Philip and carried out by MI5.

not to know or care, even though she both knew and cared, very much. "Ha, ha, it doesn't matter," was the line the mother of the groom took, and she was sticking to it.

Highlights of the wedding for me also included a puzzling mini-seminar from a fellow guest on why "fascinators"—sprigs of leafy, floral or stemlike material worn in your hair instead of a hat—count as lower class, and why the duchess of Cornwall (who wore a soaring Philip Treacy fascinator at her wedding to Prince Charles) never was and never would be an aristocrat, despite her top-drawer pedigree and status as the potential queen of England.

Aristocrats are a funny group, but probably the most easily defined: they are the ones born into aristocratic families. They remain aristocrats even if they are currently in jail, in a mental home, on welfare, or living, Monty Python–style, in shoeboxes in the middle of the road. They can be very rich and extravagant; they can be rich and act as if they are poor; they can be genuinely poor, or at least cash poor.

They can be merely cheap. My friend Lesley described visiting an older woman who lives in an exquisite country house. The ground floor was virtually off limits, its priceless furniture covered with dust sheets. The hostess had retired to a small, cramped upper apartment, where she entertained guests in a dining room the size of a small pantry. The house was surrounded by wild countryside and spectacular views; the designated dining room had no windows. The hostess boasted to Lesley about her latest money-saving regime. "It's marvelous!" she said. "You just change the bed linens every two weeks, instead of once a week!"

Another friend is the niece of one of Scotland's grandest noblemen, a lord who inherited several castles and a huge art collection (according to the cruel rules of primogeniture, her father, the younger brother, inherited no castles and no art collection). "You'll be sitting gazing at the most beautiful Van Dycks," my friend said, "passing the Blue Nun." Her uncle dresses in polyester shirts and jackets; his wife's idea of formal wear is a lavender nightgown from Marks & Spencer.

Queen Elizabeth has kept the same drab hairstyle for sixty-five years; wears sensible shoes and a dowdy scarf while tramping in the woods with her flotilla of stumpy, rotund corgis; helps herself to breakfast cereal brought to the table in Tupperware containers; and is said to go around the palace saving bits of soap. Charles, on the other hand, leads so privileged an existence that he was genuinely stymied when confronted with a cup of tea *with the bag still inside* while meeting Ronald Reagan at the White House—a terrible faux pas, especially because Charles, raised on teapots filled with hot water and loose tea leaves and operated by servants, appeared to have no idea what one does with a tea bag. After gazing uncomprehendingly at his cup, he put it down on the table and never picked it up again.* To complicate matters even further, it is a mistake to think the royal family is as exclusive or as aristocratic as they come: The Spencers, who come from ancient English stock, are said to sneer at the Windsors as nouveau-powerful Teutonic arrivistes.†

Can you still tell a person's class by the way he or she speaks? And what's so terrible about toilet, anyway? The slithery *oy* in the middle, true—that is unattractive. But to some people, particularly from the older generations, it is a virtual profanity, the biggest class marker of all. "Loo!" "Lavatory!" they admonish their children (who then laugh at them). "I'd rather my children said fuck than toilet," one woman told the *Guardian* writer Jonathan Margolis when he was researching an

---

* Tea brings up all sorts of status anxiety. Special teas like Earl Grey and English Breakfast are considered snootier than regular tea like Tetley's and PG Tips, which construction workers drink all day long, sometimes dropping three teabags at a time in single cup of hot water (they really do take tea breaks, which are kind of comical to watch: a line of burly guys in paint-splattered undershirts sipping tea side by side along a wall). Among company, guests who want to show that they don't care what kind of tea they drink, since they are so secure, request "just builder's tea."

† That was part of the fascinating subtext in Earl Spencer's rudeness to the royal family during the eulogy at his sister's funeral. Spencer pointedly referred to the fact that the family had stripped Diana of her royal title, and all but accused them of being mummified anachronisms who sucked joy and emotion out of the lives they touched. Spencer actually feels that by virtue of its ancient status, his family is superior to the queen's family, even though they get to live in all those palaces and wear crowns, and he doesn't. Another weird layer to all of this: As Tina Brown points out in her book *The Diana Chronicles*, the queen is Earl Spencer's godmother.

article about the word "fuck."* The sixty-nine-year-old Earl of Onslow wrote in *The Times* of London that he found it "almost impossible to force the word 'toilet' between my lips." (He also found it impossible to spell it. In the original draft of his essay, he wrote "toilette.")

But it's too late now. Like the Red Death in the Poe story, it has penetrated the fortress. My children say it. They also say, "Pardon?" even though the word is considered common in some circles (using the word "common" is also considered common, unless you are afraid you might be, in which case you use it to mean anyone you believe is more common than you are). People from the best families really do bark, "What?" as if they were old bad-tempered people with ear trumpets. Me? I just say, "Sorry" when I can't hear, one of the many uses of this versatile word in a nation that, judging by how often its citizens apologize, is pretty much sorry all the time.†

Britain's class system is surely less rigid now than it was when, as a child in the 1950s, my friend Hilly was required to obtain formal permission from the authorities before turning over her fork to eat her

---

* In their paper "Swearing in modern British English: the case of *fuck* in the BNC," Anthony McEnry and Zhongua Xiao, from Lancaster University, examined, among other things, the correlation between "fuck" and social class. (BNC refers to the British National Corpus, which keeps track of how often words are used in the language.) McEnry and Xiao found that people belonging to social classes A and B, particularly those over sixty, actually use "fuck" more often than those in social class C1. "One might speculate that older people from AB use *fuck* more frequently to flaunt their superiority, while those from C1 show a considerably lower rate of *fuck* because they consciously or unconsciously pay special attention to their linguistic behavior so as to appear closer to what they perceive to be the norms of AB speech," they wrote.

† "There are many, many ways of saying sorry," A. A. Gill writes in *The Angry Island*, a book about England:

There is: sorry, I apologize; sorry, I don't apologize; sorry, you can take this as an apology, but we both know it isn't one; sorry, will you shut up; sorry, empathy; sorry for your loss; sorry, I can't hear you; sorry, I don't understand you; sorry, you don't understand me; sorry, excuse me; sorry, will you hurry up; sorry, I don't believe your story; sorry, I'm interrupting; sorry, this won't do; sorry, I've reached the end of my patience. . . .

I realized it had just gone too far when I gently fell against the wall of a crowded train that had suddenly lurched as it neared the station. "Sorry," I said to the wall. "Sorry," said a lady standing several feet away.

peas. (Anything else, including MIF, was NQOCD—"not quite our class, dear.") Society is more mobile; 43 percent of people between 18 and 30 now go to college; in the early 1960s, it was more like 6 percent. When Blair left office, the House of Lords was no longer a retirement home for men with inherited titles, but a retirement home for trade unionists, self-made millionaires, former prime ministers, and political apparatchiks of both sexes. BBC announcers no longer read the news wearing evening clothes, as they had done in the 1930s (on *radio*), and somewhere along the way they swapped their classic, cut-glass pronunciation for the more exotic regional accents of places like Manchester, Liverpool, and Edinburgh.

Class distinctions are fading. Well-brought-up people—even Blair himself, demonstrating his common touch—deliberately speak Estuary English, in which consonants are muddied and *t* sounds dropped ("battle" becomes *BA'ul*, for instance). A new class has emerged outside the old class structure: the chavs, who are gaudy and tacky but who revel in their gaudy tackiness (it is unclear where the word comes from, though one theory is that it derives from *chavi*, a Romany word for "child"). Rich or poor, chavs like flashy jewelry and expensive, over-the-top, logo-studded designer clothes. Male chavs wear shiny warm-up suits and baseball caps; female chavs leave their midriffs bare and pull their hair tightly back in buns or ponytails, a style known as a "council house facelift," "council house" being the term for public housing. They go on outrageous spending sprees, have drunken brawls, exhibit inappropriate public displays of affection, embark on screaming matches in bars, destroy property and—if they are famous chavs—often appear in the gossip magazines lurching drunkenly out of nightclubs or feuding with other celebrity chavs.

Posh Spice—who got her nickname because her father drove a Rolls-Royce when she was growing up, which of course did not make her posh at all—is the quintessential chavette. So what if she wore Roland Mouret's not-yet-on-the-market Moon dress when her husband, David Beckham, made his major league soccer debut? Nothing will ever erase the amazing sight of Posh and Becks looking down on their guests from custom-built thrones at their wedding reception, wearing matching deep purple outfits—hers a tight gown that hiked her fake breasts northward toward her chin, his a three-piece suit that would not have looked amiss on Keith Partridge, ca. 1978.

The most prominent Blair-era chav, perhaps, was Michael Carroll, a onetime garbage collector and chronic criminal who leaped to public attention when he won £9.7 million in the national lottery and, in what probably constituted a first in the annals of prize-collecting ceremonies, showed up to collect his check while wearing a police-issued ankle bracelet. Carroll reveled in his chavdom and was proud of his nickname, the Lotto Lout. He affixed a "King of Chavs" banner on the window of his new Mercedes, which he called the Loutmobile (it had a vanity license plate: L111 OUT). By day he spent his lottery winnings; by night he did things like drive through town and shoot out residents' windows with an air rifle; pull a chandelier from a hotel ceiling while swinging on it; and terrorize the guests at a cocktail party for local Christians.

Carroll also experienced the traditional dark side of celebrity chavdom in a society full of newspapers willing to pay for unseemly anecdotes about the famous: his girlfriend sold him out. She told the *Sun* that the drugs were getting to him, that he believed his garden was filled with "people disguised as trees," and that he spent his nights patrolling the house, looking for phantom intruders (and trees). "I'll tell him, 'Come back to bed, you stupid twit,'" she said.

The great thing about the chavs was that they existed outside the conventional class structure—kind of like Americans. In the United States you can remake yourself in a single generation; you still can't do that in Britain, no matter what people say. Your background will always linger as a tiny asterisk beside your name, something that elicits a subtly raised eyebrow. The politician Michael Portillo, for example, served in Thatcher's cabinet, had a degree from Cambridge, and spoke perfect middle- to upper-middle-class English, but his Labour antagonists in Parliament referred to him as "the Spaniard" and pronounced his name *port-EE-oh*, because his father was originally from Spain.

Two generations ago, my friend Hilly's grandfather was a ferociously smart but modestly born businessman who founded a department-store empire and was made the Earl of Woolton. As minister of food during World War II, he was responsible for food rationing and the Dig For

Victory home-gardening campaign. He inspired the Woolton pie: root vegetables, crust, and sauce thickened with rolled oats. He had a mansion; he had butlers; he was fantastic at his job; Churchill referred to him as "trade."

It was a different era, and Churchill was teasing, sort of. Just as people are teasing now, I suppose, when they call Lord Sainsbury, the proprietor of the Sainsbury supermarket empire, a "grocer." Just as the politician Alan Clark was teasing when, quoting another politician, he ridiculed his fellow Tory MP Michael Heseltine as a man who had to "buy his own furniture." Charles Moore, a former editor of the *Daily Telegraph*, pretended to tease, too, when he wrote, apropos of Toiletgate, that "there is something intrinsically funny about the work of an air hostess." He felt the "doors to manual" remark was pretty humorous, actually. "Let us suppose that someone did make this joke — why is it, objectively, so despicable?" Moore wrote. "Surely we often make jokes about the jobs that people's parents do."

Most Britons want to move up, but feel a swamp of conflicting emotions—envy, suspicion, and resentment included—toward people who already have. You can see this on popular British soap operas like *Eastenders* and *Coronation Street*. American soaps of the *All My Children* and *One Life to Live* variety feature fabulously glamorous business tycoons, brilliant heart surgeons, gorgeous trophy wives, and idle rich people living in gracious homes with perfect hair and five outfits an hour—just the sort of world that Americans covet. No American wants to watch a soap opera about dreary poor people.

But in British soaps, the characters wear warm-up suits, live in housing projects, are bald or overweight or alcoholic, and work as builders, bartenders, fish-and-chip-shop proprietors, and salesclerks, unless they are unemployed single mothers on the dole. The neighborhood aristocrats (if there are any) tend to exist for comic effect, or to provide plotlines about the vapidity, snobbery, and fakeness of the rich. Soap operas that unironically follow the lives of the upper classes "tend to get up people's noses," one television executive told me.

One of Channel Four's most popular reality shows in 2004 was *The F***ing Fulfords*, a fly-on-the-wall account of a family of piggish, bankrupt aristocrats living in a decaying stately home in Devon. Mr. Fulford, nicknamed "Fucker," because he swore so much, played to the cameras by making offensive remarks about foreigners and "queers," complaining that he owed "lots of bastards lots of money," and pledging not to unload his three-thousand-acre estate—which had been in the family since the Crusades—to "a man called Smith from Goldman Sachs," or to the "wankers" from English Heritage, the group that takes over big estates from old families who can't afford to run them. His children played cricket in the ballroom and scampered around with loaded shotguns; his wife demonstrated her aristocratic high spirits by angrily chucking their TV set into the lake.

Is it any wonder that, when removed from their natural habitats and placed among regular people, posh Britons try to downplay their origins? "Please don't use my name—I get a hard enough time as it is from everyone I work with," a well-off man from a landowning background pleaded when I interviewed him for an article about class. He sounded as if he were a crook posing as a regular guy, determined to conceal his links to the criminal underworld.

A banker named Charles whom I met once described what happened when he went on a touchy-feely training course of which he was pretty much the only fancily-accented man in a room of 150 or so (it was "a self-actualization thing" that his wife made him go on, he explained). In one of the exercises, about breaking down prejudices, the group leader instructed everyone to go stand next to the person with whom they would least like to have lunch. When the dust settled, Charles had been joined by a total of seven people—four men and three women.

"All of the men and one of the women said they didn't expect to like me because I was too posh," Charles told me (the other two women objected to him because he reminded them of their first husbands).

This reverse snobbery can be carried to ridiculous extremes. When Prince Charles went to boarding school and was met by a wall of bullying, any boy who tried to so much as talk to him was accused of sucking up and treated to a chorus of wet slurping noises. "Those that persisted [in trying to be his friend] were either too thick-skinned to care or were indeed flatterers on the make, and were thus—in either case—undesirable companions," Jonathan Dimbleby writes in his biography of Prince Charles. As a result, Charles had no friends.

In politics, too much class provokes mistrust. David Cameron, the Tory leader, did his best to overcome the suspicion provoked by his background of easy class privilege, only to be embarrassed when the tabloids dredged up compromising photographs of him and his friends wearing white tie at an exclusive Oxford dining society, and wielding guns and wearing plus-fours at an exclusive shooting weekend. Later, when the plummy-accented Conservative MP Boris Johnson (who had also been a member of Cameron's club, the Bullingdon), ran for mayor of London, the Labour Party deployed the class card that was supposed to have been retired long before. Hazel Blears, a cabinet minister, called him a "fogeyish, bigoted and upper-class twit;" another Labour operative branded him a "tufty toff from Eton."

But, unless you are a diehard Labour politician from the old coal-mine-supporting left wing of the party, too working class is too much in the other direction. Margaret Thatcher took voice lessons as a way to smooth over her humble roots as a grocer's daughter from the sticks. But once she let her guard down. Irritated to distraction by Labour's badgering during a raucous parliamentary debate, she lost her cool and shouted that her opponents were "frit"—regional dialect for "frightened." It was an electric moment, her real self emerging the way Eliza Doolittle's does at Ascot in *My Fair Lady*, and she never lived it down. "Frit! Frit!" the Labour backbenchers used to yell at her, whenever they got the chance. MPs still occasionally use it, for old times' sake.

It's all very confusing, but I'm learning, slowly. I understand why, in a play of the Roald Dahl novella *Fantastic Mr. Fox* at my daughters' school, the children who played Mssrs. Boggis, Bean, and Bunce—the nasty, drunken farmers trying to starve and murder the nice, clever animals—affected rough working-class accents, in contrast to the upscale accents of the other actors. I understand why, when my husband displays to airline check-in clerks the faux-impressive gift I bought for him as a joke at the House of Lords gift shop—a maroon passport cover with "House of Lords" stamped on the front—he often gets upgraded to business class.

I also understand, I think, why the disembodied voice of the "speaking clock," which tells you the exact time when you call it on the telephone, uses perfect cut-glass English. And I understand why the script was changed in a little prerecorded public-service announcement played in movie theaters to warn patrons not to buy pirated videos. The narrator in the original version said that the quality of pirated videos was bad and that the picture might be ruined by "the one person who needs the toilet." After several months—and, presumably, many complaints—it was altered to, "the one person who needs the loo."

But I am too foreign and my country too young to understand properly all the nuances of the British class system. I can't, for example, sort out the layers of meaning in Mary Killen's observation that people from good backgrounds "say 'toilet' as a joke, because they know that they are above the issue." That is confusing to me—people who say what they don't mean, don't mean what they say, and use "toilet" satirically.

Once at a dinner filled with scary London intellectuals, playwrights, and novelists, I boldly pronounced the word "cretin" with a long *e*, as *CREE-tan*. An hour or so later another guest used the word with a soft *e*: *CREH-tin*. When I asked why no one had told me about the different English pronunciation, one guest said: "We thought you were being ironic."

That was a relief, unless he meant it ironically.

SEVEN

LAWMAKERS FROM ANOTHER PLANET

We are peers of highest station,
Paragons of legislation,
Pillars of the British nation!
    —W. S. Gilbert, *Iolanthe* (1882)

Until the end of the twentieth century, the best way to see an unusually large collection of aristocrats gathered together in one place was to go to the House of Lords. The place was full of legislators who had gotten there simply by virtue of birth, and it showed. The lords tended to bring whatever stray thoughts they had to the formal setting of the workplace. There was the time, for example, when they discussed the growing scourge of public spitting by celebrity sports figures. There was the time they considered the age of consent for homosexuals by swapping dismaying personal stories of traumatic incidents at boarding school. There was the time they conducted a serious debate about UFOs—do they exist, when are they coming, and are we prepared?

But one of the oddest, and certainly the most poignant, debates in the House of Lords in modern times was one that spoke to the institution's very nature—and in a way, the nature of Britain itself. The issue at hand, part of Blair's new modernization program, was a plan to strip the house's hereditary peers—the lords who inherit their titles from their fathers*—of the right to sit and vote in Parliament, a right they had enjoyed in one form or another for nearly 800 years.

The hereditaries' continued presence was so blatantly unfair that governments had been trying to evict them for more than 150 years; Walter Bagehot made his famous remark that "the cure for admiring the House of Lords is to go and look at it" all the way back in the nineteenth century. But they had never succeeded. The difference this time was that Blair finally had the votes and the political will to get rid of the hereditaries for good. The only questions were how quickly it would happen and how quietly they would go. One legislator, Earl Ferrers, thirteenth in a line of earls stretching back to 1711, said he felt like Marie Antoinette standing before the guillotine. "Naturally, one feels that it would be desirable if the guillotine were not lowered."

Reforming the Lords was part of Blair's wider agenda of constitutional overhaul.† For a prime minister wanting to pull the country from the murky marshes of the past into the fresh waters of the twenty-first century, the Lords was an obvious place to start. It was one of the few mostly hereditary legislative chambers left in the world. Many of its members were the descendants of noblemen who had been granted titles and riches by various monarchs over the centuries in exchange for such loyal acts as massacring the king's enemies and then stealing their property. "Medieval lumber," the foreign secretary, Robin Cook, called them.

For most of its history, the Lords was more powerful than the House of Commons, the lower house in Britain's two-house legislature (its members get their seats the common way, through elections). But its authority had been seeping out over time, like air from a balloon. The Parliament Act of 1911 stripped the Lords of the right to reject leg-

---

* In a few aristocratic families, women are allowed to inherit peerages.

† "Constitution" is an odd concept in Britain, in that the country doesn't have one, exactly, or at least not a written one; it has an accrual of principles, rules, and precedents. This makes what is in the constitution hard to explain to the average layperson, particularly because it is "a tangled mess," according to Peter Facey, codirector of Charter88, a political reform group.

islation, leaving it with the ability only to amend and delay bills. Even more insulting, its existence as a purely hereditary body ended forever with the Life Peerages Act of 1958, which introduced another kind of lord—one appointed by the prime minister of the day, with a title that would die when the peer did—to serve alongside the hereditaries. That made the house a hybrid: part hereditary, part appointed.*

In 1998, the House of Lords had 500 life peers (the new kind) and 750 hereditary peers (the old kind). The government was proposing to kick out the 750 and leave the other ones behind. It was not democracy at its finest, but it seemed an obvious first step, even to someone like me who had been exposed to such less-than-impressive manifestations of the nonhereditary principle as the Nassau County Legislature.

"Once you start looking at the second chamber and saying, 'The majority of these people are here because of their great-great-great grandfathers, and this is absurd, then everybody sees that the emperor has no clothes,'" Rodney Barker, a constitutional expert at the London School of Economics, told me.

The Lords sits next to the Commons in the Palace of Westminster, a hulking neo-Gothic building designed by Charles Barry and Augustus Pugin that presides in elaborate splendor over the banks of the river Thames, near Big Ben, Westminster Abbey and the Westminster Bridge. Most of the time nothing important enough happens there to warrant coverage by an American newspaper, but in October 1998, I walked over—my office is about ten minutes away—to sit in on the Lords' debate. Along with members of the British press, who on the whole are generally not interested in what the chamber is doing either, I folded myself into a severe wooden seat in an austere, dusty balcony above the chamber.

Once you made it past the metal detectors at the door and secured your official visitor's pass, it was another world in there. The Lords was full of byzantine rules, archaic customs, superfluous pageantry

---

* To make it more confusing, some of the life peers were known as "working" peers, meaning they were expected to go to the chamber and work. The implication, I guess, was that the rest were "nonworking."

THE ANGLO FILES · 129

and doddering legislators who for reasons of aristocratic convention appeared to have no need for first names.* In debates, even the most bad-tempered lord referred to his political opponents as "noble lords" and "noble ladies." The chamber's officers dressed like guests at an Elizabethan-themed costume party.

One of the main ones went by the title Black Rod; he had a deputy, the Yeoman Usher of the Black Rod. Another official was called Garter King of Arms, and when I met him once—he was wearing silk tights and tight black breeches, patent leather footwear that resembled Catherine Deneuve's chic Roger Vivier pumps in the movie *Belle de Jour*, and a red tailcoat festooned with Teutonic-style filigree—it became clear that he was to be addressed as "Garter," the same way that you would call a governor "Governor." Not even "Mr. Garter." Just "Garter." Also, he was not a king, and he had no weapons. (When I made these points to a British friend, he said: "Don't you know that his name is ironic?")†

The Lords had no retirement age, only death, so some members were over ninety. Few had offices, or even telephones. Outsiders who wanted to leave messages were encouraged to use that quaint device, the postal service. The costumed clerks at the front desk scraped and twittered obsequiously in the presence of the legislators, murmuring "My Lord" and "My Lady" as much as was physically possible in the course of any one sentence. The lord chancellor, Britain's most important legal official, a cross between the U.S. attorney general and the chief justice of the United States, wore an outfit similar to Garter's, except with a kind of undertaker's jacket instead of the filigreed one, and a big, stiff wig. He looked like a character from the trial scene in

---

* Peers by tradition use only their titles when referring to themselves, as in documents, for instance. Earl Ferrers (whose actual name is Robert Washington Shirley) would, for instance, just write "Ferrers," as if that were enough.

† The system is full of people with humorous ceremonial titles having to do with what service their holders once performed in court. There is someone known as Gold Stick-in-Waiting, for instance, who "guards" the queen at ceremonial occasions. Camilla's former husband, Andrew Parker Bowles, once served as Gold Stick's deputy, Silver Stick-in-Waiting, which led to a great many ribald jokes about sticks (and waiting) when he was still married to Camilla and Camilla was sleeping with Prince Charles.

Alice's Adventures in Wonderland, in which they suppress the guinea pigs by stuffing them into sacks and sitting on them.

In the boarding-school parlance of the chamber, the appointed peers were known as day boys, and the hereditary peers, for some obscure reason, were called binkies. A motley collection of dukes, earls, viscounts, barons, and marquesses who had always understandably considered themselves part of the furniture and fabric of the place, the hereditaries were, to put it mildly, unrepresentative of the population at large. Forty-five percent—more than three hundred of them—had gone to Eton. Less than 10 percent were members of the Labour Party. All but a handful were men. They had diverse jobs—one ran a computer consultancy, another a gas station—but a full 60 percent claimed backgrounds in landowning or farming.*

An attractive element of the job was that you didn't have to do it; you could remain at home on the farm, or at the gas station, and never go to Parliament at all. If you did choose to try your hand at legislating (gaining in the process a daily stipend, travel and housing allowances, and free parking in the crowded heart of London) you could then sit there unobtrusively—inert, silent, or asleep. Because they had not had to pass any kind of test, not even a sanity test, to get in, some lords were not possessed of a surfeit of credentials.

Lord Monteagle of Brandon, for example, took his seat in 1947 and made his maiden speech *forty-five years later,* in a debate about water shortages and droughts. He explained that he had wanted to wait until he had some experience with the subject at hand, which on this occasion he did: a pipe had once burst on his estate, wasting ten thousand gallons of water and causing, if not a general, then at least a personal shortage of water. "I have frequently been asked, 'When are you going to make your maiden speech? Surely you must be an expert on something,'" he explained. "I hasten to assure your Lordships that I am not an expert on anything."

---

* "Farmers" in this context usually means people who own vast estates and employ teams of people to do the actual farming—sowing, reaping, milking the cows, etc.

The Lords were good at amending legislation and calling the government to account—no small thing—but that was the limit of their influence. As a kind of counterweight to their lack of power, they paid vigorous attention to topics that were not necessarily at the forefront of anyone else's political agenda. They had some free time; they discussed what they liked. Subjects for debate in recent times had included the regulation of equine dentists; the chewing-gum problem ("It is far better to see a herd of cattle chewing the cud," intoned the elderly Viscount Long, in his first remark on any subject in the chamber for fifteen years, "than to see a flock of tourists and members of the British public not only chewing gum, but spitting it out or putting it around tables in restaurants"); and the causal relationship between cramped airline seats and violence in the skies.

"Perhaps I may declare an interest," the stately, generous-framed peer Baroness Trumpington announced during that debate. "I am a particularly large person."

Then there were the UFOs, the enduring passion of the eighth Earl of Clancarty (full name: William Francis Brinsley Le Poer Trench). He died in 1995, aged eighty-three, but is still remembered for his belief that humans are descended from aliens who either crawled from ancient civilizations in the earth's core or flew down to the planet in spaceships sixty-five thousand years ago.

Clancarty wrote numerous books, including *The Sky People* and *Operation Earth*, was a founder of *Flying Saucer Review* magazine, and in his spare moments could often be found in the Lords chamber, legislating. In 1979, he introduced a measure meant to force the government to conduct an official study on UFOs—a subject whose truth, he believed, had been kept hushed up by the authorities for years.

He was not the only one with an *X-Files* view of the matter, as became clear in the ensuing debate.

"Quite recently, three United States balloonists who crossed the Atlantic were followed by UFOs, but were ordered by the United States government not to discuss them," noted the Earl of Kimberley. Kimberley said he was annoyed that officials in the UK "appear reluctant to investigate . . . alleged messages from outer space," because "they say that this is the responsibility of the BBC and the Post Office."

The debate took place while Britain appeared to be falling apart. It was the middle of the Winter of Discontent, when half the country's industries were on strike, garbage was piling up in the streets, and corpses were going unburied, due to the gravediggers' having briefly joined the walkout. But the Lords were inside their little Westminster bubble debating UFOs.

"One happy thing about UFOs is that they have nothing to do with party politics!" Lord Gladwyn noted. "Another is that they take one's mind off the perfectly frightful everyday events!"

The debate was treated as a huge joke in the world at large, but the Lords took it seriously, marshaling a formidable array of scientific, philosophical, and religious arguments.

Addressing a colleague's question about how UFOs could break the sound barrier without making any noise, for example, Lord Rankeillour explained it was because they "produce a near-vacuum envelope around themselves which would allow them virtually unlimited speed." (He added that as he was not a scientist, "I cannot enlarge upon this explanation.")

If sometimes the debate had the tenor of a late-night conversation in a college dormitory during that precious window of time after the pot has been smoked but before the pizza has arrived—well, that was the Lords' prerogative. Several peers, for example, made the very excellent point that if you saw something in the sky and could not identify it, it was by definition unidentified, ergo a UFO.

"I do not know what it implies to say that you do not believe in an unidentified flying object," said the Earl of Cork and Orrery, crossly. "You do not believe in the object? You do not believe in its flying? You do not believe it is unidentified?"

A couple of them did the math and concluded that it would take so long for a spaceship to get to Earth from even the nearest star—nine hundred thousand years, by one lord's calculation, if it proceeded at the same rate as the spaceships in your average Apollo mission—that no creature could survive such a journey. Also, said Lord Gladwyn, if it was true that aliens keep coming to Earth, why was it that they seemed "content simply to hover about our atmosphere" rather than landing and making themselves known?

One of the surprising things to emerge was that Clancarty was hardly the only noble believer in alternative beings.

One peer declared that he believed in the Loch Ness monster. Lord Davies of Leek said: "We know that poltergeists exist." The Earl of Halsbury shared an interesting theory of his own devising: "I have always thought that just as mother, when baking bread, leaves a little of the dough over in order that the children may make funny little men with raisins for tummy buttons and put them into ovens and bake them alongside the bread or the cake for the day," he said, "so possibly on the day of creation a little of the Divine creative power was left in reserve for the lesser cherubim and seraphim to use and they were allowed to make funny little objects like the Abominable Snowman." The earl added that he had seen many mysterious creatures, including, when he was six, an angel.

Lord Gainford said he had seen a UFO while attending a New Year's Eve party in Scotland. He described it as a "bright white ball with a touch of red followed by a white cone." Some children saw it, too, he added, trying to bolster his argument, and they "had been drinking soft drinks."

"My Lords, of course they exist," said Lord Rankeillour. "Quite apart from the fact that the government have not admitted to the existence of UFOs, these machines are potentially dangerous. They give off blinding light, crippling rays and sometimes beams that immobilise humans; they start forest fires, eradicate crops and cause great distress to animals."

But some lords were skeptical.

"Where are these alien space craft supposed to be hiding?" Lord Strabolgi said, on behalf of the government.

"All I have seen are hazy, fudgy photographs," groused Lord Trefgarne.

The bill was defeated—"there is nothing to convince the Government that there has ever been a single visit by an alien space craft," concluded Lord Strabolgi—but it provided a happy diversion for a beaten-down nation.

• • •

Beyond the loopiness and the occasional excursion into the metaphysi-
cal, there was something magnificent about the hereditary peers. They
were beholden only to history, their ancestors, and their principles.
They felt they had a patriotic duty to look after Britain in a benign
manner from on high, as would the board of trustees of some beloved
national institution. They believed they could bring life experience and
gravitas to the job without tediously pandering to the voters.

"Because we don't have any constituents and you can't get sacked,
you are much freer to follow your own ideas," Lord Raglan told me.*

The hereditary peers were also the political embodiment of Britain's historical soul, a link to tradition and the long-ago past in a country
that had always revered those things. Their names evoked centuries
of history. Here was Earl Grey, from the tea family. Earl Sandwich,
from the sandwich family. The Marquess of Queensberry, of the box-
ing rules. Viscount Montgomery of Alamein, son of Field Marshal Bernard Montgomery, the World War II hero. The Earl of Erroll, chief of
the Hay clan in Scotland, son of a person named Sir Iain Moncreiffe
of That Ilk (what ilk would that be, you might ask); and, through his
mother, twenty-fourth in a line of noble Errolls stretching right back to
1453.

Here was Baron Strathclyde, a (relatively) young, wily and well-fed
lord who would go on to be leader of the Conservatives in the chamber, whose full name was Thomas Galloway Dunlop du Roy de Blicquy
Galbraith. And Viscount Massereene and Ferrard: John David Clotwor-
thy Whyte-Melville Foster Skeffington. And the twenty-second Earl of
Shrewsbury, known at home as Charles Henry John Benedict Crofton
Chetwynd Chetwynd-Talbot.

Secure in their places in the world, the Lords had a flair for the
kind of amusing understatement and self-deprecation at which the
British excel. The Earl of Romney, frail in body but robust in spirit,
boasted that he thriftily delayed buying a datebook until the end of
January each year, in case he died during the cold weather, and never

* Raglan was late for his own maiden speech, in 1965. "My lords, I am sorry that I have
only just arrived," he began. "I have had a series of misfortunes with my motorcar. I am
covered in oil and quite flustered."

uttered a word in twenty-five years of faithful attendance.* Describing why he was qualified to contribute to a debate on marriage, Lord Lucas of Crudwell and Dingwall once remarked that having had three wives "does not make me an expert, but it does make me an addict."

If Parliament—the House of Commons and the House of Lords together —passed Blair's proposal to eliminate the hereditaries, all these men would be sent back home. They would retain their titles, but not their right to participate in the legislature.

The day of the debate came—October 14, 1998. The chamber is often nearly empty, but it was stuffed to the brim that day. Some of the less old and less creaky members had to sit on the floor and were unfamiliar with the geography of the place. "The essential services, both outside and inside the House, were clearly strained, even to the extent that some noble Lords were unaware of their location," Lord Tanlaw said, referring to the bathrooms.†

But they came anyway, the ancient, the deaf, the retired government ministers, the gainfully employed professionals, the armchair philosophers, the landowning aristocrats, the rulers of small rural fiefs. The bishops, who automatically get to be lords, sat magisterially in their flowing black-and-white robes in a corner of the Pugin-designed room, no ornate feature of which had been omitted due to concerns it might be over the top. Looking like an extra in an amateur drama production, the lord chancellor, his face framed by his long, tightly curled wig, perched on the Woolsack, a spectacularly uncomfortable armless and backless red banquette traditionally stuffed with Commonwealth wool

---

* "Yes, that's right. The bright ones are supposed to speak, and the others are supposed to support them. That's how it works here," Romney says in Molly Dineen's documentary on the last days of the hereditaries, *The Lord's Tale.*

† A jolly-looking, portly fellow, Tanlaw was an enthusiastic amateur horologist known for his tendency to argue—even during debates on other subjects—that the UK should move its clocks forward by an hour, so that evenings would be lighter and there would be fewer gloom-related accidents.

signifying, as these things so often do, the reach and magnificence of the British Empire.

There were new arrivals, like Lord Phillips of Sudbury, who had inherited his seat just weeks earlier, following the death of his father. There were old-timers, like the Earl of Longford, celebrating fifty-three years of unpredictable, baffling, and occasionally infuriating legislative behavior. Bald except for a mad-scientist tuft of fluffy white hair on each side of his head, his face covered in liver spots, Longford was well known for his support of unpopular causes, like a pardon for Myra Hindley, the child-killing "Moors Murderer."

"Lord Longford is 92," Andrew Rawnsley wrote in the *Observer*, "but he acts like a man twice his age."

Baroness Jay of Paddington, the leader of the Lords, who had been appointed a life peer in 1992 (her affair with Carl Bernstein decades earlier had been immortalized in the novel *Heartburn* by Bernstein's cheated-on wife, Nora Ephron), opened the proceedings, saying the time had come to bid the hereditaries thank-you and good-bye.* She was not a popular figure among the old guard, having given a snippy interview to the newspapers that was indignantly circulated among her fellow lords. "Nobody is saying to them: 'We will take away your stately homes, your hunting rights, your Labradors, your gin and tonics,'" she was quoted as saying.

The debate raged for two days. The hereditaries spoke by the dozens. They were impassioned and moving, erudite and sharp, oblique and loopy, and often orbiting so far into the stratosphere of digression that the thread of their logic seemed in grave danger of unraveling. They made comments in French and Latin. They recalled conversations with Clement Attlee, Harold Wilson, and Field Marshal Lord Montgomery. They alluded to the sans-culottes, the Whigs, the Bol-

---

* Jay is tall and lovely, with soft blond hair and a patrician nose. In *Heartburn*, Ephron describes her fictional counterpart, Thelma Rice, as a "clever giant" who had "a nose as long as a thumb and walked like a penguin." There was some thought that Jay was the beneficiary of hereditary favoritism, too, in a way: her father, James Callaghan, was a former prime minister and, like his daughter, a life peer.

sheviks, the Bundesrat, and the Canadian parliament. They reminisced about how they had gone to Eton together. They quoted Yeats, Livy, and Burke; Pliny, Kipling, and Shakespeare; Gladstone, Gibbon, and Tennyson; the Roman general Fabius Cunctator; and Monty Python.

They talked of the past. "I am proud of my family, which has been represented here in various guises since the seventeenth century, and of my kinsmen and families like them, who have made a material and beneficial contribution to the country," said Baron Inglewood, a friendly-looking peer with a mop of dark hair piled on top of a section of lighter hair, like a bird's. "In Yeats's words, 'they are no petty people.'"

They invoked Runnymede, where King John signed the Magna Carta in 1215. One peer discussed sheep farming in Shetland; another mentioned *Microcosmographia Academica*, a pamphlet from 1908 he read as a student. As evidence that the general public opposed their removal from Parliament, several described conversations they had had with sympathetic taxi drivers on their way in.

The hereditaries said their feelings were hurt by criticism from people who "repeat stereotypes and make fun of us," Baron Hastings, twenty-second in a baronial line extending back to 1290, told me. The Earl of Haddington said they were not "a bunch of daisies." Baroness Strange, known for her charming habit of bringing armfuls of fresh flowers into the Lords from her house in Scotland, Megginch Castle, which is famous for its unusual collection of stuffed nineteenth-century British birds, said they were not "a collection of outmoded old buffers in red robes leaping aimlessly." Viscount Torrington said they were not "a gang of reactionary fox-hunting dukes."

"A number of Americans have been disappointed when I have told them that I cannot disembowel peasants who disagree with me," said Baron Addington, who had inherited his title when he was twenty-two, becoming the youngest serving peer in the Lords.

Many said they recognized the inevitability of change. "It would be difficult to advance in the social and cultural context of the end of the twentieth century any really convincing arguments for the survival, strictly in the legislative sense, of the hereditary principle," said Baron

Chalfont—not that he favored changing, he hastily added, "1,000 years of history in the course of a single parliamentary session."

"The simple truth is that the government have not got a clue what to do," Baron Cockfield said, posing the question on everyone's mind: What would a hereditaryless chamber look like? "They have bright ideas, but when it comes to doing anything about them, what happens?"

The hereditaries talked about the ineffable quality of the Lords, its gentle bonhomie, its exaggerated but sincere courtesies, the unusual nature and high quality of its rhetoric, the independence and unexpectedly broad experience of its members.

"I do not claim to be working class," said Earl Attlee, the grandson of the onetime prime minister Clement Attlee. "How can I, as I am public school educated? I do not like blowing my own trumpet, even quietly, but what I can claim is that I can operate a variety of machine tools. I am able to weld by gas, electric arc or metal inert gas."

They talked about how much they would miss the Lords, since in addition to its legislative functions, it had always served as a club of the highest exclusivity, a place to while away the time in London, particularly for those from out of town. They praised its ability to restrain government excess; indeed, as Blair was becoming more powerful, the Lords was taking on a welcome role as a challenger to and stern critic of his presidential style of governing. It had used the same tactic in the past. "I remind noble Lords that when my noble friend Lady Thatcher was prime minister, with a large majority in the House of Commons, it was this house . . . which kept her in check," said Baroness Flather, the first woman of Indian descent to be made a peer, whose saris made a colorful change from the grays and pinstripes of the chamber.

To illustrate their point that the government's antihereditary legislation was poorly conceived, in that it contained no follow-up plan, they wandered off on extended metaphorical tangents involving trains, boats, and buses.

"I got into a bus," said Earl Ferrers:

Your lordships may think this is surprising, but I did. Someone said to me, "Robin"—for that happens to be my name—"Do tell me what you are doing." The person used to be my commanding officer when I did my national service. At that time he was a colonel and I was terrified of him. I said, "I am moving my house in the country and I am moving my flat in London within six weeks of each other." He made a penetrating observation. "My dear man, have you forgotten the elementary principle, always keep one foot on the ground at any one time?" I recommend that to the government.

Baroness Kennedy of the Shaws, a peppery human-rights lawyer with a Scottish burr who had been appointed a life peer by Blair, set off cries of righteous indignation when she said that she would not hire a "hereditary plumber" and that she suspected "a good many people up and down the country share that view."

"No!" shouted a number of hereditaries, who did not share that view.

"What's wrong with inheritance?" asked Baron Rowallan, crossly. "Why does virtually everyone in the world try to have children if not to let them inherit? Even the Bible said the meek were to inherit the earth." ("That is a daft argument," said Baron Ponsonby of Shulbrede, whose name was pronounced *PUN-sonby*.)

Lord Buchan rebuffed Lady Kennedy with a discussion of his own plumbing arrangements.

"For many years we dealt with an excellent firm of plumbers, comprising a grandfather, a son and—wait for it—a daughter. All were excellent plumbers and they described themselves as 'family plumbers.' The word 'family' is, of course, a euphemism for 'hereditary'—and hereditary plumbers they were, and proud of it."

The debate reflected the Lords at its best and at its worst. It was a tour de force of elegant and crazy rhetoric, an elegiac, bittersweet swan song. They had such a stately and roundabout way of putting things, such a different perspective, such a memory of and respect for the past. They had such a sense of humor.

"I am reminded also that when Alec Douglas-Home became Prime Minister in 1963, he was sneered at by Harold Wilson as being the 14th Earl of Home," Baron Marlesford said (Home is prounced *Hume*). "That was repeated endlessly by the media until at length, Sir Alec, with characteristic mildness, commented, 'Come to think of it, I suppose that Harold Wilson is the 14th Mr. Wilson.'"

They spoke for two straight days and well into the night, never losing their rhetorical steam, and it was something to see. When I left the chamber to go back to the office and write my story, they were still going strong.

At the last minute, the Conservative Party in the Lords—most of whose members opposed the measure, since so many of the hereditaries were Conservatives—fashioned a backroom deal. In return for the party's support of the bill, ninety-two hereditaries would be allowed to stay behind after their colleagues had left.

There was never any doubt. The bill passed. The hereditaries would have to go.

But a host of other issues had to be resolved first, such as how to pick the lucky survivors. The Lords did something they had never done before: they held an election. It was a strange one. The electorate consisted of just 750 people, the hereditary lords who had been kicked out—truly an electorate of peers.

Almost 200 ran. They didn't campaign as such. So unattractive, self-promotion. "I do not want to proselytize my candidature," said one candidate, Lord Morris. Instead, they circulated written statements of purpose that suggested a general inexperience in the writing of job applications.

They had just seventy-five words, so they had to say it fast. Lord Pender said it fastest: "DUTY" was his statement.

Baron Seaford described himself as "a small and happy bison farmer with aspirations above his station," before lapsing into Latin. The Earl of Clanwilliam mentioned his interest in Chinese medicine. Baron Geddes unveiled an advertising-style slogan: "Brains; Breadth; Brevity."

Lord Harding of Petherton said he had always been interested in politics.

The Earl of Glasgow modestly said that he had been able to attend the Lords only about three days a month but expected to become more available in the future.

Having retired after twenty-five years as private secretary to Princess Margaret, Lord Napier and Ettrick—a descendant of the man who invented logarithms and popularized the use of the decimal point in the seventeenth century—said that he suddenly had space free on his calendar, too.

The Earl of Denbigh and Desmond noted that he was a member of the All-Party Motorcycling Group, while Baron Colwyn pointed to his experience as chairman of the Refreshment Subcommittee, as well as his civilian responsibilities as bandleader and dentist.

And Viscount Monckton of Benchley pledged that, if elected, he would campaign against animal cruelty, especially "fishing with rods," and would address the perennial problem of cats who "torture mice and small birds."

When the votes were counted, Lady Strange, Lord Colwyn, Lord Ferrers, and the Earl of Sandwich* were among those who won the right to get their seats back. The rest prepared to shuffle away for the last time in November. Winter was drawing in and the days were growing shorter. There was a restiveness in the chamber. One day, a fellow named Lord Burford (real name: Charles Francis Topham de Vere Beauclerk) bizarrely leaped onto the Woolsack, shouting, "Before us lies the wasteland: no queen, no sovereignty, no freedom!" Burford, a hotheaded thirty-four-year-old whose thick beard and mustache gave him a wolfish look, had not yet inherited his seat from his father, the fourteenth Duke of St. Albans, whose inconvenient extant status meant that he, Burford, had never spoken in the House of Lords before.

He never would again; quelled and bustled off by Black Rod, who

---

* Sandwich was elected to remain, but for a time he and his son and heir, Lord Montagu, went into the food business, producing expensive packaged sandwiches for sale in supermarkets. I did a story about it once. It was interesting to see the earl trying to adapt to the changing world. "I should think I was a bit hesitant to begin with, as I have no personal experience of going into business," Lord Sandwich told me at the time. "There's no real security in simply being from an old family anymore." As we were talking, in an ornate room in the House of Lords, Lord Montagu pointed to a grand painting of a noblewoman behind him—Queen Alexandra, I think. "She was my grandfather's godmother!" he said.

for once had to leap into unscripted action, Burford was then banned for life from the Palace of Westminster.*

The end itself—the final departure of the hereditaries—passed with little fanfare and no ceremony. There were some eulogies, not always very sympathetic ones. "What may have been appropriate 800 or even 200 years ago may not be appropriate now," Lady Jay said. "I do sincerely believe most have the grace and realism to accept this change is necessary."

The Tory hereditaries praised their ancestors and their legislature. "This House has inflicted no evil in its history, and much good has been done," Lord Strathclyde said solemnly. "Many people—the weak, the unheard, the politically unfashionable—have come to this place."

The evicted peers would go on to have varied careers, if they were young enough to start over. Ten actually returned to the Lords as life peers, appointed by the government. The Earl of Strafford took a job as a river keeper on his own estate. Viscount Exmouth said he planned to set up a House of Lords Web site and sell "items that evoke the aristocratic lifestyle."

Earl Grey said he was putting out his own line of men's leisure wear, which would include drawstring pants.

"I may not be six foot tall or have model looks," he said modestly, "but I think I have an idea what other people would wear."

Some of the outgoing lords were stoic; others bittersweet.

Caught by the BBC as he packed up his things to leave, Lord Rowallan said he was worried about the effect the loss of their seats would have on some of his friends. "I know that some of them just live for this place," he said. "I am concerned that some of them will just vegetate very quickly or get senile."

---

* Burford's family came by their title through iffy means: his ancestor the first Duke of St. Albans was the illegitimate son of Charles II and his mistress Nell Gwynn. One of Burford's preoccupations is the belief that another ancestor, Edward de Vere, the seventeenth Earl of Oxford, wrote the plays that are supposed to have been written by Shakespeare.

"I am 73, so it is all downhill from here," said Lord Stanley of Alder-ley. "I will never do anything like this again."

Then they were gone.

POSTSCRIPT

That should have been the end. But the government had not thought it through properly. Its blueprint for the reconstituted, post-hereditary chamber was vague, or, as you might say, nonexistent. Would its mem-bers now be elected? Appointed? Chosen by aliens crawling from the earth's core? Who knew?

And so the chamber lurched on, having swapped an undemocratic hereditary system for an undemocratic appointed one.

Oddly for an unelected chamber, the Lords suddenly started having frequent elections. In 2006, it elected its first official Speaker, a real job with a salary of £140,000 a year, to take over the role the lord chancellor had once held. (Though he had to give up a lot of his responsibilities, the lord chancellor also won the right to change his pants, trading his breeches-and-slippers combo for trousers and normal shoes.)

Baroness Hayman got the Speaker's job, beating off such rivals as Lord Redesdale, who had pledged that, if elected, he would "do as little as possible in the chamber, apart from sitting on the Woolsack."

There were also regular minielections to fill the seats of the heredi-taries who had been allowed to stay but who then died, which hap-pened fairly often, on account of their age.*

---

* The first to "snuff it," in the words of one lord, was the Viscount of Oxfuird, who died in 2003.

"'Prior to 1999, Lord Oxfuird would have been replaced by his boy," Lord Strathclyde told me, Oxfuird's boy being his thirty-two-year-old heir, "but as that no longer happens, we have . . . an election."

Lord Massereene, still rueful about the time "when one was chucked out," as he described the hereditaries' eviction from Parliament, was one of the 81 candidates.

"Quite obviously, I haven't got a hope of getting elected, or of getting any votes at all," he said.

Meanwhile, Lord Montgomery of Alamein, who explained that he had reluctantly

Meanwhile, the slimmed-down chamber continued to harass and annoy the government, unexpectedly making trouble by calling Blair to account on proposals that threatened to encroach on Britons' civil liberties, like one to force citizens to carry mandatory ID cards.

Debates still occasionally veered off into madness, which was, in its way, kind of comforting.

In 2004, for example, the Lords discussed a proposal to ban gay marriage.

Lord Tebbit wondered aloud what would happen if two people got married and one had a sex-change operation. Or how about if one partner "purports to be the husband and then gives birth?"

Lord Lucas helpfully pointed out that a person "who has his testicles shot off is not then compelled to become unmarried."

Earl Ferrers was worried about the possible ramifications for the principle of primogeniture, the principle upon which his entire family history was built. He used an earl with two children, a son and a daughter, as his generic example.

"Let us suppose that the daughter is older and that she has a sex change and becomes a man," he began.

"Does she then become Viscount Chump instead of her younger brother, who, up till now, was Viscount Chump? If she does become Viscount Chump, does she inherit the title of earl instead of the proper Viscount Chump, and all the cash?"

No one could answer that one, either.

---

run, only on the urging "of one or two very kind friends," failed to win the seat, either (although he would be elected later, after Baroness Strange died).

The winner was Viscount Ullswater, who also once worked as Princess Margaret's secretary. "It is a great honour to have been chosen by so many of my peers," he said.

EIGHT

FALSE MODESTY

A piece of good fortune, nothing more.
—Sir Roger Bannister, on his 1954 four-minute mile (2004)

As I have learned during a number of humiliating occasional afternoons of not-quite-soft ball in the park, British schools like to encourage the parents to participate in parent-on-parent sporting contests, for purposes of comic relief. The iconic photograph that brought to public attention one of the crueler manifestations of this tradition—the mothers' race on field day—showed a young, barefoot Princess Diana in the prime of her youthful exuberance. Wearing a full skirt and virginal high-necked blouse (she was still Shy Di, not Versace Di or Joan of Arc Di, back then) she is captured at the moment of flush-faced victory as she crosses the finish line, those long elegant arms outstretched like the wings of a self-regarding waterbird making a showstopping landing in the village pond. Gasping behind her, misery personified, are the slower, older, fatter mothers. Not only have they been unfortunate enough not to marry the future king of England, but also they have been frozen forever in their moment of failure; bit-player losers without whose trudging inferiority Diana would not have been the star of the day (along with all the other days).

You can bet that before the race, Di claimed to be really bad at running. "I'm really slow," I can imagine her murmuring to the other mothers, as they stood in a tentative clump to the side of the field, licking their dry lips and wondering whether their skirts would ride unattractively up the backs of their legs if they competed. That is what always happens. I know this from experience. "I am not good at this," I myself declared at my first field day, called sports day in Britain, as all the mothers gathered in a ragged line. This was a fact. I am slow.

The other mothers were saying the same thing. We were a chorus line of lowered expectations: "I haven't run since I played hockey in school." "I'm really out of shape." "I'll probably fall down." Go, said the teacher. But I had been fooled. My sneaky, falsely self-abasing competitors actually turned out to be incognito decathletes, retired Olympic marathon runners. They sped past me, and I came in dead last. If I'm being honest, this was kind of surprising: some of those women did look seriously out of shape.*

It is a female thing, of course, running yourself down when you're obviously wrong ("I'm so fat," the skinniest girls said in junior high, shimmying into the tiniest jeans). But it seems to me that most women do it for reassurance and praise ("No, you're so thin!" the girl's friends are supposed to trill). But British people do it as a matter of course and for more complicated reasons, mixing low self-regard with arrogance; indirectness with insincerity. They have a pathological fear of being caught bragging. Even in the thrusting twenty-first century, the country is full of spectacular overachievers passing themselves off as amateurs, halfwits, and buffoons: nuclear physicists pretending they dabble in science; famous actors attributing their success to random luck; authors who tell you their books are terrible and they don't know why anyone reads them, anyway. I saw it in the House of Lords, whose

---

* I also pulled something in my leg. But I was cheered up by the fathers' race, which came after ours. The fathers were pretending not to care one way or another, although some of them, I noticed, were wearing sneakers instead of normal shoes with their suits. There was a general air of testosterone in the air, as you get when middle-aged men are given something concrete to compete about as a way to exercise their unused aggression. At the last minute, the teachers made them race while doing the backward bunny hop.

members fall all over themselves denigrating their own credentials. And I realized I was seeing it everywhere.

When I had lunch with the unnaturally clever actor Stephen Fry, for instance, he said it was no big deal that he was an actor, novelist, memoirist, television personality, talk-show host, and amateur magician who in his spare time had written the script for a Christmas pantomime at the Old Vic, and who, when his friend Emma Thompson's book was swallowed by her computer, resurrected the lost chapters by singlehandedly repairing the hard drive (he dabbles in technology on the side). Fry suffers from manic-depressive disorder—also in his spare time, he researched and hosted a television series in which he explored his and others' experiences with the illness—and I think one of the things that distresses him is that no one else is as smart as he is. But he would never put it that way; he claims it's all a fluke.

My own husband, then the editor-in-chief of a renowned publishing house and the author of five novels and a best-selling work of nonfiction, presented himself at our first meeting as an irresponsible, drunken freelance journalist who did a little editing but was quite possibly about to be sacked.

Congratulated by an interviewer when his novel *On Chesil Beach* was short-listed for the Booker Prize, the best-selling author Ian McEwan shrugged and said, "I didn't do a thing" (in *his* spare time, McEwan writes screenplays and opera librettos).* And the British chemist Frederick Sanger, who won an almost-unheard-of two Nobel Prizes for his groundbreaking work in genome sequencing, in 1958 and 1980, once described himself as "just a chap who messed about in a lab."

Brits are supposed to pretend that achievement comes without effort; boasting is the height of poor manners. It makes you seem aggressive, ambitious, self-regarding, puffed up—verging on American. The evils of those things are ingrained in them at school, where they are

---

* McEwan has been short-listed several times for the Booker, and has won once, for his novel *Amsterdam*. He once said the award was "a wholly arbitrary matter."

discouraged from saying they are better than anyone else, even when they are. Among the drawings of flowers, dogs, and the like in the display of the children's schoolwork affixed to our refrigerator are several essays. Two are cautionary tales about the evils of boasting, in which the boasters in question—a know-it-all giraffe, a stuck-up cat—immediately lose all their friends.

There is also a sadistic tradition (now in the past) of teachers' writing strange, slyly nasty remarks disguised as home truths on children's report cards, presumably to discourage them from getting above themselves.

Stephen Fry's headmaster wrote on his report card, for example: "He has glaring faults and they certainly have glared at us this term."

"Though he seems to view his schoolmasters with amused and Olympian contempt," a teacher wrote of John Polanyi, who won the Nobel Prize in chemistry in 1986, "the present illusion of a superior mind is usually shattered by a display of abominable ignorance."

"Jilly has set herself an extremely low standard which she has failed to maintain," the novelist Jilly Cooper's report read. The writer Robert Graves's headmaster wrote: "Well, goodbye, Graves, and remember that your best friend is the waste-paper basket."

Instead of bragging, the English turn to humor and misdirection. If you ask someone, say, "How was the job interview?" she won't give you a straight answer. She will spin an amusing tale of a deadly encounter replete with gaffes, miscommunication, and uncomfortable silences in which she could barely string two words together, let alone hope to get the job. If you ask her how her latest project is going, she will laugh dully and tell you that it is barely going at all.

The horror of public displays of self-satisfaction often extends to one's own children. When children win prizes at our school's prize day, it is always interesting to see how the British parents try to resolve the terrible internal struggle between their natural pride in their kids and their natural horror of appearing to express it. At the same time, they take a cold-eyed view of those of their children who aren't likely to win prizes.

"Okay," one friend answered, after I asked him how his daughter was doing at school. He sounded as if he were talking about gravy. "Okay. She's a bit thick, you know."

Why do they do this? I think English people emphasize their faults in part as a way to demonstrate the charm of their self-deprecation. This is starkly illustrated in the personal ads section of the *London Review of Books*, where the lovelorn advertise themselves as aggressively unappealing, even actively repellent. Perhaps only someone from Britain could genuinely believe that an ad saying, "Baste me in butter and call me Slappy" might lead to romance with an actual, nonincarcerated person, but that is how one ad began.

The tradition began with the first submission the *London Review* received when it began accepting personals, in 1998: "67-year-old disaffiliated flâneur picking my toothless way through the urban sprawl," the ad said, "self-destructive, sliding towards pathos, jacked up on Viagra and on the lookout for a contortionist who plays the trumpet."

Subsequent *London Review* advertisers have described themselves as shallow, flatulent, obsessive, incontinent, hypertensive, hostile, older than 100, paranoid, pasty, plaid-festooned, sinister looking, advantage taking, and amphetamine-fueled. They have announced that they are suffering from liver disease, from drug addiction, from asthma, from compulsive gambling, from unclassified skin complaints, and from reduced sperm counts. They have presented themselves as aggressive and psychopathic. One man said he lived in a mental institution. "I've divorced better men than you," one woman announced.

Some lonelyhearts emphasize the single-loser clichés, to make themselves sound even worse: women who live with cats, men who live with their mothers, rejectees who appear to regard *Fatal Attraction* not as a cautionary horror movie about the drawbacks of adultery with a crazy person, but as a source of handy breakup tips. "Tell me I'm pretty, then watch me cling," one woman declared. There are many allusions to the heartbreak of failed former relationships: "My favorite Ben & Jerry's is Acid-Boiled Bones of Divorce Lawyer," one ad said. Some are just funny. "Woman, 38. WLTM man to 45 who doesn't name his genitals after German chancellors," one reads. "You know who you are and, no, I don't want to meet either Bismarck, Bethmann Hollweg, or Prince Chlodwig zu Hohenlohe-Schillingsfürst, however admirable the independence he gave to secretaries of state may have been."

(This being Britain, a fair percentage of men seeking women sug-

gest in their ads that, come to think of it, they might well be seek-
ing other men. One advertiser described himself as "camp as custard."
Another ad read, in its entirety: "I wrote this ad to prove I'm not gay.
Man, 29. Not gay. Absolutely not.")

The subtlety, if that is what it is, of these courtship techniques may
well be lost on people used to American-model personal ads, in which
stunning, athletic, GSOH'd characters seek soul mates for walks in the
rain and cuddles by the fire. The Americans tend to be earnest about
their desires, unshy about their accomplishments, forthright about
their physical and material attributes. But in the *London Review* those
sorts of people would be laughed out of town; unironic emotional senti-
ment (unless expressed while drunk) tends to make Britons cringe with
embarrassment.*

One advertiser I spoke to said she'd had little success with conventional ads, such as the one in which she described herself as "gentle,
curvy, tactile, educated and funny." A potential date who did respond
bragged that he was free of infection ("I did not get the feeling he was
trying to be funny," the advertiser told me). Another announced that he
lived without electricity in the woods, in a house made from trees he
had chopped down himself.

The woman changed tactics and wrote another ad: "I've got a mouth
on me that can peel paint off walls, but I can always apologize."

"That got a lot of responses from alcoholics," she reported.

The magazine's approach brings to mind the counterintuitive
advertising featuring consumers recoiling from Marmite, the curiously
popular—though controversial, because it is so vile—gloppy-as-molasses
yeast by-product with multiple functions: sandwich spread, snack, or
soup (just add boiling water). It is the favorite edible paste of British

---

* Some of my in-laws are confounded by my American habit of constantly reminding
my children that I love them. "Love ya!" they'll say, as our car pulls away from a family
lunch (British hosts often see you to the door at the end of social occasions and then
stand on the stoop, waving, until your car is out of sight. It is friendly, but it also might
be because they want to be sure that you have genuinely left). "Missing you already!" my
in-laws will say. They're being nice and trying to make me feel at home, although there
is also the possibility that they are laughing at me.

children, in much the way French children are partial to Nutella, Americans to peanut butter, and Latin Americans to dulce de leche. But Britons have a complicated relationship with Marmite. On Marmite's own official Web site, where Marmite is at one point referred to as "noxious gunk," there is a section devoted to people who hate it. "Ever taken a look at engine grease?" the Web site reads. "Ever compared the two? A pot of Marmite and a thick scraping of burnt oil? Exactly."

It sounds perverse, promoting a product by emphasizing the repugnance it inspires. But here's the trick. When Britons exaggerate their faults, they are often in fact telegraphing their attributes, practicing an *inverted form of bragging*. They do it to prove that they have a sense of humor, that they can laugh at themselves, and that they are secure enough in their achievements to pretend they have none. It takes a special kind of arrogance to surmount your own insults.

For an outsider it takes years of study to learn how to negotiate successfully all the fakes and double-fakes and insincere sincerity (or sincere insincerity?) that characterize Britons' accounts of themselves. Are you supposed to argue with them? Believe them? Pretend to believe them? Pretend to believe that they are pretending to believe?

My reporter's notebooks are full of the laconic protestations-to-the-contrary of the seriously overachieving. When I met the explorer Ranulph Fiennes (full name Sir Ranulph Twisleton-Wykeham-Fiennes; he is a distant cousin of the actors Ralph and Joseph Fiennes), he had just run seven marathons over seven days on six different continents—flying 45,000 miles and running 183.4 miles. He was fifty-nine.

Several months earlier, Fiennes had suffered a heart attack, endured emergency bypass surgery, and lain unconscious and close to death for four days. His doctors had agreed to let him go on the marathon expedition only if he promised to wear a monitor to keep his heart rate below 130.* Despite his heart troubles, age, and jet lag, Fiennes managed to do pretty well. His running companion was struck by a nasty illness, though, and barely made it through the seventh race, the New York City

---

* He left the monitor at home, claiming to have "forgotten" it.

Marathon. Fiennes, who had passed him awhile back, did the gentlemanly thing and looped back through the crowd—running against the tide of the racers like someone going up a down escalator—so that he could meet his friend, turn around again, and cross the finish line next to him.

Fiennes was straight out of *Lawrence of Arabia*: tall and lanky, weatherbeaten, with bright heather gray eyes and such a strong and silent air about him that I felt guilty for subjecting him to any questions (he said he submits to interviews only because the publicity helps him finance his expeditions). Among other things he had walked alone and without backup support across the Antarctic; parachuted onto Norwegian icecaps; traveled by hovercraft up the Nile, and circumnavigated the globe via its polar axis. He had written sixteen books and canoed up the Amazon. According to *The Guinness Book of World Records*, he was the World's Greatest Living Explorer. But he was not one to boast. "It's how I make my living financially," was the best thing he would say about himself.

We were having breakfast, a spartan meal of toast and tea. He said he had to watch his cholesterol. I noticed that he was missing the tops of the fingers and thumb of his left hand.

He explained that he had contracted frostbite three years earlier, after his sled laden with provisions slid into the frigid sea while he was on a solo trek to the North Pole, and Fiennes plunged in after it, putting himself in yet another near-death situation. The point he was trying to make was not that he had successfully hauled the sled and all his supplies out of the water on his own, nor that he had heroically kept a cool head while surviving a deadly ordeal, but that *he should not have wrecked his mission and carelessly frozen his fingers*.

The fingers turned black.

"They were very ugly, like witch's talons," he said of the frostbitten sections, speaking dispassionately, as if they belonged to someone else. The doctors told him they would have to go. "I'd been advised that you mustn't amputate for five months after the trauma, the reason being that the healthy bits that would need to be used by the surgeon were semidamaged, too." But he got sick of waiting, and sick of the pain.

After three weeks, he went to the tool shed behind his farmhouse in Somerset, got out his vise and microsaw, and performed a self-amputation.

As he was describing all this to me, Fiennes put his toast down. He spread his mangled hand on the table, and demonstrated with his bread knife. Ouch, I thought.

"Common sense," he said.

Then there is the actor Hugh Grant. Brimming with articulate intelligence, he merely has to train his lazy charm on you for a few minutes to have you in his thrall. He presents himself as hapless, talentless, bad tempered, and replete with tortured anguish and self-loathing. (Drunken, too—they all present themselves as drunken.) Grant knows that the parts that made him famous—the awkward bachelor in *Four Weddings and a Funeral*, the awkward bachelor in *Notting Hill*—present a reassuring cliché to the world.

"The roles play into a certain fantasy of what people want English people to be," he said when I interviewed him for a story (it was really fun; he flirts the whole time). "Whereas half the time, as you know, we're vomiting beer and beating people up. I know I am."

Grant claimed that he kind of lapsed into acting as a "joke detour" after graduating from Oxford with an English literature degree. He eagerly recounted the mishaps that punctuated his rise to the top, including "playing parts like Tree in Wind, and Third Shouting Peasant" at the Nottingham Playhouse, starring in a horror film called *The Lair of the White Worm*, and then falling into a "slough of unemployment" in which he tried to write a novel (working title: *Slack*) about a listless, depressed person who does nothing and cares about nothing—*L'Étranger* without the laughs.

"I used to write something in the morning and think, I'm a genius, then go out for a chicken sandwich and come back and throw it away," Grant said. A low point came when he was ordered by his agent to help the French actress Juliette Binoche improve her English in preparation for a role. After chasing her around the park shouting, "Would you like a cup of tea?" he was handed an off-the-books payment of £250 cash, "like a plumber." His foul mood was not helped when, auditioning for *Four Weddings*, he learned that the casting director had decreed: "You'll meet Hugh Grant for this part over my dead body."

Richard Curtis, the film's screenwriter, told me that Grant came to the audition "claiming that he was on his last legs, that acting was no job for an adult to do."

"He is the most disrespectful person in the world about his acting," Curtis said. He said, 'I can only do three things: normal; sexy, which is down an octave; and serious, which is up an octave.'"

But beneath all that fretting and fussing lurks a serious person, who in fact works hard and obsessively, marks up his scripts to a fault, insists on take after take, and argues with his directors and writers if he doesn't like a line or a direction.

"Hugh is a formidable person with a very strong sense of self," Julia Roberts, his *Notting Hill* costar, told me. "He's incredibly clear about who he is and what he's doing."

But would not budge from his story.

"If someone said to me, 'I'm sorry, Hugh, but a law's just been passed and you're not allowed to act any more in your life,' I'd be thrilled," he said. "I still think like an unemployed actor living in Hammersmith."

Perhaps the master of the British art of telling stories against oneself is the writer and playwright Alan Bennett, who is about the closest thing Britain has to a national treasure. He seems genetically incapable of being pleased with himself. When asked by the actor Ian McKellen in 1987 whether he was gay or straight, he responded that it was like asking a man crawling across the Sahara Desert what sort of water he preferred, Perrier or Malvern.

Bennett likes nothing better than situations in which he is pulled up short. He and his partner still use his parents' house, in a small Yorkshire village, as a weekend place. Once, when he telephoned the local coal merchant, Mr. Redhead, to order some coal, Mr. Redhead told him: "Well, I don't care how celebrated you are; you'll never be a patch on your dad."

Some time later, Bennett rang again. "Goodness me, I am consorting with higher beings!" Mr. Redhead said. Bennett reminded him of his earlier remark. "That's correct," Mr. Redhead responded, "and I reiterate it."

On another occasion, he received a free copy of the Waterstone's literary calendar, which records the birthdays of famous authors. He looked in it and found the birthdays of Dennis Potter, Michael Frayn, and Edna O'Brien. Naturally, he turned to his own birthday, May 9. It was blank except for a historical note: "The first British self-service launderette is opened on Queensway, London 1949."

Many of these anecdotes appear in *Untold Stories,* a collection of essays that is unusually candid in its revelations about Bennett's homosexuality, his mother's mental illness, and his own struggle with colon cancer. But even when he writes about gloomy subjects like imminent death, he cannot resist finding absurdity and stifling stray impulses to wallow or become sentimental. He delights in the fact, for example, that the doctor who diagnosed his cancer said his tumor was "about the size of an average rock bun."

He said that he felt uncomfortable complaining and that he had written such a revelatory book because, given a 50 percent chance of living, he had assumed he would already be dead when it was published.

"I had no objection to its being read," he said. "I just didn't want to be in the room at the time."

In person, Bennett sounds like Wallace from the *Wallace and Gromit* movies and slouches in his armchair just the way he does in the photograph on the cover of *Writing Home*, an earlier collection. He told me that when he was nominated for an Academy Award for the screenplay of *The Madness of King George*, he didn't go to Hollywood, get dressed up, or even stay up to watch the awards on television, since "it's not my sort of thing anyway."

"I didn't get one, which is quite right," he noted.

Needless to say, Bennett failed to mention that his play *The History Boys* ended up winning three Olivier Awards and, when it opened on Broadway, six Tonys.

He is much more comfortable with situations that put him in a peculiar or unflattering light. Once, he told me, he was sitting in his car in a Yorkshire parking lot when he saw a woman waving at him.

"I thought, 'I've been recognized,' he related. "She came up to the car and opened the door, which I thought was a bit strong, and I still kept a big smile on my face. Then she actually got into the car and closed the door. But I thought, 'You know, she's a fan,' and I was still smiling accommodatingly. And then she looked at me and said, 'Bloody hell, I'm in the wrong car.'"

English people are generally ill prepared for America's "I'm No. 1" attitude and do not know how to apply it themselves, even if they want to. The contrast between outlooks is portrayed nicely in the film *Chariots of Fire*, when the cocky American track stars strut into view, discomfiting the Brits with their combination of bravado and, it would appear, stupidity. (One of their missteps is to use professional coaches in a country that would later revere Roger Bannister not only because he ran the first four-minute mile but also because he did it on the side, *as an amateur*, while studying for his eventual role as one of the leading neurologists in Britain. "I trained for less than an hour a day, but it's all about quality, not quantity," Bannister said in an interview to mark the fiftieth anniversary of his achievement. "If I had had to train for two hours daily to be competitive, I would not have been running, because it would have meant I could not have been a medical student.")

A charming English friend of mine, the successful author of acclaimed historical biographies, found herself at a dinner once with some rich Americans, masters-of-the-universe types.

"I understand you write best-selling biographies," said the man sitting next to her.

"Well, I write biographies, but they don't really sell," she replied (this was not true and was supposed to be a joke). Whereupon he promptly turned his back on her and ignored her for the rest of the evening.

Similarly, I was writing one afternoon in the London Library when the fire alarm went off and all the people in the reading room were ushered outside and ordered to stand on the sidewalk. In an un-English move, we actually began to ask one another what we were working on (this is normally considered rude, in case the answer is "nothing").

One young man said he was writing a book, and I asked if it was his first one.

"I've done two others," he said, "but they're just rubbish."

We considered the rubbishness of his books, which we had not read.

Surely, I asked, there must be a less dire way to explain yourself?

Another man standing there on the sidewalk said that he didn't think so. "It is the height of tedium," he said, "to hear someone banging on about how wonderful he is."

This vast sea of self-deprecation can be exasperating. You want to shake them and tell them to shut up already. But they're generally so inept at swaggering vanity that they really shouldn't try it in the first place. English people trying to boast are typically like acrophobes walking along a cliff: It frightens them and makes them feel sick. Tim Henman, the milquetoasty tennis player who for years was a perennial loser at Wimbledon, always raising the country's hopes, only to dash them again, never seemed more foolish or more uncomfortable than, when trying to live up to his wishful-thinking tabloid nickname "Tiger Tim," he began pumping his fist in the air and emitting a kind of snarling grimace, a rictus of belligerence, at strategic moments. He was not a fierce person—he was rather colorless and modest, actually, and a better nickname would have been "Tepid Tim"—and he did not look fierce. He looked ridiculous.

By the same token, it was difficult to watch a bunch of near-hysterical young women competing in *How Do You Solve a Problem Like Maria?*, a reality-TV series that was broadcast in the spring of 2006. In the show, Andrew Lloyd Webber auditioned unknowns for the role of Maria in a West End production of *The Sound of Music*, and these women had to boast noisily while running down the competition, which did not come naturally to them.

"I've worked so hard and I've learned so much and I won't let you down and I am your Maria so please please please vote for me," they would say, wild eyed. They looked much calmer and more comfortable when they were voted off the program, a turn of events that required each loser to participate in a rousing chorus of "So Long, Farewell," while being waved off the stage by the remaining contestants.*

Self-effacement can become a self-fulfilling prophecy. When he was editor of the *Spectator*, the politician Boris Johnson took personal insouciance to absurd and wondrous heights. He was one of the cleverest men in Britain, a wonderful writer and polemicist, very funny, the former president of the Oxford Union debating society, an elegant spinner of memorable, Wodehousian phrases. At one point, he had four jobs and commuted by bicycle between three of them. He spent part of his time at the magazine, and part of his time at the House of Commons, where he was the member of Parliament for Henley and the Tory spokesman for culture. His fourth job was writing a weekly column for the *Daily Telegraph*.

But Johnson (full name: Alexander Boris de Pfeffel Johnson) exuded the shambling disorganization of an oversize adolescent. He had a shock of messy blond hair that looked like a bad wig threatening to slide altogether off his head, and an air about him of chaos and confusion. His tie was askew; his shirt was untucked. He had the stentorian voice of a carnival barker. He liked to give the impression that work flowed invisibly from him, with no actual effort. "Because I have no time to do it," he told me once, referring to his column, "I do it in no time. You just whack it out."

Don't you worry about sounding, uh, not very serious? I asked.

"Beneath the carefully constructed veneer of a blithering buffoon, there lurks a blithering buffoon," he said.

---

* By the same token, unironic boasting, of course, is considered acutely embarrassing. The actor Ben Kingsley was universally ridiculed when, proud of having been knighted, he reportedly insisted on being referred to as "Sir Ben"—even by friends of his wife (who is now his ex-wife) and even on the posters advertising his film *Lucky Number Slevin*. (While he has told interviewers that he prefers to be called Sir Ben, he has always officially denied that everyone who speaks to him is required to use his title.) In a *Daily Mail* article about the issue of what people with knighthoods should be called, the actor Sir Roger Moore was quoted as saying that he, personally, likes "Rog." "I think insisting on being called 'Sir Roger' is a load of pretentious bullshit," he said.

How blithering was he? His boss at the time, Conrad Black, said I shouldn't believe everything I heard. "There is a type in Britain who masquerades as a bumbling oaf," Black said. "But Boris is not a bumbling oaf. He is a person of great political skill and high intelligence."*

Black told me that when Boris was hired as the *Spectator* editor, he had vowed to resign from the job if he ever decided to run for public office. But Johnson failed to stick to the agreement, and got himself elected to Parliament.

"I reminded him of his promise," Black said. "He gave his usual sackcloth-and-ashes, hand-wringing response. He said his enthusiasm for political service had got the better of him and that he was motivated solely by his desire to rescue the country from the evils it had fallen into."

I asked Johnson about this. Had he really gone back on his word?

"The blessed sponge of amnesia has wiped the chalkboard of history," he answered.

Johnson rescheduled our interview several times—busy days, he said—but he finally allowed me to come to the *Spectator* editors' weekly lunch, a formal affair involving several courses, much wine, and a lot of boyish banter. Presiding over the meal, Boris held forth about his latest parliamentary activities as if he were an anthropologist describing a trip to a far-off land. If he was striving to act like something, it was something other than an elected official and the editor of a national magazine.

He had recently given a speech about a program for the disabled. "It's a jolly interesting subject," he said, "although my oration was heard by about five people. I banged on a bit—I was really very PC—and it was good as far as it went, but it wouldn't butter any parsnips." That led to a lively discussion of the origins of the phrase "buttering

---

* Black, who once showed up to a costume party dressed as Cardinal Richelieu, went on to have troubles of his own: he was convicted of mail fraud and obstruction of justice in 2007 in connection with a scheme, prosecutors said, in which he siphoned tens of millions of dollars away from shareholders of his company. His wife, who once told an interviewer that "my extravagance knows no bounds," went to the same costume party as Marie Antoinette. Black's vigorous, public self-belief was extremely un-English; in fact, he was a Canadian, although he acted more like an American.

the parsnips," which some editors claimed Boris had made up on the spot. (I looked it up later; it describes a thing that doesn't amount to much.)

The meal was becoming both merrier and more argumentative, the sort of occasion wherein you suspected that the participants might soon employ their bread rolls as weapons. Talk turned to the arts. The film *Iris* had just been released, about Iris Murdoch and her descent into Alzheimer's, and it included an account of her early romantic adventures.

"I didn't know she was such a goer," Johnson said.

He declared himself unimpressed by her writing, which could tend toward the philosophical. "Her books are pretty hard going for someone like me," he said. "I read her book *Metaphysics as a Guide to Morals*. Donnez-moi un break."

I asked him what he liked to read, and he confessed that on his bedside table rested a book of lyric Greek poetry—in Greek. (Sometime afterward, when a group of students held a rally protesting the government's decision to cut classics from the state curriculum, Johnson addressed the crowd—in Latin.)

Johnson is married, with four children. Soon after the lunch, he was removed from his Tory culture job when details of his illicit liaison with Petronella Wyatt, the *Spectator*'s fearsome "Singular Life" columnist, found their way into the papers. Like many Englishmen who have affairs, he promoted the impression that he had fallen into this one almost by chance, as if it had just sort of happened when he wasn't looking, which made it not really his fault. He tried to talk his way out of it. Confronted by a pack of reporters as he prepared to go jogging in a getup that included voluminous floral shorts—he has a generously proportioned physique—and a bandanna decorated with skulls and crossbones, he dismissed the accusations as "balderdash," "ludicrous conjecture," and "an inverted pyramid of piffle." But his edifice of denial crumbled when Wyatt's even more fearsome mother went to the news media with incontrovertible evidence of the relationship.

But it was par for the course with Boris. He was always getting into career-threatening scrapes. He upset the city of Liverpool by accusing its residents of wallowing in "victim status" after a local man was kidnapped and killed in Iraq, and had to make a groveling apology. He insulted Portsmouth by saying it was full of obese drug addicts. He upset health-food campaigners by saying that people should eat junk food if they wanted to, and had to make another groveling apology. He would eventually leave the *Spectator* job, although he continued to write his *Telegraph* column and to advance, against all expectations, in politics. He also became a television celebrity as a guest host of the satirical quiz show *Have I Got News for You*. Once, he answered his cell phone on the program. "I can't talk now," he said. "I'm on television."

After I had interviewed him, our photographer, Jonathan Player, went to the *Spectator* offices and took some pictures of Boris to go with my article.

Only it wasn't Boris. Bored with the whole thing, he had ordered a colleague to impersonate him in the photo session, to pretend that *he* was Boris. (Jonathan had never seen Johnson before but felt that something was off. "I was too polite to say anything," he recalled.) When the publisher found out what had happened, she scolded Boris as you might scold an impish boy, and ordered him to go back in there and do it properly.* My paper, meanwhile, came close to printing a profile of Boris Johnson alongside a random picture of some anonymous *Spectator* employee. That would have been some correction.

Finally, there was the annoying case of the writer Toby Young, an extreme illustration of the perils of protesting too much. Young was a shameless self-promoter who had parlayed accounts of his slapstick mishaps in America into a career. All his anecdotes were about how he had royally screwed up in various situations. His first book, *How to Lose Friends and Alienate People*, described how he blustered his way into a job at *Van-*

---

* The publisher was a vivacious American named Kimberly Quinn, whose own extramarital affair—with David Blunkett, the country's unmarried, blind home secretary—would soon find its way into the newspapers, too. They covered the story with great gusto, especially when it emerged that Quinn was pregnant and that the baby's father was not her husband, Mr. Quinn, but her lover, Mr. Blunkett.

ity Fair in New York and then offended his colleagues by, for instance, hiring a stripper to entertain a colleague in the office on what turned out to be Take Your Daughters to Work Day. He repelled the usually affable actor Nathan Lane by asking him at the outset of an interview whether he was gay and/or Jewish. He behaved so obnoxiously at *Vanity Fair's* post-Oscars party in Hollywood that Graydon Carter, the *Vanity Fair* editor, ordered him to "stop bothering the celebrities." Finally, after a long period in which Young wrote almost nothing and managed to affront nearly everyone in the tri-state area, Carter fired him.

But Young behaved like a stalker, the kind who is encouraged by any response—even rejection—from his object of obsession. He reveled in deliberate buffoonery. He wore with pride the unflattering things people had said about him. When the *Daily Mail* called him a "balding, bug-eyed, skinny-chested opportunist with the looks of a punctured beach ball, the charisma of a glove-puppet and an ego the size of a Hercules supply plane," Young was delighted enough to use it as publicity for his next project, a dramatization of the book. Every time poor Graydon Carter mentioned how bothersome it was to be a constant prop in Young's self-absorption, Young added the remark to his repertoire of putdowns and slapped it on his Web site.

When *How to Lose Friends* became a bestseller, its success jeopardized Young's carefully constructed no-hope persona. With a popular book to his name, Young was no longer the loser he claimed to be, although he told me once that it didn't matter, since Americans *did not understand the complicated semiotics of his particular type of self-deprecation.*

"The accusation of false modesty is meaningless," he declared, "because it's a form of modesty which isn't intended to be sincere in the first place."

I didn't really understand what he meant. But by the time his second book in the same vein, *The Sound of No Hands Clapping*—further accounts of his catastrophe-prone career, its details often seeming suspiciously staged—came out several years later, his act had grown old. Nobody was buying his fake haplessness any more. Having turned his failure into success, he couldn't convert his success back in to the kind of failure he needed to succeed again. Self-deprecation as self-promotion is peculiarly English, but not when you have to try too hard.

POSTSCRIPT

In 2007, Ranulph Fiennes put aside his fear of heights and complete lack of rock-climbing experience and climbed the north face of the Eiger, a six-thousand-foot peak known as the Wall of Death, at the age of sixty-three. He nearly died. "It was extremely unpleasant," he said afterward.

Toby Young went to Hollywood for a cameo appearance in the film version of *How to Lose Friends and Alienate People*. One day on set, he bounded up to the actress Kirsten Dunst, who was playing his girlfriend. "She had no idea who I was," Young bragged in the *Daily Mail*. "She looked at me as if I was some demented stalker who had somehow managed to sneak past security."

Boris Johnson decided to run for mayor of London, an unlikely move that provoked some skepticism. Telling Boris-related anecdotes onstage at a literary festival, Ian Hislop, the editor of *Private Eye*, said that he had once seen Johnson en route to a Conservative function.

"Do you know anything about Conservative foreign policy?" Hislop quoted Boris as asking.

"No," Hislop replied.

"Damn!" said Boris.

But luckily, a knowledge of foreign policy isn't an obvious prerequisite for London mayor. Boris ran a shockingly straightforward campaign and—aided by his decision to abstain from alcohol until after the election—managed to successfully keep his foot out of his mouth and to come up with plausible positions on issues like transportation and crime.

But had he really changed into a serious person?

"There is no distinction between the old Boris and the new Boris," he said huffily. "They are indivisble, co-eternal . . . consubstantial."

NINE

THE NAKED GUY AND ANGLE-GRINDER MAN

> *Stanley Green, who has died aged 78, paraded around Oxford*
> *Street for 25 years with a placard warning against the dangers*
> *of protein.*
> —Daily Telegraph Book of Obituaries: Eccentric Lives,
> Hugh Massingberd, ed. (1995)

All Vincent Bethell wanted was the right to take off his clothes. He took them off near the House of Lords. He took them off in front of New Scotland Yard. He took them off outside the Royal Courts of Justice, in Covent Garden, near Downing Street, next to the Natural History Museum, in a shopping center in Birmingham, and at the National Gallery. He climbed a lamppost in the middle of London and sat up there, naked, his only accessory a backpack with the word "freedom" written across it. Naked, he was arrested so many times he lost count, and then spent five naked months in Brixton prison, relegated to solitary confinement so that he would not upset the other prisoners.

In the scheme of protests, Bethell's nude stand did not have the authority or sweep of the American civil rights campaign or, say, the suffragettes' movement. For one thing, he had only about six followers. But as leader of a movement of his own devising called the Freedom to Be Yourself Campaign, Bethell was a free spirit in the best British tradition, a stubborn advocate for his cause, however lonely or ridiculous.

Though his movement did not exactly catch fire, it appealed to a nation with a strong libertarian streak, a sympathy for eccentric challenges to authority, and a profusion of newspapers eager to print photographs of naked people. Britain loves its oddball characters, and Bethell was a fine example.

What foreign correspondent wouldn't leap at the chance to talk to a good-looking nude human-rights campaigner? What particularly intrigued me about Bethell was that while the law frowned on his campaign, members of the public didn't; and that he seemed unperturbed by what you might imagine to be the biggest drawback of public nudity when practiced in Britain: the British weather. In any case, when I met him, early in 2001, Bethell was flush with success. Not only had he recently been acquitted of public indecency in a widely publicized trial in London, but also he had sat through the entire trial naked—becoming, apparently, the only nude defendant in English legal history. A slight, soft-spoken man who was then twenty-eight, Bethell met me in his sparely furnished apartment on an upper floor of a run-down public housing project in Coventry, a city in the west Midlands. He had shaved off his beard and all the hair he grew while in prison. Disappointingly, he was dressed. "It's about freedom of choice," he said. "And there's no heating in my flat."

His particular branch of libertarianism had evolved over time. As an art student Bethell had been struck by how difficult it was to maintain a mature attitude when confronted with the nude models in the life-drawing class.*

"I thought, 'This is interesting, that people have such a strange

---

* Whatever his reaction, it was less childish that of the nineteenth-century British author and art critic John Ruskin. Observing the nude Mrs. Ruskin for the first time on their wedding night, Ruskin—whose prior naked-woman-viewing experience had been confined to admiring classical paintings and statues—is said to have been so repulsed by the sight of pubic hair (or menstrual blood, depending on which account you read) that he never consummated the marriage. In a statement to his lawyer during the eventual, inevitable annulment proceedings, Ruskin said that "though her face was beautiful, her person was not formed to excite passion. On the contrary, there were certain circumstances in her person which completely checked it." The marriage was indeed annulled, on the grounds of Ruskin's "incurable impotency."

reaction to something that should be quite normal—the human body,'"
Bethell said. He began to see clothes as a barrier to understanding.
"It was quite a profound thing—the beauty, openness, and honesty of
it. The more you cover yourself up, the more you lose yourself as a
human being."

The weather, oddly enough, finally pushed him over the edge, a summer so unusually sweltering and so without air-conditioning that even
the skimpiest clothes felt superfluous. "I was walking around in just
shorts, and even the shorts were dripping with sweat," Bethell said. "And
then I thought: This is ridiculous. Why should I have to wear clothes?"

As a sudden thunderbolt of clarity, it did not rival Archimedes'
"Eureka" moment in the bath (although that, too, involved nudity) and
Bethell did not run, shouting, into the street. But he began stripping in
public and bombarding public figures with letters demanding to know
why it was illegal to do so. A few people replied; none were optimistic
about the likelihood that Bethell would be able to establish a new Nude
Britain.

As it happened, Bethell's home, Coventry, was also the home of the
world's most famous nude equestrienne, Lady Godiva, who rode across
town in the altogether in the eleventh century and who is now a brand
of chocolate. But he had a tough row to hoe. His friends argued that
others might not want to see him nude—what about their rights? "I
was fairly aghast," Bethell's father, Michael, a factory worker, told me.
"There was nothing like this at home at all."

Bethell conducted his first naked protest, accompanied by a handful of friends, in Piccadilly Circus in the summer of 1998, a few years
before I met him. There were some abusive comments, but nobody
physically attacked him, and some passersby smiled in what he took to
be an encouraging way. Nudeness "really does have a profound, invigorating quality that stimulates people's minds," he said.

The minds of the Metropolitan Police were stimulated in a different way, and Bethell was arrested. He was released as soon as he re-
dressed. But he did it again and again, arrested every time, until finally
he was formally charged with causing a public nuisance and sent to
Brixton Prison to await trial. His accomplices were not charged, since

they put their clothes back on. Bethell declined the authorities' offer of the same easy way out.

It was awkward for everyone. The unclothed Bethell was put in solitary confinement for five months, in a cell measuring seven feet by eleven feet. At one point a judge conducted a hearing through the cell door because Bethell refused to get dressed for his court appearance. The guards ridiculed him, muttering under their breaths that he belonged in Broadmoor, the notorious prison for the criminally insane. " 'They said, 'You're insane—why don't you get dressed?' "

But he was not insane, a prison psychiatrist ruled. His fellow prisoners admired from afar his principled challenge to the Man. "Respect!" they would shout as Bethell passed by. "Hey, naked guy! Keep fighting the system!"

The trial, in January 2001, was unique in the annals of British courtroom drama, not least because of the accommodation that had to be made for the nakedness of the defendant. When he was seated, Bethell was instructed not to stand up, so that spectators could see only his bare chest and no disturbing lower regions. When he walked to the witness stand to testify in his own defense, the judge advised the two women on the jury to "close your eyes or look away." The accused gave a ringing defense of his position, saying that his nudity was nonsexual, that he was "simply promoting the acceptance of the human skin."

Bethell had been charged with engaging in behavior that might harm public morals or "obstruct the public in the enjoyment of their rights." He called as defense witnesses several people who testified that though they had indeed seen him naked, their morals had not been harmed nor their enjoyment obstructed.

The verdict was unanimous: Not guilty.

"Being human is not a crime!" Bethell shouted from the dock, standing up and raising his arms above his head. The women jurors remained calm in the face of the suddenly full-frontal view.

"I would not go away too much with that idea," the upright (and rather uptight) judge, George Bathurst-Norman, hastily told the defendant. "It is simply not a public nuisance in these circumstances."

The nude Bethell proudly strode forth into the bracing winter air, carrying his clothes in two plastic shopping bags. He made a jubilant statement to the assembled press. Carried away with excitement, three supporters flung off their clothes in solidarity.

His victory had mixed reviews. "Hands up all those who are sick of the sight of Vincent Bethell's bare bum," Richard Williamson wrote in the *Sunday Mercury*. But several reporters from other newspapers spent time with him nude on the streets and, in the best traditions of participatory journalism, wrote first-person accounts of their naked experiences. In the *Sunday Telegraph*, Auberon Waugh, son of Evelyn, wrote (keeping his clothes on): "I think he has made a good point, even if we cannot be sure what exactly it is."

Bethell's father eventually came around—"I can see his point of view, that it has to do with freedom and so on and so forth," he told me—but it was a lonely stand, and Bethell still had a long way to go. As he left the courtroom, clothes-free and bound for home, the first taxi he tried to hail turned him down. "Not on your life, sunshine!" the driver shouted through the window.

You can't really pin down the British character, although everyone is always trying to (defining Englishness as opposed to Britishness is even harder, although people try to do that even more). In his novel *England, England*, Julian Barnes imagined England as a giant theme park embodying "the Fifty Quintessences of Englishness," a list distilled from foreigners' responses to poll questions about things they associated with the country. The list was fairly standard: the royal family, Manchester United soccer team, the BBC, Winston Churchill, snobbery, whingeing (an extra-annoying form of whining), hypocrisy, the stiff upper lip—that kind of thing.

But if, as Barnes argued, the nation's image to the world had calcified into a series of familiar English clichés, its self-image—its belief in its unity and strength of purpose—was shattered by the terrorist attacks on July 7, 2005, when four British-born Muslims blew up themselves and fifty-two others in London's tubes and buses. The incident led to a period of agonized soul-searching. There was a general fear that the lack of a strong national identity, coupled with several decades of live-and-let-be multiculturalism, was alienating immigrants—failing to instill in them the British values that would make them feel part of a greater society.

The answer, the government said, was to promote the idea of a British dream that would encourage immigrants to think of themselves as British, not Polish or Pakistani or Iranian or Brazilian and the like. But first the government had to decide what it meant by Britishness. In 2007, Jack Straw, then the leader of the House of Commons—a cabinet position whose holder organizes the government's business in the chamber—found a partial definition: "freedom, tolerance and plurality."

He wasn't the first to point out those qualities. George Orwell, in his 1941 essay "The Lion and the Unicorn," declared that while it was impossible to generalize about the English, they tended in his opinion to be hypocritical, class ridden, mistrustful of abstract thought, law abiding, enthusiastic about hobbies like stamp collecting, and instinctively prone to banding together in crises. Those qualities seem fairly random, actually. But there was a more important one on Orwell's list: the craving for liberty—"the liberty to have a home of your own, to do what you like in your spare time, to choose your own amusements instead of having them chosen for you from above."

I think that is as good a description as any, the quiet celebration of liberty. When I try to define Britishness in my own mind, I keep coming back to the unwritten constitution—the constitution made up not of concrete provisions, but of precedents built up over time. Perhaps the best we can do is to say that the British are the sum of qualities collected over the centuries, the most enduring of which is the craving for freedom. They may be conformists, but, paradoxically, they also demand the right to be left alone to practice their individuality.

A streak of anarchy, or an acceptance of it—a tolerance for letting people be themselves, within the strictures of class and other superstructures—lies beneath the country's placid surface and helps define it to itself. It is no coincidence that the British are known for their peculiar people, be they fictional, as in the work of Dickens or Trollope, or real, as in the House of Lords.

You can find them all over the place. But for a while the best place to meet good eccentric characters was in the obituaries section of the *Daily Telegraph*. There, under the stewardship of the wry, self-deprecating-to-a-fault Hugh Massingberd, who edited the section from 1986 to 1994 and who died in 2007, the conventional death notice was elevated to high, humorous art. The more peculiar the deceased, the more disgraceful, incongruous, or amusing the life, the happier Massingberd was.

Narrow escapes from death by animal mauling; bizarre sexual practices; deeply held beliefs on topics of interest only to oneself; the tendency to make outrageous remarks at the wrong time; heroic failure; insouciance in the face of sure disaster—Massingberd loved them all. He favored a good anecdote over a dreary accomplishment, a scandalous life over a worthy one. The obituaries in his time were opinionated, lively, and not always kind. "All my life, I had seen history and biography as a marvelous excuse to tell funny stories, strange anecdotes, about people," Massingberd wrote, and he applied the same principle to his obituaries, little histories of the dead.

This reflects another English attitude: the belief that the longueurs of existence—its tedium, its disappointments—can be made bearable by a bit of deft editing. One of the best things about the English sense of humor is the way they turn dreadful experiences into funny ones in the telling. Just as they embroider experiences to make themselves look bad, so they pluck the best bits out of accounts of other people, in order to amuse. Reading through the Massingberd-era obituaries, you think, Could this really have happened? Which is part of the point: adroit embellishment and a focus on the high points help make life (and death, in this case) easier to endure.

Here in *The Very Best of the Daily Telegraph Books of Obituaries*, we meet the late Bapsy, Marchioness of Winchester. "Lady Winchester was prone to circulating documents extolling her own virtues," we read. "She wrote vitriolic letters to her husband: " 'May a viper's fangs be forever around your throat . . . and may you stew in the pit of your own juice.' "

We learn that the late "Bunny" Roger was a "couturier, art collector, flâneur, wit and exotic" who, in World War II, "advanced through enemy lines with a chiffon scarf flying as he brandished a copy of *Vogue*." Meanwhile, Sir John Junor, editor of the *Sunday Express*, had a tendency toward Johnsonian-style pronouncements. "Never trust a bearded man," he liked to say. "Only poofs drink white wine."

The Welshman known as Horace the Poet recited his work while standing beside a lamppost in the town of Merthyr Tydfil for forty-five years and was often assaulted by passersby who did not care for it. Anne Cumming, a "sexual adventuress" and erotic-travelogue writer, made a man faint at a dinner party when she described a sex-change operation she had witnessed in Casablanca. Leading a bayonet charge at Arnhem in 1944 while wearing a bowler hat and carrying a battered umbrella, Digby Tatham-Warter was captured after an explosion ripped off the back of his trousers; he later escaped, disguised as a housepainter.

The third Lord Moynihan worked as a bongo drummer, confidence trickster, brothel keeper, drug smuggler, and police informer, but described himself as a "professional negotiator," "international diplomatic courier," and "authority on rock and roll." The *Daily Express* columnist Jean Rook upset the Duchess of York by comparing her to "an unbrushed red setter struggling to get out of a handknitted potato sack." Sir Ewan Forbes of Craigievar was born and raised a girl but, forty years later, successfully applied to be redesignated a man. "It has been a ghastly mistake," he said.*

As he strode along the Pennine moors, the outdoor columnist Len Chadwick "would regale the young boys who were his most frequent companions (he was homosexually inclined) with interminable but inspired monologues, often in Esperanto." Earl Russell, the Marxist son of the philosopher Bertrand Russell, declared in the House of Lords that Leonid Brezhnev, the premier of Russia, and Jimmy Carter, the American president, were "really the same person," and, greeting a visi-

---

* The circumstances were kind of murky. "I was carelessly registered as a girl, " Sir Ewan (previously known as Elizabeth) told a reporter. "The doctors in those days were mistaken, too. . . . I have been sacrificed to prudery, and the horror which our parents had about sex." Three weeks after being formally declared a man, Sir Ewan (a beloved GP, under both genders, in Scotland) married his housekeeper, Isabella Mitchell. "It was a fairly quiet ceremony," the *Telegraph* reported.

tor to his house, pointed with pride to a pair of pants hanging by a hook. "I crocheted these out of string," he said.

Untied after being beaten senseless and trussed up in the scorching sun at a Japanese POW camp during World War II, the Australian surgeon Sir Edward "Weary" Dunlop rose to his feet and declared: "And now if you will excuse me, I shall amputate the arm of the Dutchman who has been waiting all day."

One of my favorite contemporary eccentric characters was a middle-aged man who, for a time, patrolled the streets of London in a home-made outfit that included a pair of gold lamé underpants. He was not a heroic figure in the same mold as old Weary Dunlop, the redoubtable arm-amputating Australian, but in his way he was a hero of the times. He worked by stealth on behalf of a class of people who were perpetually the victims of injustice, at least in their own minds: London's downtrodden motorists.

He appeared just as war was stirring between automobile owners and the government. Drivers were showing their contempt for the speed cameras springing up like weeds across Britain by defacing them, smashing them with sledgehammers, covering them in wrapping paper, knocking them flat with industrial vehicles, and blowing them to bits with homemade explosives. In London, the Tube-riding mayor, Ken Livingstone, was putting the final touches on his plan to charge car owners a hefty fee for the right to drive into the city (a dedicated environmentalist, he also urged people not to flush the toilet each time they went to the bathroom). Parking spaces were growing ever scarcer, and the draconian parking rules were enforced by teams of vicious, implacable wardens who saw every ticket written as a step toward fulfillment of their monthly quotas.

The automotive troubles of the age gave rise to an automotive champion for the age, a shadowy, self-appointed figure who stalked the streets, helping unhappy drivers by surreptitiously removing the officially placed security boots from their illegally parked cars. He described himself as a "superhero wheel clamp vigilante" and called himself Angle-Grinder Man, after the circular saw he used in his work. He kept his identity secret, in the best tradition of superheroes. No one knew who he was or where he was from, only that, in 2003, he suddenly began popping up around London. His Web site raised more questions than it answered, although it did have a photograph of him in his superhero mask, taking a bubble bath.

I had a hard time getting hold of him. He had a special hotline number, but no backroom staff to help him field the dozens of calls he was getting a day from aggrieved citizens. But I finally tracked him down, and we arranged to meet at my office, on the fifth floor of a small red-brick building near Buckingham Palace and the St. James's Park tube station.

A tall, lanky man of forty, with long, greasy hair, Angle-Grinder Man stepped off the elevator in civilian garb—he had not wanted to wear his superhero getup on the train—and then went into the *Times* bathroom to change. He emerged in full regalia. He wore a form-fitting blue shirt; gold-lamé-covered bikini briefs on top of tight blue leggings; a pair of cowboy boots spray-painted gold; a cape, also in gold lamé; black gloves, which he had purchased from a piercing-and-fetish shop; and a black mask, similar to the one that Robin might wear in the *Batman* films.

Angle-Grinder Man was coy about his civilian identity but eager to discuss his "look," which had taken him some time and some trial and error to create. He had rejected a number of color schemes before settling on blue and gold, and trawled flea markets in search of the perfect roll of gold lamé. "There's no school you can go to learn how to be a superhero," he said modestly.

He conceded that "Angle-Grinder Man" was perhaps not the catchiest superhero name ever, particularly as *AGM*, the letters he had proudly glued across his shirt, also stands for "annual general meeting."

But he was not discouraged by setbacks, either physical or psychological. His philosophy was simple. He wanted to help the downtrodden, the drivers fed up with being abused and hassled by a hardhearted bureaucracy that regarded them as notches in the ticket books, a bottomless source of municipal revenue. He performed his services free of charge, inspired, he said, by "anger at how politicians in this country treat people in general, but particularly in regard to motoring regulations."

It was part-time work, and he was still getting the hang of it. So far, his contribution to the motorists' equivalent of the Take Back the Streets movement had been modest: when I met him, he had successfully liberated only about twenty cars. But he had left in his wake a stream of happy customers, if that is what they could be called, and was gaining a reputation for performing small miracles in the neighborhoods of south London where his efforts were concentrated.

He gave me the number of a young car owner named Petite Tendai, who had arrived home about a month earlier to find her car booted and immobilized in the street. She had parked it in a no-parking zone, which was news to her. Or so she claimed. "There were no signs saying 'no parking,'" she told me. She had barely had time to rail, even inwardly, at the unfairness of it all when Angle-Grinder Man unexpectedly materialized.

"Basically, he jumped out of his car in his outfit and said, 'If anyone can, Angle-Grinder Man can,'" Tendai recalled. "Then he just started sawing it off. It was wicked." He was gone, in the best superhero tradition, almost as quickly as he came. "It was just a 'good luck,' and whatnot, and then he was off."

Just as Peter Parker is spurred to activism in the first *Spider-Man* movie when his beloved Uncle Ben is murdered by a callous thug, so Angle-Grinder Man was inspired by an unpleasant personal experience. His own car was booted. "I was fuming inside," he said. He rented a circular saw for about £30 pounds and removed the boot himself, saving £65 on what it would have cost to have it removed legally.

He affixed a photograph of the sawed-up boot to his windshield, along with a note saying, "Please don't clamp me because I've got an extremely sensitive nature."

The sign proved a hit, though he had to remove it after "a guy on a motorbike in traffic nearly fell off his bike, he was laughing so hard," Angle-Grinder Man said. But he had struck a nerve. "There was so much injustice out there."

The police did not agree about the injustice. Angle-Grinder Man was consistently eluding them through a powerful mixture of luck, cunning, and speed: he could saw off a boot in forty-five seconds. "Both Angle-Grinder Man and the owner of the vehicle could be charged with criminal damage if the driver admitted they consented to the act," Scotland Yard warned.

Londoners took him to heart, calling his special phone number and sending him fan notes. "It's time we had a gay superhero," one man told him.

For the record, "I'm a heterosexual superhero," Angle-Grinder Man said humbly, "although I have no problem being a gay icon."

Angle-Grinder Man had someplace else to be—another distressed citizen to aid? Another interview to give?—and he strode out onto the street in full costume, wheeling his suitcase behind him like a mere mortal. In the manner of a politician reluctant to be caught on camera smoking, he asked Jonathan, the *Times* photographer, not to photograph him boarding a taxi: bad for his image.

He crossed Caxton Street and headed for the taxi stand, his gold cape glittering and swirling heroically in the afternoon light, his boots clicking on the pavement. Judith Smith, a passing salesclerk who said she had been following Angle-Grinder Man's exploits on the Internet, pronounced herself a big fan.

"I think he's extraordinarily attractive," she told me. "Especially the golden knickers."

But love of eccentricity is not the same as love of celebrity. Britain is crawling with minor celebrities—it has to be, to fill the pages of the gossip sections of its newspapers and magazines—and people see them as the stars of long-running soap operas with frivolous plot-lines: getting drunk at nightclubs, kissing the wrong person, gaining weight, losing weight, having plastic surgery, wearing clothes that are too skimpy; shopping with your friends, stealing the husbands of your friends; checking into rehab. But these celebrities are expendable, and the public can turn against them and shoot them down as quickly as it builds them up. So Jade Goody, a former dental nurse who became a gossip-magazine staple after being propelled to fame by her ridiculous observations on the *Big Brother* reality-television program (she believed East Anglia, the region in England encompassing Cambridge, was called "East Angular," for instance), was seen as diverting, but absurd. The ludicrously expensive wedding of the enormous-breasted model Jordan, in which she arrived in a Cinderella-style carriage shaped like a pumpkin and drawn by six white horses? Mesmerizing but risible.

Contrast that with the late Isabella Blow, a fashion editor known for exotic habits like doing the gardening in Manolo Blahnik heels and for wearing spectacularly impractical hats—hats with horns, hats whose tendrils crept down and completely covered her face, a hat shaped like an erect penis. She was absurd but marvelous, and when she committed suicide, suffering from cancer and depression, it was her eccentricity rather than her tragedy that was remembered and celebrated. The obituaries recorded how she had once shown up for lunch with her boss, the managing director of Condé Nast UK, wearing a pair of antlers. When he asked her how she intended to eat, given that swooping down from the antlers was a heavy black lace veil that obscured her face, she replied, "Nicholas, that is of no concern to me whatsoever."

The best part about Blow was that she was able to laugh at herself, which was why she fit in so well.* No such luck for the American showman and illusionist David Blaine, a pseudoeccentric who took himself far too seriously and made the mistake of doing so in the heart of London.

Blaine was a street-magician-turned-enactor-of-unlikely-feats whose previous stunts, performed in the warm embrace of New York, had included standing for a spell at the top of a tall plinth, burying himself

---

* Her husband, Detmar—who wore the same old-fashioned military costume to his wife's funeral as he did to their wedding—was just as colorful. After Blow's death, he told an interviewer that he would miss her terribly, in part because she was so alluring. "Of all the girls I've made love to, she was the best," he said. "She was super-sexy! She had the most beautiful knickers! She was my soul mate."

in a Plexiglas coffin, and encasing himself in a block of ice in Times Square. His plan this time was to spend forty-four days in a see-through Plexiglas box, dangling from a crane near London Bridge, subsisting on nothing but water. He called the endeavor "Above the Below," which some observers considered a bit much.

The British were not impressed. They were not impressed when Blaine pronounced his venture "the most extreme exercise in isolation and physical deprivation ever attempted, " or when he said: "I'm a great artist: nothing more, nothing less." They were not impressed by the multimillion-pound deal he struck with Sky TV, and they were not impressed that he had decided to confine himself to a glass prison and voluntarily starve when so many people were actually incarcerated in real prisons, and actually starving. Mayor Livingstone said it was disrespectful to the IRA members who died on hunger strikes in the 1980s.

Blaine duly took his place in his box. But the stunt totally backfired: it was as if it were the eighteenth century and Blaine was in the stocks. Crowds of cynical Londoners gathered underneath the box and laughed at him. They pelted him with bananas, French fries, and eggs. They made such a mess that his girlfriend, the unusually named German model Manon von Gerkan, had to be cranked up on a crane to wash the food detritus off the box with a cloth. "We never had anything like this in New York," she said.

Blaine's helpers raised the box, so it would not be within egg-throwing distance. A group of men positioned themselves on Tower Bridge and tried to hit it with golf balls. A hamburger van pulled up and began ostentatiously frying onions and other foods whose enticing aroma was designed to upset Blaine, starving as he was. A man tried to cut off his water supply. Some youths frightened him by shining laser pens into his eyes. A homeless person sat nearby, behind a sign saying, "Please give generously. I am attempting 44 days on continuous alcohol alone."

Women took off their tops and flashed their breasts at Blaine; men pulled down their pants and mooned at him; people stayed up all night playing the drums so as to disturb the tranquillity of anyone who might be trying to sleep in an overhead box. A radio station urged its listeners to stand in the cold chanting, "Ding, ding, ding" in an obnoxious fashion. Someone blasted the song "Living in a Box" by the British pop-funk group Living in A Box. A remote-control helicopter buzzed by, dangling a juicy-looking cheeseburger on a string.

There was unpleasant speculation about Blaine's bathroom arrangements, in keeping with Britons' well-known lavatorial obsessions. Blaine's explanation of his plans for his liquid waste—that it would be expelled via a tube leading out of the plastic box—had left the solid waste situation deliberately vague. Adult diapers were mentioned. A radio host took to calling Blaine "Nappy Man."

Newspaper columnists speculated that the illusionist had been eating on the sly, saying that he actually looked kind of fat, considering. In the *Sun*, Jane Moore referred to him as "that total twerp currently dangling in a glass box over the Thames." In the *Guardian*, Catherine Bennett said that the satirical response to Blaine illustrated the temperamental gulf between Britain and America, because Britons know how to "tell the difference between a huckster and a hero." She urged Londoners to engage in mass public ridicule by taunting Blaine with food. "Even a blob of oily ice-cream tastes exquisite when consumed in the suspended company of the preposterous, faux-starving Blaine," she said.

True, he did have his supporters, including American tourists; regular visitors who believed that they had telepathic connections to him and that he was sending them special signals from the box; people who felt sorry for him; and the paranormalist Uri Geller, who announced: "He has the quality of Rasputin."

When Blaine finally came down, thin and weak and with his major organs on the verge of collapse (or so he said), the general feeling was that "Above the Below" had been beyond the absurd, a huge pretentious failure. But what was it that made ordinary Britons tease and resent Blaine so much? Because he was making such a big deal about it. Because he had revealed himself to be a puffed-up self-promoter rather than the friendly kind of eccentric who does what he does for himself rather than for public acclaim, and who is capable of going to the pub and laughing at himself over a few pints. Because he did not know when enough was enough.

POSTSCRIPT

The issue of how to describe Britain—and how to define what it meant to be a British citizen—continued to rumble on after the end of the Blair era. When Gordon Brown became prime minister in mid-2007, the government announced that it wanted to formulate a statement of "British values" as a way to foster good community relations and national cohesion.

That led to a certain degree of mirth, since one defining trait of the British is their tendency to make fun of worthy government proposals. Detractors spread the rumor that the government was looking not for a considered statement but for a snappy, pithy, "liberté, égalité, fraternité"–style slogan that it could plaster across government buildings in a kind of branding exercise.

The government denied there were plans for a motto, but *The Times* of London held a motto-writing contest anyway.

The finalists included: "Dipso, Fatso, Bingo, Asbo, Tesco" ("Asbo" stands for antisocial behavior order, a law-enforcement tool, while "Tesco" is a pervasive supermarket chain); "Once mighty empire, slightly used"; "At least we're not French"; and "We apologize for the inconvenience." The winner, favored by 20.9 percent of voting *Times* readers, was "No motto please, we're British."

"The point I was making is, this idea of a statement of Britishness; I cannot think of anything less British than that," said twenty-five-year-old David Bishop, author of the winning motto.

In the House of Lords, there was a surreal debate on the nonmotto, even after Lord Hunt of Kings Heath, an official in the Ministry of Justice, said flatly that there were no plans to have one.

"I do not think I will go down that route," he said. "But I will say that the motto of Birmingham City Football Club is 'Keep right on 'til the end of the road.'"

Earl Ferrers asked: "If the Minister finds it difficult to provide a motto for the whole country, would he be prepared to consider a motto for your Lordships' House: 'Questions and answers ought to be short'?"

The Earl of Mar and Kellie suggested employing the Scottish heraldic motto "Nemo me impecune lacessit," which he translated as "Do not sit on a thistle" (actually, it means "No one provokes me with impunity"). Lord Roberts of Conwy asked: "My Lords, what is wrong with the excellent words which face us daily, 'Dieu et mon droit,' and 'Honi soit qui mal y pense'?"

Well, lots of things, now that you ask. "As the noble Lord will know, that represents the divine right of kings," Lord Hunt responded. "While it is of course a well-known phrase, one would need to reflect on whether that would be entirely relevant to a motto that we are not going to have."

TEN

INVASION OF THE HEDGEHOG PEOPLE

Are hedgehogs intelligent?
Basically, the answer to that question has to be "No."
　　　　　—Pat Morris, *Hedgehogs* (1987)

Hedgehogs are native to many parts of Great Britain, but not to the Hebrides, a wild and sparsely populated group of tiny islands off Scotland's west coast. The Outer Hebrides, which include North and South Uist and Benbecula, are known for severe weather, severe religion, and spectacular birds—lapwings, snipe, redshank, plovers, and oystercatchers, among others—who stop off to build their nests in the scrub brush there each year. This is the kind of place generally described as "unforgiving," where the winds pushing against your car door create a vacuum effect that impedes your ability to disembark; where a village means half a dozen cottages and a flock of sheep; and where a day that the landscape is not lashed by torrential rain and/or buffeted by tornadoesque wind patterns is considered a pleasant surprise.

It is unclear who brought the first hedgehogs—two males and two females, in a box, as legend has it—to the Hebrides in the early 1970s. Some believe it was a doctor, and others a schoolteacher, but the consensus seems to be that whoever it was hoped to find a cheap and easy slug-destroying device for the garden. But the move had unforeseen consequences. Free of such natural predators as badgers, the hedge-hogs multiplied like Tribbles, the fuzzy, furry, rapidly procreating fictional creatures in *Star Trek*. Although it is hard to get an actual figure, on account of how many hogs are hiding in the brush, resting, or hiber-nating at any one time, the rough estimate is that there are between four thousand and ten thousand hedgehogs on the islands (there are about four thousand people). And because hedgehogs eat everything they come across, whenever they run into the eggs of the nesting birds (which is often, because the birds lay their eggs on the ground), they gobble them up—a habit that has severely reduced the bird numbers.

Hedgehogs are curious creatures. Small and covered in one-inch spines, they look like ambulatory toilet brushes without the han-dles, or like turtles, if turtles were a little bit taller and had prickles glued on their shells. But the pragmatic Hebridean islanders have no romantic notions about their spiny garden friends. The only time they generally notice them is when they see their flattened corpses on the roads. If it came down to a contest, they would tend to choose the birds over the hogs. "Rats with prickles," is how one islander described hedgehogs to me.

Such hardheartedness is very much the exception in Britain, a place where sentimental attachment to animals, including abstract ones fea-tured in the newspapers, can often surpass genuine attachment to liv-ing people featured in one's own home. This seems like an eccentricity, but I don't think it is; I think it is a fact of life.

It is really striking. When my daughters were babies and I was pushing them in their stroller through London, no one ever stopped to chat, or offered to help, or asked any questions about them. But when I got a puppy, I became the Pied Piper of Kensington. People began following me around the park, swooning about the puppy's cuteness, offering helpful dog-rearing tips, and trying to schedule playdates with their own puppies.

Every British animal has its cheerleaders. The country has so many badger-support groups that it was deemed necessary to create an umbrella organization, the National Federation of Badger Groups, now known as the Badger Trust, to coordinate all the disparate badger-related activity. The National Bat Hotline takes ten thousand calls a year, providing "free information and advice to anyone who needs help with a bat," its Web site says. Every year, during the toad mating season, hundreds of volunteers put on orange fluorescent vests and help amorous toads cross the street in Wales, using the two most popular toad-helping methods: escorting them or transporting them in buckets.

A 1980s television show called *One Man and His Dog*—in which audiences watched taciturn, weatherbeaten shepherds use high-pitched whistles to issue instructions to dogs attempting to herd sheep into pens—attracted eight million viewers a time. "It doesn't kowtow to the idea that people can only concentrate for 30 seconds," said the actor Stephen Fry, who in addition to his other jobs and interests was a fan of the program. "And I love the idea that it sometimes takes place in the rain."

At Brook Gate on Park Lane in London, just east of Hyde Park, visitors can admire the £1 million Animals in War Memorial, erected in 2004 to commemorate the animals who aided the British in various armed conflicts. These include, according to the bas-relief sculpture on the side of the memorial, donkeys, horses, monkeys, pigeons, mules, camels, and glowworms—the last apparently used as flashlights by soldiers in World War II trenches. Chiseled on the side is an indisputable observation about the animals' participation in the wars: They Had No Choice.

U.K. HONORS GLOW WORM HEROES, read the headline on the CNN Web site when the memorial was erected.*

Britons are particularly keen on contributing to charities supporting animal causes. In 2003, a rest home for abused, retired and elderly donkeys in Devon took in £13 million in donations, more than was given that year to charities supporting the elderly and the mentally ill. (Seventy percent of the money came in the form of bequests in the wills of deceased donkey lovers.)

"What's quite hard to swallow is the fact that lots of people out

---

* In addition to his position as the queen's Silver Stick-in-Waiting, Andrew Parker Bowles, the Duchess of Cornwall's ex-husband, was the vice chairman of the Animals in War Memorial Fund, which raised the money to pay for the memorial.

there would rather give money and sympathy to donkeys than to, for example, the children of refugees," an executive at Ideal Creative, a charity marketing group, said at the time.

But even with all those support groups and competing interests, hedgehogs have a special position in the British animal hierarchy.

They don't make the most affectionate of pets, in part because they are naturally wild animals, and in part because their IQs seem to be only slightly higher than those of, say, flashlights (over time, however, housebound hedgehogs have been known to learn to raise their heads in a slightly alert manner when their owners arrive with breakfast). When threatened, a hog responds by rolling itself into a prickly ball and pretending it is not there, like a small child who believes that if she covers her eyes with her fingers, no one will be able to see her. While rolling into a ball helps shield hedgehogs from other animals, it provides little protection against their greatest threat, the automobile.

Nor were hedgehogs always so popular. Neolithic pre-Britons liked to eat them, roasted. Farmers in medieval times believed that hogs crept into fields in the middle of the night and surreptitiously siphoned milk from cows. In Ireland they were known as "graineeogs," or "ugly ones." Shakespeare mentioned them unfavorably on several occasions, calling them "urchins" and "hedgepigs"; in *A Midsummer Night's Dream*, he put them on a list of vile creatures—including newts, blindworms, and spotted snakes—meant to stay away from Titania, the queen of the fairies.

But hedgehogs were rehabilitated in the popular imagination by Beatrix Potter, who made one the protagonist of *The Tale of Mrs. Tiggy-Winkle*, a book about the difficulties of running a woodland laundry service. The eponymous heroine, whose prickles jut alarmingly through her headscarf, works as a washerwoman and, though not a hog of obvious intellect, does manage successfully to juggle the taxing linen demands of Cock Robin, Squirrel Nutkin, and Peter Rabbit, among others. She displays an admirable work ethic, even when the job is difficult. "That one belongs to old Mrs. Rabbit; and it did so smell of onions!" she frets, about a pocket handkerchief. "I've had to wash it separately."

In real life, even the grumpy, misanthropic poet Philip Larkin

developed in his later years an affectionate rapport with a hedgehog that regularly visited his garden, probably one of the few of his
acquaintances who was as prickly as Larkin himself. Tragically, Larkin
inadvertently murdered the hedgehog by running it over with his lawn
mower. The incident inspired the tender poem "The Mower," in which
he described the anguish of examining the lawn mower and finding the
ex-hog "jammed up against the blades."

It's not just Larkin who appeared to find hedgehogs more sympathetic than people. The *Daily Mail* once printed an article about a man
in New Zealand who allegedly threw a hedgehog at a teenager in anger,
hitting him (the teenager) in the leg and causing a "large red welt and
several puncture wounds." "The man was arrested shortly afterwards
and he's been charged with assault with a weapon, namely a hedgehog,"
an official told the paper. The hedgehog was dead—it was unclear for
how long—when the police arrived.

In comments on the *Mail*'s Web site, several dozen British readers
expressed their dismay.

"When will people learn that they cannot and should not use animals in this callous and cruel way?" wrote Abi from Shropshire. "I would
hope this man gets five years for killing the hedgehog, not assaulting the
teenager!"

People always have something to say about hedgehogs.

"If you go to a party and say, 'I study anal glands or biochemical
pathways,' that would be the end of the conversation," Pat Morris, a
retired lecturer in zoology at the Royal Holloway College who spent
more than thirty years studying hedgehogs and is the author of *The
Hedgehog*, a comprehensive work on the species, told me. "Whereas if
you talk about hedgehogs, everybody's an expert." His colleagues have
not always understood his obsession. "In the zoological community, I
think hedgehogs are regarded as a bit of a joke," he said.*

---

* Morris was modest about his accomplishments, but he is generally regarded as the
world authority on the European hedgehog. "There was a German chap who published
a monograph in 1938 on hedgehogs, and his publishers described him as the world
expert," he said. "But it was a title I was glad to take over."

Why do the British care about them so much?

They are cute, with adorably snuffly noses and attractively frosted quills. They sleep most of the day and hibernate for months at a time, making them a perfect object of adoration for the intimacy averse. They provide the benefits of a satisfying personal relationship without the fuss of emotional engagement. If you leave some food—dog or cat food is fine, although discerning hogs enjoy Spike's Dinner hedgehog chow —in the corner of the garden, you can see the hedgehogs come scuttling around at dusk, before they go away again. Although they are promiscuous, visiting many gardens a night, they don't make any trouble.

"You can't find fault with a hedgehog," Lisa Frost, a veterinary nurse at Tiggywinkles, a hospital for wild animals in Buckinghamshire that treats thousands of sick hedgehogs a year, told me. (For those who are particularly enthusiastic, it has a hedgehog museum on the top floor.) "Literally, they come in and eat all the slugs and snails in a garden, and then leave." They make good patients, too, she said, except for the curling-into-a-ball part.*

Hedgehogs naturally have their own lobbying organization, the British Hedgehog Preservation Society. The group raises money, agitates on hog-related matters, and provides support to the wide network of volunteers who run shelters for disabled, ill, and orphaned hedgehogs across the country.

He became interested in hogs as an undergraduate at Exeter University when, looking for rabbits under some brushwood, he happened upon a trove of rolled-up prickly balls. They looked like giant Spanish chestnuts, but they were really hedgehogs, fast asleep. Not just sleeping but hibernating. It was at the time a rare sight in the history of hedgehog study—they were hard to catch in the act. "There'd been a lot of research on hibernating in the laboratory, but nobody knew about their ecology," Morris said.

Morris studied the sleeping hedgehogs for six winters and, one summer in the early 1960s, installed tiny radio tracking devices on his subjects to find out where they went when they were not in bed. He wrote his doctoral dissertation on hedgehogs and continued his research over the following decades, cementing his position in hedgehog circles.

* My husband and I took our daughters to the hospital one summer. We were directed to the handsome grounds outside where, we were told, we would be able to spot recuperating hedgehogs snuffling around the fenced enclosures. Alas, they were all hiding in the bushes, or somewhere, and we didn't see any.

I met one of these volunteers once, a hedgehog devotee named Mavis Righini. She had converted a room in her suburban London house into a kind of hedgehog dormitory, caring for as many as forty at a time, some suffering from brain damage after car accidents.* When I visited the house, her hogs were mostly just resting, obscured by their bedding.

She explained that she had always loved animals. But it was only when a coworker unexpectedly entrusted her with five sickly baby hedgehogs, or hoglets, pink and frosted with coats of delicate white prickles, that she finally found her true life's calling. Her husband, a shy postal worker, was more skeptical. It took him years before he could bring himself to physically touch one of his wife's patients. "I like animals, in the abstract," he told me.

I picked up one of Righini's patients, which immediately prickled at me in a sea-urchinesque manner. There is a protocol for uncurling them, explained in detail in a hedgehog society pamphlet, but I had not yet seen it and was at a loss. It was an exciting moment. I had never been close to a real hedgehog before, although I had once seen one shuffling noisily in the bushes at dusk at our cottage in Cambridgeshire. But it was a bit of an anticlimax, and the prickles were gouging uncomfortably into the skin on my hand. As I stood there wondering what to do with the hog—the method favored by Lewis Carroll's Queen of Hearts, using it as a ball in a croquet game, was not an immediate option—Righini began to describe some of the difficulties of hedgehog care, like their smell (bad) and their tendency to attract fleas and other unwanted visitors. The most pressing quandary for the proprietor of a hedgehog sanctuary, though, has to do with hibernation.

The issue is this: Come wintertime, should rescued hedgehogs be encouraged to hibernate indoors, under blankets, or should they be allowed to stay up all winter, doing the hog equivalent of partying through the night?

---

* Brain-damaged hedgehogs tend to wander around in circles, which is always distressing to watch.

Like an indulgent mother of an American child, Righini believed in not setting too many hard-and-fast bedtime rules. "As far as hibernating goes, some do and some don't," she said. "It's their choice."

In the spring of 2003, while the island of North Uist was minding its own business and getting on with the grimness of daily existence, it was suddenly invaded by a swarm of outsiders. "Hedgehog people," was the unadmiring way the proprietor of a local store, James Matheson, described them to me. He also said that he was "brought up not knowing what hedgehogs were," which described the islanders' attitude in a nutshell.

When I arrived on North Uist, on a blustery afternoon, several things immediately became clear. First, it was not a good day to be outside, even if you define "outside" as "the area between the car and the hotel." Second, the islanders were people of few words. If the English are laconic, then Hebridean Scots are virtually mute.

Third, the last thing anyone wanted to talk about was the hedgehog situation.

But it was important, whether or not the natives wanted to admit it. It had come to a showdown between two animal groups: the hedgehogs and the wading birds. Studies had shown that that on South Uist and Benbecula, which were teeming with alien hedgehogs, the bird population had been declining steadily and severely—in some cases, by as much as 50 percent over fifteen years, due to the hogs' bird-egg-eating habit.

A government agency called Scottish Natural Heritage concluded that the hogs were hurting not just the South Uist ecology, but also the economy, which was heavily dependent on birdwatching tourists. It had to intervene, the agency decided, before the same thing happened on North Uist, where the hedgehog population had not yet taken hold. The idea was to get rid of as many hedgehogs as possible.

There were two potential methods of doing so. Option A: round up the hedgehogs and airlift them to freedom on the mainland. Option B: catch them, put them on the hedgehog equivalent of Death Row, without the long wait or chance of appeal, and then kill them by lethal injection.

After more studies and more debating, the agency decided that relocation would traumatize the hogs and cause many of them to die of shock anyway, so the best bet was Option B, killing (or "culling," as it is called by the people doing it).

But the government had not reckoned on the powerful hedgehog lobby, led by the British Hedgehog Preservation Society. The hogs should not be killed, the preservation society said; they should be rescued. They offered to fly the animals off the island themselves, at their own expense, and place them in hedgehog-hospitable gardens on the mainland. They said they would vet potential adopters with detailed questionnaires and onsite inspections. (They went ahead and began accepting applications. Thousands of people applied to be hedgehog guardians; most were turned down as unsuitable.)

The two camps tried to reach some kind of compromise, but negotiations broke down in discord. An un-Solomonic solution was devised, wherein each side—the cullers and the rescuers—decided to go forward with its own scheme, racing to collect the most hedgehogs and keep them out of the other's clutches. The government would kill its hogs; the hedgehog groups, which had coalesced into a special team called Uist Hedgehog Rescue, would pack them into cardboard boxes and ship them to rehabilitation centers on the mainland before releasing them to freedom.

In the greater battle for hearts and minds beyond the small confines of the Hebrides, Uist Hedgehog Rescue had the psychological advantage. What sadistic sort of person would want to inject a cute little hedghog with lethal poison? In no time at all, the group had raised some £40,000 and gathered support from as far away as Australia. After someone gave out his e-mail address, George Anderson, then the press officer for Scottish Natural Heritage and, unhappily for him, the human face behind the government plan, began receiving unfriendly notes in his in-box.

"This is downright disguisting [sic]!" wrote a woman from Bellflower, California. From Kent in England, another woman compared the government to the Nazis. "This is the animal version of destroying the Jews to protect the Aryan races!" she said.

Anderson appeared to be unfazed by all the abuse, though there were times when he wished that the hedgehogs were a little less winsome.

"For over a year, we've been killing hundreds of mink here for exactly the same reason, and nobody has batted an eyelid about it," he told me as he unlocked his car in a parking lot on the island, shouting above the wind. But minks smell *really* terrible and have unpleasant personalities, in addition to mean little faces and sharp little claws, and had never been the subject of a well-known children's book.

"I sometimes wonder if Beatrix Potter had had a character called Mindy Mink, if we'd be having similar reactions to the mink cull," Anderson said. The rain misted through the wind, and his hair whipped around his face as if someone were slapping him with wet spaghetti.

The two groups set up their opposing camps, pointedly pretending to ignore each other, like rival teams of explorers racing to the North Pole. The biggest problem they faced was in actually catching the hedgehogs. They had to work at night, since hedgehogs are nocturnal. The going was slow, on account of the gloom, the uneven terrain, and the wet. Also, when the would-be hedgehog-catchers started their operations, many hedgehogs had not yet woken up from their long winter's nap.

On the positive side, the hogs lived up to their reputation as inveterate curlers-into-balls rather than runners-away, thus proving easy to grab, as long as the grabber was wearing gloves.

Each group had its own advantages. Scottish Natural Heritage had the advantage of money, experience, and being able to conduct its search with flashlights and floodlights. Using artificial lights to look for wild animals in the dark in Scotland requires a permit, and Scottish Heritage, as it happens, is the very agency that issues the permits. Not surprisingly, it turned down Uist Hedgehog Rescue's application.*

But Uist Hedgehog Rescue had the advantage of a well-developed sense of moral superiority and a messianic passion for the sanctity of hedgehog life. Also, it pledged to pay local residents £5 for each live hedgehog they brought in.

---

* Some of the rescuers used flashlights anyway, "for their own personal safety," Ross Minett, a spokesman for Uist Hedgehog Rescue, told me. "If they happened to come across a hedgehog, they'd pick it up."

The rescuers, a rotating band of veterinary nurses and general enthusiasts, settled into a number of cabins in a deserted trailer park. One cabin became the hedgehog center; the other was the command center, where rescuers warmed up, drank tea, and ate cookies. They needed all the cookies they could get. After three nights, they had rescued just five hogs. They named the first one Hamish. Another, whose name I did not catch, was found impaled on a fence and required nose surgery. The rescuers all smelled like canned dog food, the tasty treat they had been laying out in an effort to lure the hedgehogs. But their enthusiasm remained undiminished.

The government, now trying to put a better spin on things by calling its effort the Uist Wader Project, was just as determined to go ahead with its plan to stamp out the hedgehogs. Both groups worked steadily for the next two months. The rescue group caught 150 hogs and airlifted them to safety. The government caught 66 and killed them all. The numbers raised an interesting question: Since at least that many hogs would be born the following year, thus replacing the lost population, didn't the whole thing—the elaborate catching methods, the anesthesia, the boxes, the food, the injections—seem rather quixotic?

Well, exactly. Even as the two hedgehog groups worked in opposition to each other, what linked them was that both operations were patently absurd. You can no sooner catch an entire population of several thousand hedgehogs in a hostile strip of grass and sand than you could capture all the individual ants in an anthill, or all the mosquitoes on a swamp.

"There's no long-term solution, unless they manage to remove every single one, which is pretty damn unlikely," admitted Ross Minett, the hedgehog-rescue spokesman. "It's come down to a real point of principle."

The prospect of dozens of government workers and volunteers coming back regularly, with their cardboard boxes and their crazy schemes and their bowls of dog food, had one shopper at Matheson's store muttering unkindly about "nut cases."

But even nut cases have to spend money on places to stay and things to eat, and here was hope that the influx of outsiders would provide a small boost to the local economy. Hedgehogs, no hedgehogs—it was all the same to them, the islanders said, as long as they themselves didn't have to participate.

And they didn't. The next year, the two groups came back and did it all over again.

POSTSCRIPT

The government put about seven hundred hedgehogs to death over the next few years. In the spring of 2007, under relentless pressure from the hedgehog lobby, it stopped killing and instead turned over the hogs it caught to Uist Hedgehog Rescue for relocation to the mainland.

ELEVEN

"I SNAPPED IT OUT MYSELF"

*When you put [the fact that 12 percent of Britons say they
brush their teeth 'a few times a week' or 'never'] alongside the
fact that people are using anything from drill bits and ham-
mers to fish bones and toe nails to pick their teeth, then you
can see that there is still a long way to go in improving oral
healthcare in this country.*
>   —Dr. Nigel Carter, chief executive of the
>   British Dental Health Foundation (2007)

*It's simply astonishing in this day and age that we have people
pulling their own teeth out.*
>   —Dr. Anthony Halperin, chairman of the
>   Patients' Association (2007)

One winter's evening, I found myself standing on the edges of
a book party in a shabby, cavernous room at a club on Pall Mall,
in central London. The party was full of important figures from
the publishing world, but scant attention had been paid to the care and
feeding of the guests. It was as if someone had thrown us all in to a high-
school gym with poor acoustics and poor heating and told us to talk amongst
ourselves. The hors d'oeuvres were mostly small bowls of potato chips laid
out along the windowsills. Once I spotted a waiter carrying a tray of sau-

sage rolls—sausage meat enrobed in pastry—but then he vanished, as if there were piranhas and they had gotten to him (and the sausage rolls).

I had been making a big effort, really I had, to get over my shallow obsession with my personal comfort, a holdover from my old life. I tried to focus on the conversation: it was so much better than it would have been in New York. There was no chatter on the topics of My Therapeutic Epiphany, for instance, or My Hamptons Traffic Nightmare. No one was bragging about his accomplishments or being earnest about her problems. I don't even remember what clever arguments they marshaled, what personal disasters they spun into sharp anecdotes, but they were dropping the sort of witty offhand remarks that make listening to Britons in full humorous mode one of life's great pleasures.

But I was kind of cold, and kind of hungry, and I was doing more listening than talking, and after a while even the good stories weren't enough to keep me from mentally drifting off. Just as a weary commuter riding the subway late at night might become entranced by the flickering lights in the tunnels, I became fixated on something entirely different.

Something scary had happened to their mouths.

The BBC producer? Her teeth were a revolting grayish yellow, stained from decades of smoking and tea drinking.

The distinguished novelist? His gums had receded so completely that it looked as if, were you to quietly tap one of his teeth with a small Q-tip, the tooth would topple over like a rotten gravestone.

The woman in the sexy top describing her racy romantic past? Her teeth were not only gray and mottled, packed at the gums with old unflossed bits of food that had calcified into fixed cementlike structures, but also they pointed in all directions, so that one had carved a permanent indentation into her lip.

I looked around—at mouths whose upper teeth had grown unusually long, traveling down to join stunted lower teeth; at teeth flecked at the top with black bits, a side effect of smoking and failing to brush after meals; at ancient crowns where gum recession had deposited what looked like dirty watermarks on the teeth, as if the tide had come in and then retreated.

THE ANGLO FILES • 195

It wasn't very nice of me. In 1941, Orwell described "the crowds in the big towns, with their mild knobby faces, their bad teeth and gentle manners," and the truth is that many of the unkind cliches about British dental care are, in fact, dead accurate. Especially from the point of view of the tooth-obsessed foreigner. An American friend in New York sent her British husband to her dentist soon after they got married. The dentist reported back. "A typical English mouth," he told her grimly. "Disaster."

Think of Mike Myers's mouth, with its crooked, yellow teeth that look like a horse's, a visual joke in the *Austin Powers* movies. Think of the classic *Simpsons* episode in which dental-phobic children are forced to read *The Big Book of British Teeth*, a cautionary collection of distressing photographs of people like Princess Margaret (the idea is that exposure to these sorry oral specimens would propel anyone double-quick into the dental chair). In Mexico bad teeth are known as *dientes de ingles*. Johnny Rotten of the Sex Pistols may or may not have been named for his grubby, algae-colored teeth, antiadvertisements for his country, but if he wasn't, he should have been.

The state of Britons' teeth increasingly has to do with money. People who can afford to pay, go to expensive dentists, while people who can't, take pot luck with the state-financed system, the National Health Service. But it's generational, too. Many older Britons grew up regarding anything other than basic dentistry—the kind that prevents all your teeth from falling out, and that's about it—as excessive self-indulgence. They are still suspicious of and even repulsed by American teeth, their unnatural sparkle and aggressively expensive evenness, their self-regarding sheen; away from London such teeth would seem as obvious and fake as bad breast implants. Every British actor I've interviewed has grumbled about the demeaning American tooth job, the transforming ritual of crowns, veneers, and whitening treatments that Hollywood producers insist on as a casting prerequisite.

When my friend Damian arrived for graduate school at Harvard, his mouth gave him away before his voice did.

"I assumed that good teeth were part of the Harvard admissions policy," he says, "until I noticed the other dentally challenged people speaking with English accents."

In *The Information*, Martin Amis imagines the American city as "a monstrous acreage of wedged dentition": "With those big teeth they have, no wonder their gums whine with permanent maintenance and repair, all the deep scaling and root-canal work, the cappings, bridgings, excruciating extractions."*

You could pity the Brits for their bad teeth. But you could also say that it is possibly their own fault. Most parts of the country still refuse to fluoridate the water, considering fluoride a dangerous drug and an example of government mind control. While most drugstores stock an array of affordable dental products, like dental floss, which people could use if they wanted to, Britons tend to consider the removal of food from between one's teeth an optional activity.

"Prevention and having nice white shiny teeth is a huge priority for us from the moment we're born," Jennifer Stone, the sales and marketing manager for an American dental products company in Britain, told me. (She's American, too, which is why she said "us.") "That doesn't seem to be the culture here. You've got a lot of tea drinkers; you've got a lot of staining. In the U.S., we go through a spool of dental floss in six weeks, on average. Here it's a year and a half."

Let me repeat that: *The average Briton takes one and a half years to use up a pack of dental floss.*

Generally speaking, foreigners have always been more obsessed with British teeth than Britons have themselves. But in his book *British Teeth*, the journalist William Leith turns the spotlight inward, examin-

---

* Amis's teeth became a cause célèbre in 1994 when it emerged that he had received a huge, un-British advance for *The Information* while also undergoing a huge amount of un-British dental work in Manhattan. It became a scandal, the issue of dental improvement. Was it necessary, or just narcissistic? Was it unpatriotic, even hostile?

But it was a false debate. Amis had not self-indulgently treated himself to a spot of cosmetic enhancement. His teeth were a catastrophe. They always had been, since he was a child at the mercy of the local practitioner, and they were an underlying theme of his work. From his first novel, *The Rachel Papers*, Amis's books feature characters suffering from a thousand different kinds of toothaches. The unfortunate category "dental problems" takes up five lines in the index of *Experience,* his 2000 memoir.

The world "thinks I'm after a Liberace effect, that what I want is a dazzling smile," Amis said later. But, able to use only about 11 percent of his mouth by the time he made it to that American dentist, all he wanted, he said, was to be able to eat.

ing tooth as metaphor by equating the decline and fall of one of his molars with the disintegration of Britain itself.

Leith's book describes how the tooth is not only hurting, but also cracking and splintering in new and frightening ways. The pain and its wider connotations make him feel bad about himself, and bad about his country. His molar seems to be just one more example of Britain's deterioration, on a par with other national failings. He thinks about former prime minister John Major, who "had spent the day before he decided to stand as leader of the Conservative Party at the dentist, having a tooth pulled to facilitate the drainage of an abscess." He thinks about how British people regard their nationality as "something awkward and difficult, something that must be handled with tact and discretion, and preferably hidden or masked."

> [Britain] was a place of bitterness and envy, a place that had become ashamed of itself, a place where educated people hid their knowledge, where the middle classes grew up trying to imitate the voices of the poor. We had developed a taste for failure. . . . We had become known, and knew ourselves, as a nation of losers.

British Teeth was published in 2001, just as it was becoming apparent that the crisis affecting Leith's mouth was also affecting the mouths of many others. A strange thing began to happen, so strange that at first no one could understand what was going on. People began to report seeing groups of citizens lining up at seemingly random locations around the country, often very early in the morning. The British can be good at, even excited about, queuing—"An Englishman, even if he is alone, forms an orderly queue of one," the writer George Mikes observed in 1946— but this was something completely new. Suddenly there were queues in places few people had ever queued before, like rural Wales.

What was happening was this: People were trying to sign up for dental care.

"I said this couldn't be for us—no, this couldn't be for us," said Nelson Kernahan, a National Health dentist in the tiny Welsh town of Carmarthen, who arrived for work one day and found one of these

198 · SARAH LYALL

queues, a ragged line of citizens extending out from the front door of the office to some spot far into the distant netherworld. They looked wretched, even despondent. There were perhaps six hundred of them. "It was like a breadline."

Then he realized. They *were* there for him. They were there because, in a practically unheard-of development, his dental practice had announced that it had extra space for three hundred new patients.

The prospective patients outside Kernahan's door were desperate, the trauma of their bad teeth having been aggravated by the unpleasantness of camping out overnight in the harsh Welsh rain. They had been turned away from dentists before, and many of them were about to be turned away again.

It was unlikely, for instance, that fifty-six-year-old Steve Acworth, who had traveled by bus for seventy-five minutes, would make the cut. He was too far back in the line, which was a shame, "considering he does not really have any teeth to speak of," my colleague Lizette Alvarez wrote in an article in the *New York Times*.

"My crowns all fell off," Acworth explained. "I got some really bad dentistry and it ruined all my root work. I have no front teeth and one pair of molars, which meet on the right side of my mouth. I can't bite anything."

As in Carmarthen, so it was around the country. The queues stretched everywhere, evoking Depression-era runs on banks, Deadheads camping out for tickets, shoppers lining up for the Harrods post-Christmas sale, vagrants massing at soup kitchens. It was an embarrassing phenomenon for a government that had pledged to make dental care accessible to everyone.

Legislators said that aching teeth, and no one to treat them, were among their constituents' biggest complaints, up there with rising gas prices, shrinking pensions, and lawlessness in the streets.

"You could argue that Britain has not seen lines like this since World War II," Mark Pritchard, a Conservative member of Parliament from Shropshire, told me. "Churchill once said that the British are great queuers, but I don't think he meant that in connection to dental care."

"Their teeth are going rotten," said Paul Rowen, the Labour MP for Rochdale.

The National Health Service (NHS), perhaps the world's greatest experiment in nationalized health, was founded in 1948, instantly improving the health of a nation and altering forever, as did other provisions of the new welfare state, the relationship between the government and the people. Then, everyone had access to free, or nearly free, dental care—at least in theory. The treatment was not necessarily thorough or comprehensive, but it was better than nothing.*

But a system that worked in the middle of the century had become overstretched by the end of it. By the time John Major's government left office, in 1997, many NHS dentists had become disillusioned and restive, even more so than other national-health workers. They earned too little money, they complained; they spent too much of their day filling out forms and meeting quotas; they were forced to see too many patients in too short a time. In 2006, the government introduced a new system designed to rationalize the payment structure by assigning to each procedure a set number of "dental units" that would be worth a certain amount of money. But that failed to solve the problem—in fact, it made many dentists even more fed up—and large numbers simply left the NHS and went into private practice or quit the business altogether.

From the patients' point of view, this was a disaster, because there were far fewer NHS dentists to go around. Also, few of those were eager, or even willing, to take on new patients. If your dentist went private, leaving you stranded and in search of a replacement, forget it. If you moved to a different neighborhood with different dentists, forget it. If you angered your dentist by missing your appointments, she might easily strike you from her books. You would be disappeared, a dental

---

* In *Vanity Fair*, Christopher Hitchens once described his own early experience "stretched on the grim rack" of NHS dentistry, "with its gray-and-yellow fangs, its steely-wire braces, its dark and crumbly fillings, its shriveled and bleeding gums."

refusenik, like Dubček in Czechoslovakia, airbrushed from history. Your unsavory options included: hoping for an opening somewhere, paying out of pocket (dental care is not reimbursable under most private insurance plans in Britain), and waiting for hell to freeze over, whichever came first.

At the end of 2005, just 49 percent of the adults and 63 percent of the children in England and Wales were registered with public dentists. A survey conducted two years later found that only half the dentists in the country were accepting new NHS patients.

Some patients began traveling far away to seek treatment.

"It's quite a small country and I thought, they specialize in dentistry —so that's what I might do," a woman named Josie Johnson told me. She was speaking of Hungary, where she planned to get the dental care she couldn't get in Britain.

I talked to her in the airy, air-conditioned offices of a company called Vital Europe, a travel agency-cum-dental-screening center that matched Britons desperate for treatment with Hungarian dentists eager for patients to treat. At forty-two, Johnson had four rotten teeth that were on their last legs. It would be half as cheap to get the implants she needed in Budapest, she said; plus, she reasoned, she could take in a few castles and eat a little goulash on the side.

There was a third way: autoextraction. I had heard rumors about it when I visited my own dentist, Mr. Glynn, a reassuringly expert private practitioner with plush offices near Harley Street, the Upper East Side of London medicine.* To cheer me up as I lay back in the chair, incapacitated and bleeding, the hygienist, Claire Dacey, told me grisly anecdotes about her days with the NHS. The dentist she worked for had spent five minutes per patient per cleaning, she said; his biggest priority was getting the patients out the

---

* One difference between private dentists in New York and those in London is that the British ones are much gentler and less scolding. They don't lecture you about eating too much candy or failing to brush the requisite four minutes a day. Mr. Glynn, who could not be nicer, calls my teeth "chaps," as in, "Let's have a look at that chap."

door before unearthing anything wrong that might require noncursory treatment.

Some patients had difficulty getting attention.

"I had a lady who was in so much pain, and had to wait so long [for an appointment] that she got herself drunk," Dacey said, "and had her friend take out her tooth with a pair of pliers."

"*Mmmughph&&&**@#@#!*," I said, in my chair.

But Dacey wasn't exaggerating. I took the train to Rochdale, a down-on-its-luck community up north, to work on an article about the national dental crisis. There, I met a man named William Kelly, whose mouth had large gaps in it where the teeth were supposed to be. He directed my attention to an area in the upper left quadrant.

"I snapped it out myself," he said.

I looked in his mouth. He had done a poor job, actually. In the spot that used to belong to his tooth, there was a jagged stump, black as charcoal, from which jutted scary little shards of semi-decayed dental material.

Kelly had a history of run-ins with his own teeth: he had extracted four of them in the previous six years. His experiences had turned him into an amateur dentist spouting amateur dental philosophy. "If you don't get them out," he explained gravely, "they'll eventually get some sort of infection and result in gum disease."

Kelly was just forty-three, but looked much older, with his wizened skin, wrinkly eyes, lack of hair, and general air of world-weary defeat. He said he had once had a dentist in Sussex, where he used to live, but had been unable to find one since moving to Rochdale. He was a veteran of the lines-to-nowhere situation. No one wanted to treat him. He didn't understand why his teeth were in such poor condition, he said: he brushed them, once a day.

Having dispatched the upper left tooth, Kelly was now concerned about one on the other side. He was already waggling it around in its socket at various times during the day in preparation for its eventual extraction.

"It's the worst kind of pain, dental pain," he said expansively. "It's a nagging, gnawing pain." He was popping paracetamol tablets like breath mints and was sure he had become addicted. Kelly had little hope for the rest of his mouth. "These ones," he said, gesturing vaguely toward the back: "I'll just rip them out eventually."*

The clinic, called the Dental Access Center, was full of pain and suffering the day I visited. It was supposed to be a place of last resort— one step short of the no-hope saloon—for the mouths of 123,000 people. But when you have nowhere else to go, an emergency clinic becomes a primary-care center.

I wandered over to a corner of the room, near the windows. It was a sea of oral discomfort. There was Shahana Begum, a twenty-seven-year-old Bangladeshi immigrant, whose aspirin-resistant toothache had kept her awake for a month and was currently driving her insane. There was Mr. Miah, her elderly translator, who grabbed my notebook, wrote down his telephone number as if he were a Burmese dissident communicating important information to the outside world, and told me to call him later. He was looking forward to sharing with me his collection of horror stories about his teeth and the teeth of his friends, relatives, and neighbors, he said, and also had some broader thoughts about the health-care system in Britain.

There was sixteen-year-old Sanya Karim, Begum's stepdaughter, who had come along to help Begum negotiate the difficulties of, for instance, taking three different buses to get to the dentist if you don't speak English and half your face is swollen like that of a chipmunk preparing for winter. Sanya herself was suffering from a low-grade twinge, but the appointment that day wasn't for her; she'd been unable to secure one. She was doing her best to ignore the pain. "It normally goes away in a couple of days," she said.

* Pulling your own teeth is, admittedly, an extreme solution. But a survey of 5,200 patients and 750 dentists in 2007 found that 6 percent of patients were resorting to do-it-yourself treatment of one kind or another. The company that employed Jennifer Stone, the floss-loving American, sold at-home tooth-fixing kits that people could use to alleviate their gum pain, reattach their fallen-out crowns, or replace their lost fillings. In a single week in 2006, British drugstores sold six thousand jars of the filling replacement and six thousand of the crown-and-cap replacement—a 40 percent increase from a year earlier.

George Glasper, eighty-one, sat nearby. One of his teeth had crumbled and broken off a week earlier (he needed it, he said, because he had only two other ones). When he called his longtime dentist and told him about his emergency, Glasper was informed that the practice had gone private and that the dentist no longer regarded him as a patient. None of the dentists in the four other practices he telephoned wanted to regard him as a patient, either, or to regard him at all. He had run out of people to call.

Glasper's wife, Lillian, was not currently having any troubles, possibly because she had no upper teeth. When she was young, her NHS dentist had yanked them all out, saying that toothlessness would save her a lifetime of bother. She had had no choice, and she began to cry as she recalled the shame of it, decades later.

She snuggled next to her husband. "We're getting used to this sort of thing in this country now," she said. "We're resigned to it."

My teeth began to hurt, too. They hurt more when the secretaries at the emergency clinic explained how to secure an appointment. It wasn't a drop-in center—if it was, the would-be patients would have been spilling out into the streets and down the block—and nor could you book appointments for future days. People had to call first thing in the morning on the day they wanted to come in. If the line was busy, they had to keep calling. Ten minutes after the clinic opened, all the appointments would be gone.

Rochdale is a poor area, with a high percentage of Pakistani and Bangladeshi immigrants, many of whom speak little or no English. Dental care is not high on their personal agendas, said Dr. Khalid Anis, the clinical leader of the dental emergency center. I asked him if that meant it was difficult to convince residents of the importance of flossing between meals. Anis's answer, following a low snort of hollow laughter, made me cringe at my gaucheness.

"Flossing?" he said. "That's a good one."

Anis was a vigorous, earnest idealist growing somewhat exasperated by the reality he found himself in. He described how in 2006, just 33 percent of the Rochdale population was signed up with a public dentist, down from 58 percent in 1997. He explained that the clinic's initial mission when it opened five years earlier—treating patients in crisis and then passing them on to public dentists for continuing care—had changed because no local dentist had taken on a new NHS patient for the past two years. He described how hard it was to promote dental health in a place where the water is unfluoridated and where people chain-smoke home-rolled cigarettes.

"We see toothaches through trauma, toothaches through neglect, dental caries, dental abscesses, gum disease," Anis told me. "What we see is shocking."

He laid out some positive dental developments in Rochdale: a second clinic, opening soon; an aggressive community health program that reached out in blighted neighborhoods; a political will, among some people, at least, to fluoridate the water (only 11 percent of the water in the country currently contained fluoride). But, he said, "Sometimes I feel as if I'm hitting my head against a brick wall."

Things looked bad. But the government claimed that the overall situation was actually better. Improvements in diet and general health, and a greater understanding of the importance of using a toothbrush regularly, had helped bolster the national statistics. In 1979, 28 percent of adults surveyed by the British Dental Association were missing all of their teeth. When the same survey was done again in 1991, the number of no-teeth adults had fallen to 17 percent.

But as the poor struggled, the rich were going in the opposite direction. They were starting to pay for good teeth—not just the medical part, but the esthetic part. They were starting to care about their appearance. Television personalities would go away "on vacation" and come back with whole new sets of gleaming white teeth, as if they were Americans. Harley Street was suddenly overrun with new offices specializing in cosmetic dentistry, which, by 2007, had become a £360 million-a-year business.

Politicians realized that it is easier to get elected when your mouth is not full of gaping holes, yellowed incisors, and inflamed gums. They began, quietly, to seek cosmetic help.

Blair began sprucing up his teeth while he was prime minister, so that they sparkled forth in House of Commons debates and gave him added authority when he met with even-teethed White House officials and plotted the invasion of Iraq. (For some reason, he neglected to address a bad lower tooth, which turned a foul dark color at some point, and stayed that way, distracting from his shiny chirpiness at Prime Minister's Questions.)

His successor, Gordon Brown, the son of a Scottish Presbyterian minister and a man who dressed as though he believed that the vanity involved in wearing a correctly fitting suit was the work of the devil, had a poorer baseline standard. His teeth were basically brown, with large unappealing gaps between them, matching his severe, plain demeanor. But as Blair's power waned and Brown began his long campaign to seize control, Brown embarked on what (for him) amounted to a charm offensive. Not only did his grimy teeth become suddenly, gleamingly white, nestled evenly side by side like pieces of corn on a cob, but also this dour, frugal man began regularly to do something he had rarely done before.

He smiled in public.

TWELVE

WINE FROM WEEDS

*Just one last word of warning. Bronco toilet paper. That hard,
shiny stuff, designed for minimum adherence and absorption.*
—"Bog Standards," *Oxford Student*, April 26, 2001

n his classic *Miami Herald Magazine* article "Can New York Save
Itself?" Dave Barry imagined a list of rules that ought to be posted
inside every taxi in the city, the most important being: "Driver Hates
You." That would sum up the general attitude in traditional Britain,
too—driver hates you—if you took the word "driver" to mean "any person who answers a telephone, operates a cash register, waits on a table,
or manufactures, distributes, or sells a good or service" (and if you took
the word "you" to mean "you").

But the country has lived through something of a consumer revolution, and I am happy to report that the hate has turned, mostly, to
mild dislike. Somehow over the last fifteen years, almost despite itself,
when no one was looking, Britain became a modern, attentive society.
Consumers stopped accepting so little, and began demanding a lot. The
service industry began actively pursuing that previously unimportant
goal, customer satisfaction, and sometimes they got it right.

But how did it happen? Why did it change when it did, and not
before? And was it a wholesale transformation—or just a shiny new
veneer on top of what, at heart, had remained essentially the same?

There is no arguing that the country started from a very low base. Shockingly poor dental care was just the beginning. Sometimes, Britain seemed so lost in the past as to belong to the Third World. A Formerly Industrialized Nation—that's what an American friend who studied political science at Oxford in the 1980s jokingly called it, due to the general grimness he encountered, the inedible food, the lack of heating, the way the stores seemed so devoid of useful products (and were so often closed). Another friend remembers the selection of fruit offered by mid-eighties supermarkets: apples, oranges, and bananas.

Even when I moved to Britain, after the Thatcher financial revolution had come and gone, the place still had the feel of a sleepy backwater. Products were shoddy, and no one seemed to care. When you bought a lamp, you had to wire it yourself. Surly service was part of the national experience, like winter damp: the centerpiece of a drama starring hostile shopkeepers, insufferable waiters, slovenly receptionists, and resentful hotel clerks who could convey self-loathing and class contempt in the mere act of asking for your credit card (assuming they accepted credit cards—an innovation that the huge department store chain John Lewis, for one, did not embrace until 1999). If they could draw you into their world of seething, insulted, persecuted servitude, in which a person like them should not have to work in a place like this, they would do it.

Graham Greene once made fun of the sprightly manner in which customers are greeted in American banks, where the teller seems "overjoyed at the lucky chance of the encounter," but I was homesick for that unabashed enthusiasm. I wasn't used to having to apologize to a salesclerk for asking where the shirts were, for instance, or to facing open antagonism from people trying to sell me things, like the fruit vendor near my office. He had placed his ancient little wooden stand across from the St. James's Park tube station, presumably to entice commuters with fresh fruit as they went in to work.

But he was not a relaxed salesperson. He had an eclectic, abundant supply; it was just the demand he couldn't deal with. His main goal, it seemed, was to keep his potential clientele away from the goods. Do Not Touch, Finger, Poke, Handle, Jab, Prod or Stroke the

Fruit, the stand warned, every place you looked. Once I lost my concentration and gave a peach I was considering buying a mild squeeze,
only to be drawn into an unpleasant verbal exchange one line of which
was: "Sorry, yes, I do know how to read." But I had proved his point:
the customer is the enemy.

When people you dealt with weren't rude, they were dozy. Directory
Assistance, for example. The system was demonstrably bad. It was bad
when it was a monopoly. It was still bad when it was deregulated and
half a dozen companies began competing for the exciting opportunity to
provide you, a member of the public, with the correct telephone number.

Instead of being spurred to improvement, the companies sank to a
new low in baseline incompetence. Dealing with an operator was like
asking for information from the world's worst computer: no imagination, and no access to a decent data base. Or ability to spell. Let's say I
was looking for my telephone number, and I said, "I am looking for the
number of Sarah Lyall—L-Y-A-L-L, a residence in west London," the
operators always repeated the information back in the form of a question, every single thing you had just said: "Is that a business or a residence?" "What city?" "How do you spell it?" "Do you have an address?"
and "Is there a first name?" A perverse feature of the system was that it
was hard to find a number *unless you provided the operator with an exact
address.*

Once I was trying to find a friend's number. I gave his name. I
spelled the name. I gave the exact street address.

"What part of London is that?" the operator asked.

I thought she was kidding. I was not at my most patient and I think,
too, that my foreign accent put her off. "I've given you the address!
Shouldn't that be enough?" I asked.

"Well," she answered, "London is a very big place."*

---

* I was left so cowed and beaten down by these tussles that once when I was back in
New York on vacation, I asked Directory Assistance for the number of the Guggenheim
Museum by saying, "The Guggenheim Museum, please, spelled G-U-G-G—" Over-
riding the automated system, an operator came on and snapped, "I *know* how to spell
Guggenheim!"

As for consumer goods, some were just inexplicable. The cling film, what back home I knew as Saran Wrap: it seemed unable to adhere to the side of anything, like a bowl, meaning it had failed in the one job it was supposed to do, adhere. Some places still used Bronco toilet paper, which old ads proclaimed was for the "hygienically minded," but which resembled waxed paper and had a nonabsorbent slipperiness that tended to defeat its very purpose (practical wartime-era children learned it could also be used as tracing paper). Our British-manufactured washing machine was twice as small, twice as expensive, and four times as slow as the ones back home; the wash cycle took so long it may as well have been called the Ring Cycle.

It seemed perverse to me. Why make, sell, or buy products that blatantly don't function?

On the other hand, their electric kettles boiled water in less than a minute, so you could always get a cup of tea right away.

With the exception of the large supermarkets, which were bigger and better than the ones in New York (maybe because the restaurants were so much worse), the stores were poorly laid out, clumsily organized, badly lit—designed for maximum inconvenience. They were legally prevented from opening on Sundays, and by Saturday evening, supermarkets would be picked dry of goods like fruit, vegetables, and milk, as a store might have been in the dark days of the Soviet Union. In country villages, local shops opened at obscure hours and were stocked with moldering, obsolete items according to the particular whims of the shopkeepers, who looked like the country folk in *Tess of the D'Urbervilles*. It was hard to know how the stores stayed in business, unless they were tax shelters or fronts for rural heroin-smuggling operations.*

Inured to this regime, Britons were pathetically grateful for what little they had. In the early 1990s, for instance, there were few places

---

* My daughters really liked the penny candy you could buy at small village stores—things like Gummi Worms and solidified sucrose molded in the shape of flying saucers. They didn't mind that it was often covered in dust and seemed to have been undisturbed for several years. There was one shop we visited a lot on weekends, and I could have sworn that the candy there was at least as old as the children.

where motorists could stop and eat during long car trips. There was Happy Eater, a chain of restaurants whose logo was a smiley face wherein the face's hand was pointing down its throat, as if it needed the Heimlich Maneuver or was about to be sick. Then there was Little Chef, one of Britain's last great bad-service, bad-product institutions. That it was visited by millions of loyal customers every year said a lot about the nation's low expectations and high endurance threshold.

Distinguished by its angry waitpersons, 1950s mental-home decor, and overboiled, overfried, and overgreased food, Little Chef was a throwback to a simple, easy time—a time without options. A time when a single slice of white bread qualified as a legitimate side dish (you could get one if you paid *an extra pound*, in 2004) and a glass of reconstituted grapefruit juice counted as an appetizer. A time when you were ridiculously glad of the existence of any place thoughtful enough to enable you to possibly get some lunch.

With its famous logo of a fat little man in a chef's hat, the chain had been a fixture on Britain's roads since 1958. It radiated comforting familiarity, which was why people like my husband and so many others loved it. My friend Ben, whose family used to drive far out of their way to find a Little Chef when he was a child, thus adding hours to their journey, says that he has "measured out his life in Little Chefs."

But many customers have a hard time articulating their passion.

"The food is bad, the service is terrible, the prices are overpriced, and they haven't kept up with the times in terms of menu, style, or cleanliness," admitted Roy Gibbens, a thirty-two-year-old salesman, when I caught him eating lunch once at the Little Chef outside Newmarket. He was wolfing it down: a thin slab of cheeseburger on a puffy bun, accessorized by sickly beige French fries and a clump of iceberg lettuce, known on the menu as "salad." He grew slightly defensive. "We're in a rush, and it's right by the side of the road."

His coworker, Matthew Melly, called Little Chef "a necessary evil," as if it were dental work, or taxation.

"If they closed it," said June Starkey, another diner, "there wouldn't be anywhere to go to the toilet on the motorway."

As if determined to make no concessions to the health concerns

of its customers, the restaurant featured food that was deep-fried, battered, or smothered in sauce, sometimes all three at once. One dish
consisted of warm bacon and black pudding—black pudding being a
breakfast delicacy made of pig's blood, pork fat, and cereal filler. If you
ordered a "bacon bap," you got a flat white roll filled with limp, sweaty,
fatty bacon.*

"I don't think anyone would come here out of choice," said Leslie
Millman, another diner, whose fried-egg-and-baked-bean lunch had
pooled together to form a gloppy yellowish-red puddle on his plate. He
was heading for a funeral. He said the food was rubbery, but at least
it was food, and the best part was that if you had baked beans, they
drowned out the taste of everything else.

Little Chef was the missing link between a past of privation and a
future of abundance. The highways of the new millennium would be
filled with enormous rest-stop complexes teeming with shops, video
arcades, cafés, and other temples to restless consumerism; Little Chef
would struggle under a series of new owners who didn't understand
how to modernize an unmodernizable brand. But that was yet to come.
Back in the mid-nineties, Britain still thought of itself as a place of less,
not a place of more.

I didn't understand why, at first; I was too busy being irritated. But
gradually it became clear. Like so many other things, it had to do with
World War II. I had known that the older generations in Britain were
still obsessed with the war, which represented the last time the country
was able to think of itself as a true international power, a force to be
reckoned with. The war reminded them of themselves at their best—
their self-reliance, their self-sacrifice, their stoicism—and it filled them
with a terrible nostalgia for the time when they still had their empire
and were sure of their place in the world.

But they clung to memories of World War II for another reason:
because what happened at home then had been so terrible, and had

---

* For some mysterious reason, the default bacon in Britain is what Americans call
Canadian-style bacon—the flabby kind.

taken so long to overcome. While we in America celebrated the postwar years as the beginning of a golden era of affluence and prosperity, Britain was still struggling in a miserable, gray period of extended privation. When my husband was born, in 1953, rationing was still in effect. For his first year, he had a ration book that set out how much food he, an infant, was allotted per week.

It is almost inconceivable now, how little the people of the war generation had and how long their period of wanting would last, many years after the war had ended. They didn't have enough clothes, or enough fuel, or enough food. They were supposed to be basking in the glory of victory and celebrating the end of that terrible conflict, but instead they were struggling to keep warm and get enough to eat. My mother-in-law, who lived during that era, said that at one point as a student, she was subsisting on two slices of bread a day.

"We still bathed in water that wouldn't come over your knees unless you flattened them," writes Susan Cooper in "Snoek Piquante," an essay about postwar hardship. "Chewing carrots for sweets, we still said avidly to our parents: 'Tell us about your pre-war days,' and wondered at stories of chocolate cigars and real pineapple that didn't come out of tins."

Life was all about making do, making the best of things. In 1948, rations had fallen to *below* wartime levels.* Housewives made cakes from reconstituted dehydrated eggs, hot chocolate from dried milk, and "cream" from cornflour and margarine. The bread tasted like chalk. A typical recipe called for baking hot mashed potatoes together with lard, sugar, dried fruit, and flour, and calling it dessert.

The winter of 1947 was so cold that parsnips in the ground had to be excavated with pneumatic drills. Postwar imports grew so expensive that the government tried to persuade families to eat canned snoek, a cheap South African fish that tasted disgusting, no matter how you dressed it up ("Snoek Piquante" was one of the recipes it came up

---

* That year the average man was allotted a weekly thirteen ounces of meat, an ounce and a half of cheese, six ounces of butter and margarine, an ounce of cooking fat, eight ounces of sugar, two pints of milk, and a single egg. Every two months, he got a can of dried milk.

with). The housewives rebelled, preferring that wartime delicacy, and Monty Python favorite, Spam. Beer was watered down and whiskey impossible to get hold of. The *Daily Mirror* printed a how-to article entitled "Wine from Weeds."

In his memoir *"Will This Do?"* Evelyn Waugh's son Auberon recalls the sudden reappearance of bananas years after the war ended. To a shell-shocked, deprived generation, they were the epitome of luxury and indulgence. The government munificently decreed that every child should be allowed his own banana, and duly doled them out to the families, a banana per child. At the Waugh household, the great writer took the three allotted to his offspring and put them on a plate, his son writes in a poignant passage in the book. "Before the anguished eyes of his children, he poured on cream, which was almost unprocurable, and sugar, which was heavily rationed, and ate all three."

All that privation becomes hardwired in the system. People from the war generation are incredibly careful with their resources. They reuse old envelopes and old tea bags. They wear their clothes until the clothes wear out. An elderly friend of our family wore, for his entire adult life, the handed-down evening clothes of a relative who died before World War II. According to her former daughter-in-law, the Duchess of York, Queen Elizabeth is so frugal that she insists on using forty-watt lightbulbs in all her many houses.

Older-generation Britons might wait until darkness has settled outside and begun to creep through the house before finally switching on the lights.* They might wait until the last moment—say, November 15, no matter what—before turning on the heat. During the war, civilians marked lines in their bathtubs designating acceptable water levels; even now people who lived in that era might leave their water behind after taking a bath, so it can be used again by someone else. I have an American friend whose English husband graciously offers to leave

---

* An unusual number of British people I've interviewed don't seem to keep the lights on as a matter of course. As the dark tendrils of the late afternoon begin to creep into the darkened room, sometimes I can't help myself, and I ask that they switch on at least a lamp. It makes me feel really extravagant, wanting to have enough light to be able to see.

his postbath water—he calls it "gravy"—in the tub for her own bath. (No, she graciously answers.) They care less than we do about creature comforts, such as the necessity of sleeping on mattresses purchased sometime in the last half century. Surprisingly often, Robert and I have stayed in smart houses where, when you sit on the bed, the mattress sags down to the floor, and when you lie down, it folds up like a U, propelling you both into a little heap in the center. It's not that they can't afford new beds; it's that they think it's frivolous and self-indulgent to buy them.

Older people might cook just enough food so that there is not quite enough for everyone. They were raised to believe that hunger was greed, and that greed was the height of bad manners. "FHB," their parents would declare when company came to eat and the food was laid tantalizingly on the table—"Family Hold Back." Waste distresses them. If there are leftovers, even a lone potato or a bit of cheese, they wrap them up and store them in the larder for later. The mother-in-law of one of my friends boils vegetables in water, then throws in a stock cube, and serves the water the next day as soup. Some of my husband's favorite desserts have stale white bread as a major ingredient.

The attitude that food was not a matter of sensual pleasure but of necessity persisted long after the end of rationing, despite the efforts of pioneering cooks like Elizabeth David.* Everyone laughs about the cliched food—the tough meat, overboiled vegetables, murky sauces, and suet-filled desserts with quaint and occasionally obscene names—that still form the classic image of British food to foreigners, and they are right to mention them. Even British people never tried to pretend they particularly enjoyed what they cooked. "Boiled cabbage à l'Anglaise is something compared with which steamed coarse newsprint bought from bankrupt Finnish salvage dealers and heated over smoky oil stoves

---

* Now sophisticated cooks and three-star restaurants are everywhere. But when I arrived, the country was still in thrall to a TV chef named Delia Smith whose whole repertoire was big on traditional British food. One of her shows was devoted to the correct method of boiling eggs.

is an exquisite delicacy," William Connor wrote in the "Cassandra" column in the *Daily Mirror* in 1950.

When I got to London, coffee was still mainly instant and came in two varieties, white (with milk) and black (black). The best restaurants were Indian. At London sandwich shops (which tended to close by 2:30 p.m., in any case), the potential fillings—things like egg salad, ham salad, tuna salad, chicken salad, prawn salad, mystery salad, all drenched in evil-looking "sauce"—were laid out in vats behind glass counters so you could see them congealing, crusting, and browning before your eyes. Sometimes I'd walk out of the office to try to scrounge up some lunch, and find nothing that seemed remotely edible, except baked potatoes—a cheap, nutritious, and reasonable meal, as long as you avoided the advertised toppings: canned corn, tuna-and-mayonnaise salad, shrimp drenched in Russian dressing.

Cheap foods were popular foods. My husband liked Scotch eggs, hard-boiled eggs rolled in a mélange of bread crumbs, ground pork bits, and hardened fat, and then deep-fried in oil; he used to buy them from the refrigerated-food section of the gas station down the street from our house, a bargain at two for eighty-nine pence. For dinner, he liked to heat up a can of baked beans—for him they were the ultimate comfort food. In the North, they fancied chip butties—French fries on buttered bread—and crackling and dripping sandwiches, bread filled with crispy pork fat and spread with solidified grease from the roasting pan. Everyone liked Brown Sauce, which is sauce that is brown. A concoction of vinegar, molasses, dates, glucose-fructose syrup, tomato paste, and other ingredients, Brown Sauce can be put on any food so as to conceal the food's underlying taste. People also fancied Marmite, which not only smells funny but is made of yeast. Yeast. They ate it out of the jar; they spread it on crackers; it was a snack and an appetizer and a meal.

This mindset—low expectations, a sense of making do, a sense of enduring rather than enjoying—carried straight through into the 1970s and 1980s. When my husband went to college, the only way you could get heat in your dorm room was by putting coins into the gas meter. No change, no heat. Coal miners' strikes in 1974 sent the country into what was called the three-day week, meaning that power was drastically cut, and offices, stores, and other commercial users of electricity were allowed to open only for three days each week, for a specified number of hours. Four years later, my husband lived through the Winter of Discontent, when pretty much everyone was on strike.

The country was still traumatized by all that when I got here—all those reduced expectations—and it meant I was in for some unhappy experiences when I arrived, on account of my foreign standards. The provincial hotels, like one near Stonehenge, where breakfast, left on a tray outside my door *the night before*, was a carton of milk and two slices of buttered white bread cut into triangles (and wrapped in coming-off cling film). The place in Bournemouth, where the receptionist went quiet after I placed my room-service order, from the menu, at 8:30 or so. There was a scuffling noise, a whispering. And then she returned. "The chef has gone home for the night," she said. The guesthouse in Blackpool, where the walls were dotted with water stains and the room had a large damp spot on the floor, as if some wet thing was oozing permanently upward. My blanket was as thin as Kleenex and my towel as rough as a cat's tongue. But it was all relative. Breakfast (served with ketchup and Brown Sauce) was so spectacularly bad that I began to think nostalgically about the eggs at Little Chef.

But then it all began to change. A lot of it had to do with money, a sudden infusion of it. Buoyed by the largest sustained period of economic growth in modern history, Britain from the late 1990s onward became awash in excess. The City, London's financial district, turned into a teeming hub of round-the-clock Eurobankers and thrusting American hedge fund managers, who brought with them a novel work ethic, in which workers stayed in the office for more than the customary eight hours a day. Lured by liberal tax policies and the freedom to settle in a place so thrilled to have new money that it didn't ask many questions about where it had come from, Arab sheikhs, Russian oligarchs, and Indian magnates began buying up megaproperties for upwards of £20 million cash, in central London.

Property prices went through the roof. In July 2007, the average house price in London was £344,000, compared with £266,000 pounds three years before. High-end stores sprang up across London, filled with preposterously expensive items catering to a tiny sliver of the very rich and dedicated to their customers' every petulant whim.

The new prosperity brought a new attitude, and not just for the well-off. It trickled down to the whole population, a generation for whom wartime privation was something in a history book rather than a personal memory. Suddenly, people who never expected much began to want everything.

The Internet exposed the public to endless new possibilities and endless new sources of fidgety dissatisfaction. When I got to London, there were just four television channels, and two of them were the BBC. Now there are hundreds. Consumers are spoiled for choice. A reporter for the *Times* of London tallied up some of the items at her local Tesco: 38 types of milk, including soy, goats', and banana flavored; 154 flavors of jam; 107 varieties of pasta; 98 kinds of fruit cordial.

Prices rose and rose, and the public stopping queuing and began to make demands.

Britain, with its sense of gratitude for what little it had, had never had a Ralph Nader figure or any tradition of consumer revolt.

But that started to change, too. In their small way, a group of disgruntled passengers on the Bath-Bristol railway line struck a blow for consumer activism one morning in the winter of 2007. The passengers had been pushed to the brink of their patience by train service they found terrible. They had had enough. They were upset that ticket prices had gone up, far past the rate of inflation. They were upset that the morning trains were so crowded that often they could not get on at all, never mind getting their own seat. They were upset that no one listened to them when they complained. So they boiled over in what counted as a revolutionary roar of outrage (for them): They refused to pay for their tickets.

The ringleader, Peter Andrews, issued fake tickets on which the printed destination was not Bristol, but To Hell and Back, the class was "cattle class," and the seats, "standing room only." The commuters massed in the station and surged illegally past the ticket collector. Andrews brandished his ersatz ticket in triumph.

"And then everyone else raised their tickets high," he told me later, still excited from his small brush with civil disobedience. "It was like something from *Henry V*."

The protest was over as quickly as it began—no need for tear gas or the dragging of limp protesters down the street—and the commuters returned to their daily lives. But the protest had exposed the issue of train overcrowding to a wider audience. Parliament hastily scheduled a debate. "We need an efficient railway system, not something that closely resembles a succession of cattle trucks," Grant Snapps, a Tory MP, declared. The *Evening Standard* started a new campaign that was almost poignant in the humility of its demand: "A Seat for Every Commuter." In Bristol Temple Meads, a rush-hour commuter showed up at the station wearing a sardine costume, with a sign saying: "I'm gutted by rail overcrowding."

In a way the government had built a rod for its own back, to use a British expression that means "become the agent of its own trouble": it had handed the passengers the very sense of entitlement they were now using against it. The Conservatives had established a Citizens' Charter in the 1990s that called for greater accountability in public services, and suddenly schools, hospitals, train companies, and the like were setting out targets, promises, pledges, statements of responsibility, and declarations of performance. National Health Service hospitals were ordered to reduce waiting times for treatment, and were fined if they failed to meet the targets. In London, the subway introduced a policy under which passengers were informed in a running commentary which lines were operating smoothly, which were subject to scattered delays, and which had simply ceased to operate.*

---

* It's hard not to feel that this system causes more problems for the subway operators than it solves, by exposing the network's failings to the daily naked gaze of the commuters. By the same token, when you go to work and are told that the District Line, the one you need to take, is running normally, it fills you with a great and irrational sense of relief, always a pleasant way to start the day.

In 1994, stores became legally allowed to open on Sundays—for just six hours, but that was six hours longer than before. Shopping stopped being so masochistic. Clerks greeted customers not with traditional sullen resentment, but with modern in-your-face cheerfulness: occasionally you got the feeling that they sincerely wanted you to buy something. Old-fashioned stores like Marks & Spencer remade themselves into all-purpose arcades of convenience, replacing their dreary old products with new, contemporary lines. They worried about what the customers thought of them and conducted surveys to find out.

The government passed its first-ever minimum-wage law in 1998. Armies of migrants from the European Union—from Croatia, from Slovakia, from Italy, from Poland—took the low-paying jobs that working-class Britons no longer wanted to do. London became a center of blatant consumer spending. Cheap clothes from chain stores; expensive clothes from the Gucci, Dolce e Gabbana, and Prada boutiques that sprang up like mushrooms across town—anything you wanted. Handbags for £20,000. Upscale sandwich shops on every corner. Bread from Poilâne bakery in Paris. Home delivery. Armies of house-call-making yoga instructors, manicurists, masseuses, personal trainers, closet organizers, and lifestyle coaches: an effusion of goods and services that had never existed before. Pret à Manger, the first in an explosion of fast-food lunch places offering fresh, healthful food, was so committed to consumer satisfaction that it printed the real phone number and e-mail address of its president on its bags. Pubs reinvented themselves as "gastropubs," swept the musty bags of peanuts and old potato chips off the counter, and put up blackboards listing the specials of the day, which often involved radicchio, truffle oil, and similar nouveau delicacies.

Restaurants got seriously good. In 2005 *Gourmet* magazine declared London the world's food capital. Four of the top ten restaurants, and fourteen restaurants in all, were included in its list of the fifty best restaurants to be found anywhere.

Consumers took home more pay, but they also threw aside their traditional frugality and borrowed as if borrowing were going out of fashion. Banks offered dubiously financed mortgages that sometimes equaled 125 percent of the value of the house. A country that used to pride itself on thrift became awash in debt, about £1.35 trillion of it by 2007—giving it the highest ratio of debt to personal income in the developed world. "It's changed the culture and the way people use their money and spend here—it's become a 'buy now, pay later' culture," Chris Tapp, deputy director of Credit Action, a nonprofit group that helps people deal with debts, told me. The general standard of living increased; at the same time, the gap between the very rich and the very poor widened more than it ever had. Prices rose out of control. The cost of a one-way subway ride in the center of town—80 pence when I arrived—quietly increased to £4, about $8, in 2007.

To someone of the war generation, the abundance and disposability of everything must have seemed obscene. Sometimes it seemed obscene to me, all the worst of American excess. Before it had been too slow; now it felt too fast. It wasn't just Starbucks on every block, it was Marks & Spencer food stores, Carphone Warehouse cell-phone shops, Boots drugstores, EAT lunch shops, L.K. Bennet clothing stores—"a mind-boggling parade of clothes, gadgets, financial products, holidays and entertainment," Liz Hollis wrote in the *Times* of London. At lunchtime now, I can step out of my office and find dozens of cafés and takeout restaurants, including three separate Pret à Manger outlets, two EAT shops, and two different places selling gourmet lunch pies at $12 a pie.

It felt frenzied and out of control, all this new consumer greed, and indeed, it would all begin to unravel when the economy began to fail in 2008. But in 2007, people were still partying like it was 1929. Some three thousand shoppers massed outside at the opening of the new Primark discount clothing store on Oxford Street, surging into the door so that it came off its hinges and trampling over each other in an effort to be the first inside. Order was restored by the arrival of the mounted police. (There was already a huge Primark store in Hammersmith, which is also in London, but, for some reason, consumers wanted to shop in this one.) Thousands of jostling, combative women began lining up at 2 a.m. at Sainsbury's stores one night for the chance to buy five-pound shopping bags—flimsy cotton sacks, really—that had been advertised in various fashion magazines and were printed with the words: "I am not a plastic bag." "You know I'll fight for one of these bags, don't you?" one woman said. The city's first Whole Foods Market opened in Kensington, a symbol of American abundance. "Those are vegetables of mass destruction," said a friend's mother, horrified at the sky-high pyramids of produce and simple salads that could cost £15—$30, by then—for a regular portion.

But even as consumers and products and services danced in an endless circle of wanting and providing more, there were problems of adjustment. The service industry had to catch up with the new philosophy. And the services they provided had to meet the new expectations.

Still caught in the old mindset, many of the workers weren't used to all the enforced cheeriness, all the mandatory goodwill. They struggled to change their ways. At one point the newly refurbished Virgin Trains company offered first-class passengers an elaborate in-seat drink and snack service. This required teams of attendants in snappy, happy red uniforms to place and then remove fresh sets of silverware and dishes at each seat throughout the trip. It was a bit of a pain—all that fiddling with cups and spoons—and the new task taxed the goodwill of the attendants, whose responsibilities in the past had been confined to punching the passengers' tickets and then retreating to the café car, where they could complain about the horrors of the job in customer-free comfort.

They resented their supersized workload. Wielding the new snacks menacingly, they faced the passengers with all the enthusiasm of gulag inmates press-ganged into digging holes in the tundra using rusty spoons and shards of old glass. "Coffee?" they would snarl, slapping the coffee into your cup as if to say, "One false move, and you will wake up with third-degree burns over 90 percent of your body."

Despite the promises, things didn't always work. British Airways had an annual summer ritual of shutting down on account of strikes, terrorist attacks, and the weather, and miserable passengers had an annual summer ritual of having to camp out like refugees in huge tents set up outside the terminals at Heathrow, one of the world's busiest airports. (BA kept them quiet one year with an oompah band.) It was a sight to behold. Airline employees would wander into the tents, where literally hundreds of displaced passengers were slumped in conditions of unspeakable misery, and say things like: "Does anyone wish to go to

Zurich who does not have a reservation?" Bag handlers regularly went on strike; the baggage system regularly broke down; every other bag seemed to go missing; on any given day more than half the planes would be late. Thomas Harris, a businessman, wrote in the *Evening Standard* that even on a normal day, it was so overcrowded, so understaffed, and so inefficient that "many international executives I meet will do almost anything to avoid traveling through Heathrow."

Other parts of the infrastructure failed, too, like the roads and the subways. The trains were hopeless, even though Blair's government was pouring some £4.5 billion a year into the industry. They were forever stopping, midtrip, at places that were not stations, like old deserted fields in the middle of nowhere. Or they were just canceled.

There were plenty of reasons for the trouble with the trains, and the public was treated to an account of them in pointillistic detail. The autumn leaf fall. Rain. Snow. Ice. Heat. Once, when a light dusting of snow fell across London, the whole network—subways as well as trains—seized up, thwarting the valiant efforts of hundreds of thousands of commuters to make it to work that day. "Inch of Snow Causes Chaos," the *Evening Standard* reported.

Under the new, transparent system, the consumer was always informed exactly what had gone wrong, just as consumers were in the subway, which had its pluses and minuses. "It's always something different," said Daniel Rolph, a passenger I spoke to once in Waterloo Station, when I was researching an article about railway troubles (strictly speaking, I didn't need to do much research, given how often trains I was riding broke down). "One excuse was that the train was delayed because it took too long for the passengers to get on and off," Rolph told me. "Once they announced, 'Due to staff shortages, your train has been cancelled.'"

I have been collecting excuses. Here are some I have heard myself, heard from friends, or read about: "leaves on the line," "trees on the line," "debris on the line," "cows on the line," "dew on the line," "horse on the line," "the wrong kind of snow," "high levels of pollen," "extreme sunlight," "signal failures," "switching failures," "person attempting suicide on the line," "nonarrival of staff," "overhead line problems," "non-availability of rolling stock," "a problem with the door-locking mechanism," "passenger incident," "customer incident," "operational reasons," "boarding flow problems," "poor rail adhesion," "adverse weather conditions," and "extreme weather conditions."

Also: because the train had to "follow a freight train from York"; because the train was "held at the station for rationalization"; because the train "has completely broken down"; because "children are throwing stones at the train"; because of "a death at Clapham Junction"; because "the driver has issues to raise with the signalman"; because "we need to carry out safety checks with some of the track workers"; because "we've been stuck behind a slow Connex train, when they know we're an express service"; because "the train wasn't getting traction, so a second locomotive had to be got, and this locomotive had to be hired from another company"; because "a pigeon dropping landed on a vital electrical component, causing a short circuit"; because "we've run out of fuel"; and "as a result of the driver having had his car wheel clamped."*

On the tube I heard "shortage of trains." One commuter reported on a railway-complaint Web site that when he asked when his usual train was coming, the conductor replied: " 'Train???? There be no trains tonight, Sir!' " Another, stranded at a rural station at night for hours, finally spotted a staff member—who, stricken with panic at the sight of a live, irate customer, immediately ran away and hid in a closet.

Once my train was idling at a station in London when a woman's voice came over the loudspeaker: "If you are the driver, please make yourself known to staff." Passengers on another train felt it shudder to a halt and heard the conductor say: "Is there anyone on board who knows the way to our destination?" On one train, the conductor informed passengers that they had stopped moving "because the driver is only 5 ft. 1 in. and his swivel chair has broken, and he's too short to reach the pedals." On another occasion, the windscreen wipers broke, the train

---

* These excuses are always preceded and followed by abject apologies that you hear at each new stop. Once, as I traveled between London and York, on a train that accrued minutes and then hours of delay for different reasons along the way, I counted thirteen apologies in the first hour and a half alone.

could not move, and a staff member asked: "If anyone has some nuts and bolts with them, will they come forward?"

"Willing passengers gathered together a rudimentary tool kit and one even clambered on to the front of the engine in attempt to get it running again, but to no avail," the *Daily Telegraph* reported.

When things went wrong, the feeling of disappointment was compounded by the higher expectations. The public was no longer inclined to overlook incompetence or poor service. You felt as if the workers were trying, but just didn't know how to do it right. One summer I went to a fancy wedding in rural Northamptonshire. Several hundred guests fanned out to the most expensive, five-star hotels in the area. The American guests were bitterly disappointed. In one such hotel, one friend said, it appeared as if the staff was surprised that people actually wanted their food that same day. "I have never paid as much or waited so long for food that bad," she said.

In 2003, I had to travel to the Midlands for an article about the Conservative Party, headed for yet another disastrous defeat at the hands of Blair's Labour juggernaut. I booked myself into a hotel offering sleek, modern efficiency tailored to the needs of the discerning business traveler. It had televisions that worked, real hairdryers, the promise of decent room service. What it did not have was heat. I had run into this before in other hotels, and in places like pubs, where it was standard practice to heat some of the rooms but not others, like the bathrooms. But this hotel had presented itself as something different.

My radiator could have been a Duchampian installation, a decorative urinal or bicycle wheel, for all the good it did, inert in the corner. I could see my breath.

I called the front desk.

"We don't turn the heating on until four," the clerk said. It was three forty-five.

I waited forty-five minutes. The heat did not come on.

I called the front desk. "It's coming on soon," the clerk said. Nothing happened. I called again. Nobody answered.

I went downstairs, but the clerk was not interested in the heating situation. "It should be on by now," he said. I went back upstairs. My nose was red and the coldness was wafting between my pants and my legs. I lay down on the bed under a nest I had fashioned out of my coat and a pile of blankets and towels, sealed at the top with some extra pillows to lock in the warmth.

The phone at the front desk was permanently busy; they had taken it off the hook. I decided to go down to the lobby, where at least there was body heat from the people waiting to check in, a huge scrum of workers on some kind of retreat, many of whom were carrying open beer bottles they had brought with them from the bus.

The elevator came. But as I stepped onto it, my wedding ring suddenly flung off my finger, a first in nearly a decade of marriage. In the space of an hour, my frozen fingers had shriveled to the size of a nine-year-old child's.

The ring fell into the space between the elevator and the floor before disappearing into the void. I went down to the front desk, where the manager at first said, "too bad," and then, after I went American on him, promised he would try to find someone to look for it on Monday. It was Friday.

It seemed I had fallen victim to Bad Hotel Syndrome, but there was more to come when I left the next day; a great karmic convergence of incidents that represented something bigger: "Britain hates you." In the morning, no taxis were available because every single person in the country was watching England play Australia in the Rugby Union World Cup final, a rare event in that England never gets that far, and also never wins.

I offered to pay double, and eventually a sullen, mute adolescent appeared in a beat-up old car. The road was deserted. It was like the *Twilight Zone* episode from season five, "Stopover in a Quiet Town," when Barry Nelson and Nancy Malone wake up in a strange, empty community only to find that they have been kidnapped by giants and are now pets in a doll village.

The youth drove toward the station in such a manner that I began to wonder if he meant for me to disembark while the cab was still moving, as would happen to someone who had fallen afoul of the Mob. When we reached the station, we discovered it had closed since the day before, apparently for good. It had a padlock on the front door and an air of musty neglect. We drove to the next station. The teenager drove off, back to his television set.*

I waited. After an hour, someone announced that the line had been crippled by signal failures. I took a bus, waited some more, took a train, was evicted because of a switching problem, and got on another train. I arrived home five hours late, without my wedding ring, which was hard to explain to my husband.

The hotel manager called on Monday to say that he had found the ring and would send it through the Royal Mail, in a special registered-mail category.

This was a fatal decision, and I should have known better. No one should trust the Royal Mail, whose service had gone from really good to indifferent to shockingly bad in the space of a decade. While it had no instances of workplace rampages ending in multiple deaths, as in the U.S. Postal Service, it had a history of postal workers' succumbing to existential despair and throwing the mail away or stashing it in the closet for years at a time instead of delivering it.

The previous year the Royal Mail had failed to meet any of the fifteen performance targets set out in its contract. An undercover documentary filmed mail carriers stealing items from packages, doing drugs, and setting fire to the mail. One newspaper sent out ten letters around the country, and only one got to where it was supposed to go when it was supposed to get there. I once wrote a story about a street in Newcastle where for three months, only the people on the even-numbered side of the street got mail, because the post office had failed to notice that people also lived on the odd-numbered side of the street.

One of the residents went to the post office to complain, only to be informed that the house she lived in didn't exist. She finally blustered her way to the place where they sort the mail and found a pile of her old letters, stuffed behind a table.

---

* England won. Days of national celebration ensued.

Anyway, the mail service worked for me on this occasion, in that my special-delivery package departed on time. It arrived on time. I signed for it. Things were looking up for me domestically. I called my husband.

But my good mood was premature. The ring was missing from the envelope. It had been stolen.

"BY GOD, SIR, I'VE LOST MY LEG!"

It is not that the Englishman can't feel—it is that he is afraid to feel. . . . He must bottle up his emotions, or let them out only on a very special occasion.
—E. M. Forster, "Notes on the English Character" (1920)

There is a lovely essay in Anne Fadiman's book *Ex Libris* about the failed British explorers of the Victorian era, the honorable, hopeless men who embarked on expeditions to the unknown and came to unfortunate ends. Sir John Franklin, for instance, who died of illness and starvation along with 129 other men, "in a region of the Canadian Arctic whose game had supported an Eskimo colony for centuries." Although they left their guns behind, Franklin and his team brought along items like monogrammed silver, a cigar case, a clothes brush, a backgammon board, some button polish, and a copy of Oliver Goldsmith's 1766 novel *The Vicar of Wakefield*.

"These men may have been incompetent bunglers," Fadiman writes, "but, by God, they were gentlemen."

They were also the sort who wore their stiff upper lips on their sleeves and cultivated the impression that they would rather die than complain, literally. The early-twentieth-century adventurer Robert Falcon Scott, the greatest of the great exploring failures—who arrived at the South Pole a full month behind the Norwegian explorer Roald

Amundsen, and who then perished trying to get back—kept up his brave, stoical journal entries to the bitter end.

As he lay dying, did Scott write about how sorry he felt for himself? Did he say, "I wish I'd stayed at home with my family and never heard of the bloody South Pole, or annoying Roald Amundsen?" No. He struck a dignified pose, and he thought about his country. "I do not regret this journey," he declared, "which has shown that Englishmen can endure hardships, help one another, and meet death with as great a fortitude as ever in the past." Some months later, a search party found him and two comrades, their frozen corpses huddled inside sleeping bags, in a small canvas tent just eleven miles from a depot of food supplies.

My husband's generation, born in the early 1950s, was raised on the details of Scott's doom—the ferocious weather, the dwindling food, the frostbite, the gangrene, the shoddy equipment, the futility, the jolly bad luck of it all—and the fortitude with which he bore it. Honorable mention, of course, always went to Scott's upstanding companion Captain Oates, who, ill, lame, and using up valuable resources, demonstrated the elegant selflessness with which Britons are known around the world.

"I am just going outside and may be some time," he announced, advancing into the blizzard, never to return. Oates epitomized the ideal Englishman: uncomplaining and understated, a man who, if he had to speed along his own demise for the good of his companions, would damn well do it while tossing out a neat parting line for posterity.

America has its share of self-sacrificing heroes, like Nathan Hale, regretting that he had but one life to lose for his country, but our history tends to emphasize the overcoming of the adversity, rather than adversity for adversity's sake. Our iconic figures are people like Abraham Lincoln in his uncomfortable log cabin, traipsing twenty miles through a blizzard to return a library book (or to get to school, or to pay back a nickel, depending on which version you prefer). But one of the positive things about Lincoln, in addition to his leading the country through the Civil War and liberating the slaves, is that he did not carelessly freeze to death because of poor planning, poor luck, and a failure to pack the right gear.

But self-denying Britons are part of the national identity. Fiction is full of them, too, characters like Sydney Carton, the brilliant ne'er-do-well from *A Tale of Two Cities*, who sacrifices himself for the sake of his friend Charles Darnay and the woman they both love, Lucie Manette. Carton takes time en route to the guillotine to proclaim his eleventh-hour redemption "a far, far better thing that I do, than I have ever done." That is all very well, and I cried bitterly when I first read it (not to mention when I saw the movie; who wouldn't prefer racy Ronald Colman, playing Carton, to Donald Woods, in the role of the, let's face it, drippy Darnay?). But sometimes these paragons of virtuous self-denial went a little too far, in my opinion.

After I moved to England, everyone recommended the 1945 film *Brief Encounter* for its helpful insights into the national psyche. In the movie, Celia Johnson and Trevor Howard—married, but not to each other—tumble headlong in love, suffer pangs of lust and conscience, and naturally sacrifice happiness together for dull lives of duty with their tedious spouses. Only in Britain in the postwar era of blood and tears, toil and sweat could it have been considered the height of nobility to gaze longingly into someone else's eyes, agonize in a brittle accent about the tragic hopelessness of the situation, and not even get to have sex. In the end, Trevor goes to Africa and Celia goes home, where her husband, a dullard played by Cyril Raymond, sits prissily by the fire, doing the crossword puzzle.

Unlike, say, the nearly contemporaneous film *Gone With the Wind* (1939), that great American celebration of triumphing over adversity, making dresses from curtains, and stealing other women's men, *Brief Encounter* celebrates the virtues of repressed emotions and self-sacrificing responsibility. It is my English friend Ian's favorite movie. He loves Celia and Trevor's goodness and their frustration. "You've got Rachmaninoff sounding away in the background—but all the emotion is in the music," he said. "When you cut back to the people, they're saying, 'My dear, have you got something in your eye?'" The film, he believes, expresses "a particular facet of Englishness which we don't have any more, but that we can just trace some vestige of in ourselves."

Sometimes they could have it both ways: endure the sacrifice, suf-

fer the discomfort and love to tell the tale. One of my personal favor-
ites in the who-cares-how-bleak-this-is-I'm-an-Englishman genre was
the Earl of Uxbridge, who fought alongside the Duke of Wellington
at the Battle of Waterloo. At one point, Uxbridge, commanding the
Anglo-Belgian cavalry, happened to notice that his leg had been blown
off by a cannonball. The story goes that he then turned to Wellington
and announced: "By God, Sir, I've lost my leg!" To which Wellington is
said to have replied, "By God, Sir, so you have!" Following the convention that you are supposed to pretend your complaint doesn't matter,
or laugh it off with amusing tales, Uxbridge later had the amputated
leg buried with full military honors in France and thereafter enjoyed
the nickname "One-Leg," in the approved eccentric manner. The leg
was exhumed after his death and sent to England, where it was buried
beside him.

But like shopping-free Sundays, all that is receding into the past. In
twenty-first-century Britain, this idea of accepting your fate without complaint, sacrificing yourself for others, and keeping your troubles to yourself (to the extent that you admit you have any) is going quickly, if it has
not already gone. The heroes of today are intimately familiar with their
own swings of unhappiness; they flaunt their feelings instead of repressing them. Perhaps the greatest legacy of the late Princess Diana was to
open the floodgates in Britain to naked displays of unedited emotion. She
would have understood the collective hysteria her death inspired; the
country was only following the example she set so vividly in life.

For those bizarre two weeks after Diana died, in 1997, Britons
seemed to teeter between two poles of behavior and two types of
people—the stoics versus the emoters, the strong and silent versus the
tragic and noisy. At one extreme was the queen, taking the view that
dropping her mask of dignified reticence would be betraying the duty
she had always held sacred. She had been raised never to show weakness or falter in her adherence to tradition; and that is the approach
she took this time. *The Queen,* the meticulously researched 2006
movie about the aftermath of Diana's death—a strange, heady time

when it seemed as if Britain's deepest values were being thrown up in the air like sticks in the children's game, and who knew where they would fall—used the elderly Elizabeth as the embodiment of old-school virtues.

Peter Morgan, the screenwriter, told me that he based the queen's character in part on that of his own mother, who comes from the same wartime era.

"My mother is uncomplaining, stoic, never sees a doctor, would be in incredible pain and never mention it, thinks aspirin is decadent, walks around turning the lights off and wears clothes that are thirty years old," he said. He contrasted that approach—the queen's, and his mother's—with the "narcissism and intolerance of pain of our generation, to whom happiness is a God-given right."

Diana was a product of that younger generation; in her world, Celia and Trevor would have run off together after meeting at the train station, and *Brief Encounter* would have been called *The Great Love Affair Which Was Consummated on the First Date (And Which Broke up Two Marriages, But Who Cares).* Diana preferred talking to repressing, sharing her pain to keeping it to herself, having her own way to ceding to others. It's hard even now to overestimate the shock to the system that her entry into the royal family caused.

Who can forget the sight of Diana at one of her great emotional coming-out moments, her 1995 interview with Martin Bashir on the BBC's *Panorama* program? Her face deathly pale, her eyes pandalike with black makeup, and her hair framing her face in a bizarrely unattractive style that she had insisted on doing herself, Diana talked freely about her eating problems, her estranged husband, his girlfriend ("there were three of us in this marriage, so it was a bit crowded" was how she alluded to his affair with Camilla Parker Bowles), her own affair with

---

* Three of Elizabeth's children—Princess Anne, Prince Charles, and Prince Andrew—divorced their spouses in the 1990s. Only a generation earlier, divorce had been so frowned on that Princess Margaret, the queen's sister, was told that unless she gave up her divorced boyfriend, Group Capt. Peter Townsend, she would have to renounce all her royal privileges and become a common person (she gave him up.). She married someone else, but ended up divorcing him.

James Hewitt, and her view that the royal family had bullied, repressed, and tried to break her.

It was riveting television. It also neatly established the terms of the division that would widen after she died: Us (normal people who have emotions) vs. Them (the cold, inhibited, repressed royal family). Diana set it all out: "Maybe I was the first person ever to be in this family who ever had a depression or was ever openly tearful," she said. She said that "the establishment that I married into" put her down "because I do things differently, because I don't go by the rule book, because I lead from the heart, not the head."

Diana made it safe to have feelings; she democratized, and feminized, emotion, she gave the country license to mourn and weep and gnash its teeth and to set itself up in opposition, as she had, to the royal family, so chilly and out of touch in those weeks at the turn of the century.* "The Floral Revolution," the *Observer* called it, in an account of the flowers blanketing London left by people who wanted to be part of it somehow. Diana surely did Britain a favor, by helping it to remember it had feelings, even if she did so while wallowing in narcissistic self-pity and casting herself as the perpetual victim in the dramatic rendering of her life.

Diana was not, as it happened, the only one. Her husband had tried it, too. A year before the *Panorama* interview, Charles, in a move that contradicted his entire upbringing and background, provided an extraordinarily candid, and extraordinarily self-pitying, account of his own life for his biographer, Jonathan Dimbleby. His childhood was lonely; his parents were unfeeling; he had had a very rough time, he told the nation via the book and in a companion television interview—the princely equivalent of appearing on *Oprah*.

---

* In *The Queen*, Elizabeth's bewilderment at a country she suddenly feels she doesn't understand is best seen when she is forced by the government to lower the flag on Buckingham Palace to half staff (completely unprecedented) and to address the nation on television (also completely unprecedented, except for her annual anodyne Christmas address). Her speech was typically reserved and stiff, with one exception, when she mentioned that she was speaking to the nation as their queen and "as a grandmother." According to the film, Tony Blair's spokesman and image spinner, Alastair Campbell, thought up the phrase and inserted it into the address.

The early parts of *The Prince of Wales* (1994) are grim reading—
he might as well have called the childhood section *A Prince Called
"It,"* after Dave Pelzer's book about his own abused past. By any normal standard, Charles had indeed had a terrible time. His mother
had been formal and remote and prone to such unmaternal moves as
leaving her toddler son at home while she went on an extended business trip around the world. The Duke of Edinburgh, Charles's athletic, macho father, despised his son's softness as sniveling weakness.
He was from the "no crying" school of parenting. But his methods—
shouting at the prince in front of company, ridiculing and criticizing
him for his fears and lack of athletic ability—only made the tears
come harder and faster.

Things were lonely at home, but they got worse when Charles was
dispatched to Cheam prep school at the age of eight.* Cheam was followed by Gordonstoun, a severe institution in deepest, darkest north-
eastern Scotland whose attitude toward the treatment of adolescent
boys might best be described as "bracing." The students wore shorts,
even in winter (and northern Scotland is really cold). Boys who slept
near the window, propped open round the clock according to school
policy, frequently woke up soaked from the rain or covered with a light
dusting of snow.† The traditional way to welcome new pupils was "by
taking a pair of pliers to their arms and twisting until their flesh tore

---

* A lot of British boarding schools have unpleasant or strange names. There is a prep
school in Oxford called the Dragon (its graduates are called Old Dragons, just as Har-
row's are called Old Harrovians and Winchester's Wykehamists, as if they were members of the occult). Maybe it's just me, but "Cheam" sounds like a kind of inedible
cheese by-product.

† This was totally normal. In *How to Be Topp* (1954), Geoffrey Willans and Ronald
Searle ungrammatically lampooned the situation at Eton, the country's premier boarding
school. "Welcome sir," they imagine "the maître d'hotel" saying: "We have to put you in
suite number 2 this is only temporary sir you understand no bathroom no shower your
toothpaste will be waiting for you frozen in the wash-basin." At my husband's school,
ice formed on the inside of the windows on winter nights. The boys took enforced cold
baths every morning, and they would line up in the bathroom, one behind the other, and
jump in and out, like wicks being dipped in wax. It is a measure of the wretchedness of
this ritual that the boys wanted to be the last in the tub—the water might be dirty by
then, but at least it would not be so cold.

open," according to a former student. Charles's schoolmates relentlessly mocked his juglike ears, set upon him on the rugby field in an effort to injure him, and disrupted his slumber by pelting him with weapons like pillows and slippers as he lay in bed at night.

"Last night was hell, literal hell," Charles wrote at the time. He begged to be allowed out. Certainly not, his father said: Buck up and shut up.

People of Charles's class and background weren't supposed to acknowledge, let alone grumble about, the vicissitudes of any aspect of existence. But if he had been trying to elicit friendly attention to counter the sympathy the public felt for his wife, with her accounts of how terribly she had been treated, Charles was bound to be disappointed. The book had almost the opposite effect. The general response was, What a total loser.

"No sensible person could possibly complain about the Prince of Wales experiencing these various traumas," the former MP Roy Hattersley wrote in a review. "What is, however, inexcusable is his decision to make them public."

Another reviewer, John Grigg, found Charles's victim mentality "ludicrously unconvincing." "He had some nasty experiences at Gordonstoun, but no nastier than many others who went to boarding school."

But wittingly or not, Charles was on the cutting edge of a new trend. Wallowing didn't work for him, but it did little harm to the soccer star David Beckham, Britain's turn-of-the-millennium hero and, along with Diana, the country's only truly international superstar. Beckham was blessed with a lethal right foot, a stratospheric salary, a pointlessly opulent house known as Beckingham Palace, and a reputation as a fashion trendsetter who looked as fetching in soccer shorts as he did in a sarong, a pirate-style do-rag, and a tight all-leather ensemble. He was a metrosexual sports hero. His shirt "smelled only of perfume," the Brazilian star Ronaldo noted in wonder after the two exchanged jerseys when Brazil beat England in 2002.

In his early career, when he was mostly just a soccer star and not yet the preening, tight-underpants-promoting celebrity superstar he would become, Beckham also had a chronic petulance problem. He felt very sorry for himself. He believed he was perennially hard done by. Upset that he had botched a play in the 1998 World Cup tournament in France, Beckham churlishly kicked an opponent from Argentina and was ejected from the match, leaving his team a man short (they lost).*

Then, in 2003, he was involved in an unseemly locker-room incident with the Manchester United coach, Alex Ferguson, who was annoyed at his flashy player's outside interests, like hanging out with Elton John, and also at the team's loss to its bitter rival Arsenal. In the midst of berating the squad, Ferguson angrily kicked a soccer shoe, which then flew up and struck Beckham just above his eye.

Rather than taking it on the chin (or leg) like Lord Uxbridge, or even Trevor Howard, Beckham scraped his highlighted hair back into a girly hairband and strode into the path of the waiting flashbulbs. He made sure the photographers got a good shot of his forehead with its sad injury and its reproachful Band-Aid. He spread around the story that the wound had needed stitches.

But perhaps the biggest sign of how things had changed came three years later, during the World Cup in Germany. For the England fans, this tournament is a perennial exercise in futility and disappointment that forces them perpetually to carry two conflicting emotions in their heads: the hope that the team will win, and the realization that it probably never will. Following an ancient script, England failed to live up to its early promise and was heading toward elimination from the tournament. Beckham scored a goal against Ecuador, but then threw up on the field, which was embarrassing enough. In the quarter final against Portugal, he hurt his foot—which meant that the game and the tournament were over for him. He ripped off his captain's armband and, instead of passing it on to the substitute captain, the way he was supposed to, flung it to the ground in a fit of pique. He limped to the stands and flamboyantly burst into tears.

---

* They always lose, eventually.

It was a very un-old-school performance, particularly when you compare it to the behavior of the players on the 1966 national soccer team, the only England team that has ever managed to win the World Cup. They are still considered possibly the best thing to happen to English sports in world history, and are still the benchmark of achievement against every subsequent team that has always lost. These players were devoted to the game, not to themselves. Most earned less than £100 a week. They took in a total of £300 in sponsorship money each, for wearing Adidas shoes during the tournament. Their bonus for winning was £1,000 apiece. (By contrast, Beckham made about $27 million in 2003–4, according to a French soccer magazine.)

Unlike the pampered, cosseted, spoiled 2006 team, whose wives and girlfriends—the WAGs, the papers called them—were shipped out to Germany to party, shop, and distract the players with their skimpy outfits, the 1966 team had to forego conjugal relations for six weeks before the tournament. They were expected to abide by the old standards of courtesy and fair play that had long been ingrained in British schoolchildren. Their manager, Alf Ramsey, kept them under a tight rein. "He expected you to act like a professional, and if anyone stepped out of line, he couldn't understand why. He expected people to do the right thing by the English public," one player, George Cohen, said.

People disagree about why tearfulness and self-pity are so common in modern Britain. Some blame Diana. Others blame, variously, the media, the welfare system, the self-indulgence of celebrities, the collapse of family values, weedy European legislation, political correctness, too much therapy, and the United States. Frank Furedi, a professor of sociology at the University of Kent and the author of books like *Therapy Culture* and *Paranoid Parenting*, once told me he blamed Mrs. Thatcher, whose efforts to wean the country from the welfare state and promote the idea of "clients" rather than "citizens" promoted, paradoxically, the notion of being owed rather than owing.

"There is no such thing as society," Thatcher said, encouraging a sense of greedy individualism to replace the collective responsibility of the past. The Blair government took the notion further in 1999 by incorporating the European Convention on Human Rights into British

238 • SARAH LYALL

law (it's similar to the American Bill of Rights, with provisions like the right to privacy and the right to freedom of expression). Britons, who had never had such a formal assertion of rights before, suddenly had a new tool of legal entitlement.

The mood changed to match the new laws, right down to the way students are taught. In my husband's and Prince Charles's day, students were threatened, humiliated, and browbeaten into achievement. Praise came grudgingly, and any kid who wondered who the dumbest kid in the class was didn't have to wonder for long, because the teacher told everyone, straight out. John Lennon once got a report card announcing that he was "certainly on the road to failure."

Not anymore. Teachers spray praise around like air freshener to make all the students and parents feel good. I'm used to it—that's what they do in New York, and I have always appreciated a bit of insincere positive reinforcement—but my husband isn't. We once went to our daughters' school's mandatory annual poetry recital. Not all the small children were natural public speakers. They whispered, they forgot their lines, they cried; they lapsed into unintelligibility. But we all burst into ecstatic applause after each poem, after which the teacher announced that the performance had been fantastic, even when it obviously hadn't been.

I thought this was fine; they were only seven; well done for not wetting their pants. But I noticed that Robert was not clapping along with the other parents. He explained on the way home. "When I went to school, no one got praised for doing a bad job," he said. He looked upset as he remembered the overly honest, overly mean teachers of his youth but had to think that maybe they had been right.

"How are the good students supposed to know they are any good, if everyone is told how wonderful they are?" he asked. "How are the bad ones supposed to know how badly they did?"

He has a point, and it feels at times as if the pendulum has swung too far, too fast. At field day, the younger kids all get certificates for good sportsmanship, even if they cheat or cry. A friend actually witnessed a kindergarten teacher leading the kids in the self-enriching group exercise of patting themselves on the back and chanting, "Well done, me!" At graduation, every child in the graduating class gets a cup for something, even if it is just for doing a credible job in his beginner's karate lessons. "Do you think he's hurting my self-esteem?" one of our children asked in all seriousness about a teacher, apropos of the teacher's having given her a not-so-great grade on a paper.

Our kids' school has not gone completely over to the American side. It still terrorizes the children with a constant state-mandated barrage of exams and demands the sort of slavish attention to the correct uniform and "kit," meaning equipment, that would be familiar to anyone who has read Enid Blyton's Malory Towers books, set in a fictional girls' boarding school in Cornwall. School mornings are frenzied hunts for elusive regulation items—the right shin pads, sweatshirt, schoolbag, coat, sweater, or shorts—without the presence of which my children face the possibility of being slapped with demerits to be deducted from their house points, as Harry's mishaps cause points to be deducted from Gryffindor in the Harry Potter books. Now, that is something my husband can understand.

My children go to a private school in West London. In overcrowded, cash-strapped state schools (what Americans would call public schools), the new sense of personal entitlement manifests itself differently: in children who are obstreperous, hostile, and out of control, and in teachers who, because of changing attitudes and the fear that they will be sued or fired, are afraid to discipline them.

"Back in the 1970s, at a parents' evening, if you said, 'John's doing rather well, but perhaps he could work a little harder,' Dad would support the system, as it were," Martin Ward, deputy general director of the Secondary Heads Association, which represents secondary school principals, told me. "Now if you say something like that, you're likely to get the reaction: 'It must be your fault. What are you going to do about it?'"

The new entitled attitude goes far beyond education. It is permeating the whole society. "The philosophy used to be that you would take things in your own hands and deal with them in your own way," Paul Murphy, a member of the Manchester city council, told me. "You'd stand in the queue—that was the British way."

But an American-style tendency not just to complain and demand, but also to sue—supported, as it happens, by the legal scaffolding of the

Human Rights Act—has infiltrated the national approach. Schoolchildren who blame their troubles on the teacher are growing into adults who blame their troubles on the government, or anyone else who is handy. In 1966, when a waste tip slid down a mountain in the South Wales mining village of Aberfan, killing 144 people, 116 of them children, the survivors and families decided not to sue for compensation, saying it would be unseemly and undignified. But that was then. Now, in big cities with deep pockets, would-be litigants lurk around construction sites, take photographs of sidewalks undergoing repairs, and use the pictures later in court, claiming they fell down and hurt themselves.

The National Health Service spent £466 million dealing with clinical negligence claims in 2002, compared with 1 million in 1974; by 2007, the figure was £579 million. The NHS estimated that the theoretical cost of paying all the outstanding claims would be £9.09 billion (90 percent of the cases are settled out of court; the NHS tends to just pay off the complainants rather than go to trial).

The tabloids call this the "compensation culture" and the "blame culture," and use it as evidence that Britain is going to hell, and quick. "Increasingly, people in Britain have begun to develop an idea that a lot of the adverse, negative experiences they encounter are the fault of another institution or individual," Furedi told me. "There's been a fundamental recasting of ideas about responsibility, blame, and whose fault it is."

Some of their arguments fall in to the category of nostalgic fretting about five-pence ice cream cones and children who had no toys except bits of old string, with which they happily entertained themselves for hours on end, but people like Furedi make a good case. Now police officers sue after having witnessed traumatic events in the course of their work or because they claim to have been discriminated against on account of race, gender or, in one case, dyslexia. An obese man successfully sued a florist's shop for damages in 2007, after he slipped on a stray petal outside its front door. "Since the 1980s, we've pretty much achieved in twenty years what took the United States fifty years," Furedi said.

Britons still file far fewer lawsuits than Americans do, and most lawsuits are dismissed before getting to trial. But fear of them has led to so much prophylactic planning, and such higher insurance premiums, that people and businesses have radically changed the way they operate in order to minimize risk whenever possible. Some schools have canceled field trips and outdoor recess. "Health and Safety" rules—many of them required by Europe, and despised by the British as Continental weakness, like taking overly long vacations and carrying "man bags"—are invoked everywhere, to the point of foolishness.

Passengers buying tea on trains are ordered, whether they want to or not, to carry the cups in paper bags so they won't spill. Notices in supermarkets warn that fallen grapes can cause accidents. At the indoor climbing center where I learned how to rock climb, a door leading to a tiny courtyard outside is kept permanently locked; a sign warns people that no one is allowed to go outside because of "health and safety regulations."

Speeding across the Thames in a motorboat, flanked by a pair of heavies from the British security services, the actor Daniel Craig affected a suave and dangerous air for a news conference announcing that he had been cast as James Bond in the latest Bond film. The effect was somewhat spoiled by the bulky life preserver he was wearing over his superbly tailored dinner jacket; apparently, even MI6 agents with licenses to kill need to follow civilian safety laws.

Tabloid newspapers love stories about absurd precautions and frivolous lawsuits, and use them as examples of the "nanny state" and "political correctness gone mad." (Sometimes, true to the nature of the tabloids, their reports are true. Sometimes they're partially true, and sometimes they're completely false.) We read that local pony clubs are closing because too many children sue after hurting their thumbs. We read that a village in Devon canceled its annual Pancake Day race, in which the local children race along the streets balancing pancakes in frying pans, because the insurance was too expensive. And we read that villages across Britain have stopped building their traditional Guy Fawkes bonfires on November 5—commemorating the failure of Fawkes to blow up Parliament five hundred years ago—because fire is dangerous. Some places have replaced the live flames with fake flames made of beanpoles, straw, and flaps of orange paper; others simply show movies of bonfires, akin to the old Yule Log broadcast on TV.

It can seem as if the British have melted into a collective puddle of whingeing, weeping lightweights. But the story is more complicated than that. I don't think the stiff upper lip is dead, not completely. It comes out again at times of genuine crisis.

Fifty-six people were killed, including the four bombers, and hundreds more were injured in the bombings that tore through London's transportation system in July 2005. For several heart-stopping hours, it looked as if this might be Britain's 9/11. There were the same panicky reports—an explosion here, a power outage there, an unexploded bomb somewhere else, blood-soaked casualties pouring into the streets, hundreds missing—and no way to tell what was true, and what was rumor. Cell phones were permanently busy, and the transportation system was crippled. There was the same terrible sense that events were unfolding almost too quickly for understanding, and that there might be worse to come.

But 7/7 was markedly different from 9/11, both because of the physical dissimilarities—no skyscrapers fell in London, the deaths were fewer, the air was not poisoned, and the sun was not erased by clouds of smoke and ash—and because of the ineffable thing that is the British character. These are the times that Britons invoke the Dunkirk Spirit, in honor of the great outpouring of civilian boats which crossed the English Channel in 1940 to help carry the country's dispirited, wounded soldiers back home after their disastrous retreat from France. It happens every time—whether the disaster is explosion, flood, or fire.

"I tenderly love this city with its wounds," the French philosopher Simone Weil wrote about London during World War II, as an earlier set of bombs rained down on the city from the skies, night after night. "What strikes me most about these people, in their present situation, is a good humor that is neither spontaneous nor artificial, but that comes from a feeling of fraternal and tender comradeship in a common ordeal." As 7/7 wore on and the accounting of casualties and damage and danger was almost over, London's first instinct was to seek normalcy. To get on with it, in that prosaic phrase Britons use so often.

The prime minister, presiding over a meeting of the Group of Eight nations in Scotland, broke off briefly to travel to London, but returned that night to resume discussions of global warming and aid to Africa. In the House of Commons, legislators doggedly debated the scheduled issues of the day before turning their attention to the terrorist attacks.

Two days after the bombings, London went ahead with a long-planned commemoration of the sixtieth anniversary of the end of World War II. Thousands of frail, elderly veterans wearing too-tight uniforms heavy with medals traveled to the city from across the country—many braving the train system and then walking on unsteady feet from Victoria Station. They gathered in front of Buckingham Palace and down the Mall, the broad boulevard that stretches out in front of it, shaking off any worries that such a large gathering might tempt further terrorist attacks. There was a defiant determination to show that Britain would not be cowed, as it had not been cowed during the Blitz, or during thirty years of terrorist bombings by the Irish Republican Army.

Two days earlier, I had been in a wounded, frightened city. Now it was celebrating the essence of a nation. "Look how marvelous this all is," Maj. Alan Frost, a reservist in the British army who was on crowd-control duty, told me. "There's something about Londoners—about the British." He used the familiar phrase: "We just tend to get on with it."

Nonveterans had gathered, too, in a show of courtesy for the past and respect for a dwindling generation that represents Britain as it still likes to see itself. Lorraine Barrett, forty-one, a supermarket cashier, was there to honor the memory of her father, a World War II veteran who had died of cancer in 1989. Barrett, who had once been down the street from a nail bomb that killed two people in Soho, said that the latest terrorist attacks had made her afraid to ride the subway, but that she had ridden it anyway.

"I was determined to come, no matter what," she said. "I'm not going to let what happened in the last few days stop me from doing what I want."

I walked along and tried to get the veterans to talk about their wartime experiences. But they were from the pre-Diana generation, the one that recoils from the self-indulgence of articulating terrible memories, and they would not say much. I chatted for a few minutes with eighty-one-year-old Fred Reed, who was walking toward the Mall from St. James's Park with his wife, Connie.

Both had medals pinned to their jackets, and I asked what Mrs. Reed's were for. "They were my older brother's," Mr. Reed said, won posthumously after his brother was killed, in 1941. Mr. Reed enlisted in the Royal Navy a year later, when he turned eighteen. He went to fight even though he was the only son his parents had left.

Weren't his parents worried about losing him, too?

"They never said so," he said. "You wanted to get the war over and done with."

He said he had been "stationed all over the shop," in North Africa, in Europe, but didn't want to go into it. Really, his time had not been any worse than anyone else's, the battles he fought not particularly difficult, none that stood out, none worth dwelling on now.

"Well, D-day," his wife said.

I once gave my husband for Christmas a copy of the *New Yorker* cartoon that shows a businessman lying on a couch and saying to his shrink: "Call me in denial if you like, but I think what goes on in my personal life is none of my own damn business." I honestly think many old-school Britons believe that. I think that people in the war generation believe that self-preservation depends on a commitment not to examine unpleasant emotions or rake over distressing times from the past.

I also think that the British stiff upper lip comes in handy in times of traditional crisis: you are about to be massacred by a mob of Indians who don't, for some reason, appreciate the benefits of British rule; you have a week's supply of food, but a month's journey ahead through polar-bear-infested ice; the Battle of the Somme is starting in five minutes. The system fell apart when Diana died because her death wasn't a real disaster, but a time of emotional catharsis, a time to let centuries of pent-up feelings out in an inchoate howl of anger and nonspecific grief. The anguish was real, but the cause was a fantasy, something safe, in its way, to cry about.

I also think there is a quiet and dark underside to all this, that the

British pay a terrible price for suppressing their emotions. This is a very American view. But Pat Barker says much the same thing in her *Regeneration* trilogy, novels that explore the psychological wounds inflicted on Britons by World War I. This was a war in which three hundred young men, deserters who for the most part were suffering from shell shock, were executed by firing squad for cowardice.

Barker sets much of the first book in the Craiglockhart War Hospital, where the emotionally wounded are sent for help with problems which manifest themselves in an array of terrible symptoms, from stuttering, bed-wetting, and nervous tics to the psychosomatic inability to walk, talk, or—in the case of a soldier knocked unconscious by an explosion that propelled him headfirst onto the corpse of a decomposing German soldier, filling his mouth, nose, and eyes with putrefying flesh—eat.

The treatment involves the kind of talking, remembering, and grieving that runs counter to the "whole tenor of their upbringing," Barker writes. "They had been trained to identify emotional repression as the essence of manliness. Men who broke down, or cried, or admitted to feeling fear, were sissies, weaklings, failures." The father of one officer, Billy Prior—traumatized by watching men under his command die and then scraping body parts, including a stray eyeball, out of trenches—is puzzled and angry that his son has ended up in a mental hospital. "He'd get a damn sight more sympathy from me if he had a bullet up his arse," the father says.

A British psychiatrist I asked about this told me that the same attitude persists in old-school Britons even today. It is a legacy of "generations after generations sending their children away to be educated at boarding school," she said; people use it as a way to "pretend that bad things don't happen." A way to make yourself feel better by anesthetizing yourself from the awful possibility of feeling terrible.

I once interviewed a distinguished elderly Englishman, a man whose mind was still as subtle, sharp, and delightful as ever, but whose body was beginning to fail him. His eyesight was going, his legs, his teeth, his hearing. But he regaled me with funny stories, behaved as if his complaints were minor nuisances, and claimed that he was neither afraid nor angry, that this was just getting old.

We finished the interview, and his wife walked me to the front door. I mentioned how much I admired her husband's fortitude and uncomplaining common sense, what a good role model he was of cheerful old age.

I had caught her in a low moment.

"When we're alone, he complains all the time about how much it hurts, and how hard it is, and how scared he is of dying," she said. And I realized I had been given a small glimpse, just for a minute, of the private struggle that allowed him to keep up the public pretense that was so essential to him.

FOURTEEN

THE BEST OF THE DAY

*No climate in the world is less propitious than the climate of
England, yet with a recklessness which is almost sublime, the
English rush out of doors to eat a meal on every possible and
impossible occasion.*
          —Georgina Battiscombe, *English Picnics* (1951)

The summer after I moved to England, my husband took me on
a romantic weekend to St. Ives, on the southern tip of Cornwall, purportedly one of the loveliest spots in the country.
St. Ives could well be lovely—its magically changeable light inspired
a golden period of British art in the mid-twentieth century—but on
that particular occasion it was hard to tell, on account of the storm.
The weather had just taken a turn for the worse. The temperature
plummeted, and the skies filled with evil-looking black clouds emitting relentless rain. It was just too much, coming after a wet, freezing
spring, and I burst into tears and yelled at Robert in a way that suggested that I planned to move back to New York and blame it on him.
At the hotel bar, a grizzled man dressed in what looked like an old sea
captain's costume gazed lugubriously into his beer and said: "The sun
was shining until yesterday."

I heard this so often the first couple of years that I started secretly
to think that maybe, in some pathetic-fallacy sort of way, I was carrying

the poor weather with me, like Pigpen with his traveling cloud of dust. On a trip to Trebetherick, the beautiful village on the wilder north coast of Cornwall where Robert had, according to his own accounts, spent his entire childhood frolicking on the beach in conditions of idyllic perfection, I was greeted by gusts of snow and volleys of hail the size of golf balls.

He claimed to be surprised: "It never snows here at Easter."

As I researched an article for a magazine about the sports events that make up society's annual summer "Season," I encountered different gradations of rain at each stop. A light drizzle at the Derby, where I sat miserably in the pavilion, watching the horses on TV and feeling slightly delicate. A deluge at the Henley regatta, which ruined my high-heeled slingbacks as I sprinted through the mud to the beverage industry's "hospitality tents," where everyone got tanked and forgot about the race (the rowers, rain cascading from their hair, had to go ahead anyway, but by that time the number of spectators in my general vicinity who actually cared was small indeed).

Then there was Wimbledon, an annual vexation for players, tennis fans, and television schedulers. Holding a tennis tournament on grass courts is a wonderful old-fashioned notion; holding it in a place where it always rains is willfully perverse, because when it rains, you can't use the courts. Even a suggestion of rain, and play ceases instantly, as groundskeepers hurl themselves forward and cover the grass with protective tarpaulins. For the courts to be considered ready again, the rain has to stop and to remain stopped for twenty consecutive minutes, which is harder to pull off than it sounds. A drop of water falls, the tarp rolls out, you repair to the strawberries-and-cream-selling café, the rain stops, you come back, twenty minutes pass, the tarp is removed, play resumes, another drop falls, and it begins all over again. It tends to break the concentration.

It rained so often and so relentlessly in the summer of 2007 that the men's third-round match between Rafael Nadal and Robin Soderling took five days and more than ninety-two hours to complete, only four hours of which were spent playing tennis. They had to stop for rain eight, or possibly nine, times, according to varying accounts. "Is this the worst Wimbledon ever?" one of the papers said, over a photograph of two wretched spectators sitting in the empty grandstand, water streaming down the sides of the garbage bags they had fashioned into makeshift raincoats.

Every time it rains during scheduled events, the people around you shake their heads in sorrow and act as if they are surprised. This is perfectly normal, including the part where the people are surprised. No matter what anyone says, no matter how hopeful they are, no matter how many fair-weather activities they plan, no matter how shiny and blue the day is when morning comes, there is always something, if not at that moment, then at a moment sometime soon. And everyone knows it. So rare are unbroken weeks of summer warmth and sunshine that the English remember them with the nostalgic awe that New Yorkers reserve for exceptionally cold and snowy winters. We had the blizzard of '83; they had the heat wave of '95.

In spite of this, or maybe because of it, it takes a lot to keep a British person indoors. This is partly due to the tradition of "getting some fresh air." Mothers leave their babies to sleep in prams in the garden, for fresh-air purposes. After lunch in the country, it is common practice for everyone to haul themselves outside for a brisk walk in the driving rain, so that they can get some fresh air.

But in the summer so many activities are dependent on good weather—from the fancy picnics at Glyndebourne opera house to the hotdog-and-cotton-candy weekend excursions to Brighton—that, when the day is inevitably spoiled by rain, a little question wells up in the mind of the outsider. What exactly did you expect?

The answer is multi-pronged. Britons like living on the edge of disappointment. Having their hopes thwarted bolsters the legitimacy of their congenital pessimism. They enjoy an excuse for a grumble. They prefer bad weather because it reflects the national mood—gray (grey, really) and misty—and allows them to get more things done. They don't really care if it's raining, as long as it's not too cold (or, possibly, they don't really care if it's cold, as long as it's not raining).

Most Britons would go mad in a bright, cheerful climate like Southern California's. Warm, sunny weather makes them happy for about a day, but then it makes them nervous. The spells of ninety-plus weather that global warming has brought with it upset the natives as thoroughly as a bitter cold snap does in winter. Most people don't have air-conditioning, anyway. When you order a drink, they still ask you if you want ice in it, as if ice cubes were exotic delicacies.

But it's not that straightforward. Britons' relationship to the weather is a complicated psychological dance that I only began to appreciate after years of enforced acclimatization and some active studying. As part of my effort to understand, I took Robert and the children to the south coast on a late-May weekend one year when I was researching an article about British beaches. The British love of their own seaside—the scene of 27.5 million visits by natives in 2002—has, interestingly enough, not been wrecked by the arrival of cheap plane tickets and holiday packages to fairer places on the Continent. Those places have better weather and better sand, and you can swim in the water without slathering yourself in grease, dressing like a Navy SEAL, and having to gulp down buckets of hot tea afterward. But for reasons known only to themselves, the British still love their traditional bucket-and-spade day trips to the coast.

"While the weeklong holiday has gone, the day out at the seaside has never been as popular," Peter Gibson, a spokesman for Encams, an environmental group that gives awards to the cleanest beaches in England, told me. I didn't really get it. Having been raised near the vast, warm, gentle beaches of Long Island, I was rather frightened of the challenging conditions on English beaches, where people cram miserably together in the cold on strips of rocky sand. Why would they go to the beach, when the beach could be so unpleasant?

We got to Camber Sands near Hastings (the scene of 1066 and all that) in the middle of a bank holiday weekend, bank holidays being days off that commemorate nothing except that you get the day off. It was a typical late-spring morning. Pockets of black clouds massed ominously in the east and the west. The wind propelled the sand in a horizontal direction, along with moisture that may have been rain or drops from the sea; it was all merging together. The beachgoers had found shelter, some huddling in trenchlike depressions among the dunes, others behind elaborate plastic shelters they had brought from home and erected on the sand.

These devices, called windbreaks (as opposed to windbreakers, water-resistant jackets we Americans wear over our sweaters and which are known in Britain as "windcheaters"), were meant to protect the beachgoers from the wind, rain, and cold; some people also used them as racks to dry their wet clothes, making it look as if they were itinerants at a makeshift camp for displaced persons.

I thought it was unusual, setting out for the beach when you fully expected to need to shield yourself from the wind and rain by sitting behind a portable shack, but that is what they were doing.

Far up the beach, Jackie Hancock, forty-three, shivered, fully dressed, in front of her windbreak, sweaters draped on her legs, drinking something hot from a Thermos. The ragged pile of wet towels beside her turned out on closer examination to be her older daughter, Katherine, curled in the fetal position.

Why exactly were they there?

"It's nice to get some fresh air," Mrs. Hancock said, adding, a little sharply: "It was sunny when we got out of the car." Katherine said something, but I could not catch it, since her head was buried in the towels and some kind of howling wind tunnel had developed in the corridor of air between us.

Nestled behind some large dunes, nearer to the parking lot than to the water, another couple, Tim and Kate Nash, tried to explain what led them to the beach after a morning spent monitoring the Weather Channel on television. The day's forecast, as usual, did not leave much room for either certainty or dispute, covering pretty much every meteorological possibility, delivered with so many qualifiers that it would have been impossible to argue later that the predictions had been inaccurate.

"Many eastern and central regions will start cloudy with rain, heaviest in Scotland," *The Times* had reported that morning. "Most western regions will become brighter with sunny spells, spreading into the east. However, showers will develop, heavy over Northern Ireland."

Unsure of what that entailed—did "brighter with sunny spells" mean "it will rain all day, but occasionally there might be a ray of sunshine?" What was "brighter" anyway? Brighter than what?—the Nashes, who were celebrating their daughter's birthday with a posse of adolescents, had planned for every eventuality. They had their barbecue equipment, their cricket bats, their bathing suits, and their towels, but they also had their windbreak, their heavy jackets, their sweaters, their raincoats, and their formidable collection of golf umbrellas, which they planned to fashion into a seamless rain-repelling canopy should the need arise.

"You have to be positive!" said Mrs. Nash, who was dressed for autumn.

"I believe that after this chunk of gray cloud passes, there's a big chunk of sunshine coming," said Mr. Nash.

"It's a very British thing," his wife continued. "Because we don't get that many sunny days, we have to make the most of them."

"We will assess the situation and remain here even if it looks thoroughly miserable," Mr. Nash concluded. He was looking forward to the day's beach activities. "The girls will have a sand castle competition. They'll bury Edward"—Edward being the Nashes' son, his legs already disappearing under the sand—"and then they'll be going to play cricket. We are going to read the newspaper." He gestured to his *Times*, a little damp already, but still hanging together.

I talked to a few more people, but my daughters were starting to lose heart—they were, I'm sorry to say, affected at that moment by my poor morale—and they couldn't make sand castles because they had lost all feeling in their hands, so we got back in the car.

Things were grimmer still down the coast at Bexhill beach, a forbidding collection of uncomfortable rocks in medium sizes—much bigger than pebbles, but not quite as large as boulders. The beach was slanted down at a sharp angle leading to the English Channel. The sky was darker, grayer there, muffled under fog and heavy with expectant rain. George Horn, fifty-nine, was slumped out of the wind against a jetty dividing the beach into sections, eating buttered rolls with his wife, Janet. He pronounced the conditions perfect.

"Fine weather in this country means it's not raining," he told me. "It's either fine, or it's raining. Of course, if it's not raining, it soon will be."

Nearby, thirty-seven-year-old Kath Hamilton, wearing a fleecy jacket, had planted herself on some other rocks with her children and mother-in-law. One of her daughters had on a bathing suit, and her skin had turned that pale white you see when you take off your gloves on a freezing day in winter. "I suppose you're used to really hot weather," she added accusingly. "I'm not keen on the heat. I like this much better."

It started to rain a little, so we left them there and walked to the top of the beach, where there was a handsome bleached-wood boardwalk. There I observed another British beach phenomenon, following directly from the customary rainfall: the customary impromptu indoor picnic. A group of people ate bacon-and-butter sandwiches, known as bacon butties, under a bus shelter. Another family crammed inside their car— mother, two children, two dogs—munching on oat biscuits and waiting for the sky to clear.

This was nothing to be embarrassed about; they were making the best of things.

"I wouldn't go out of my way to say, 'Right, we're eating in the car,' but if it was raining that's what we would do," the mother said. Peter Gibson, the Encams spokesman, told me that he had lived through many similar mealtime events from his own childhood in the North, where summers are as cold and forbidding as they come.

"What we would do, to be honest, is sit in the car and look out to the sea," Gibson said. "We loved to go to the seaside."

When forced to give the unvarnished truth about what really went on during the perfect summers of his youth, my husband recalls beach picnics as desperate searches for shelter followed by the quick inhaling of a few cheese sandwiches followed by a rapid rainy retreat to the car. At that point my stoic, practical mother-in-law, shepherding her four small children along, would sweep the food into the picnic basket and announce brightly, "Well, at least we got the best of the day."

My friend Victoria spent many of her early summers eating lunch in parking lots in the family's little white Ford Poplar—she and her sister in the back, her parents in front, spilling hot tea onto their legs as they passed the Thermos back and forth. "It was either stay in the car, or get out and freeze," she said. "It was rather cozy. My father used to get piping bags that my mother used for icing, and he'd inject pork pies with mustard."

You can see Britons eating in cars all over the country, especially in rest areas beside the highway, where, in a perverse move, they remain inside even on sunny days (conversely, on days of poor weather, people in pubs think nothing of standing outside on the sidewalk, drinking their pints and chatting in the cold and damp).

Peter Gibbs, a BBC weatherman and an old hand at deciphering the semiotics of British weather psychology, once tried to explain it to me. The inherent delightfulness of sunshine is by no means a matter of faith in a country with such changeable weather and such independently minded citizens, he said.

"We have to be very careful not to make value judgments," he said. "'If we say, 'It's going to be a fantastically nice sunny day' "—here he mimicked a gung-ho American-style weatherman, perhaps the sort whose on-screen persona might include sunglasses and a "fun" Hawaiian T-shirt—"then we will get letters from people who don't like the sunshine, or who have asthma, or who need the rain because their gardens are dying."

Gibbs and his coworkers waded into a full-blown weather controversy in 2005, when the BBC unveiled a £1 million redesign of its weather-map graphics. The idea was that it would be more like a moving commentary, to reflect the rapid fluctuations in the climate, and less like the old-style static slide show.

The changes were radical, if such a word can be used in connection with a daily weather report. Out went the old fixed map of the British Isles, dotted with cute, straightforward little glyphs. In came a constantly moving picture swooping panoramically across a 3-D map in which sun and clouds were represented not by familiar symbols of sun and clouds, but by splotches of color: dark gray for cloudy sections, light gray for sunny ones. The new rain in the picture looked as if it were really falling, beating down on the ground, or at least on the map.

But far from being thrilled, viewers reacted as if New Coke had come, unbidden, on the market again. Four thousand people filed official complaints, grumbling that the new broadcasts were confusing, ugly, simplistic, and London-centric. They said that all the moving around was making them queasy and sick to their stomachs.

Fishermen said that the BBC had failed them by omitting information about barometric pressure. Groups representing black-and-white TV owners and the partially sighted said that the BBC had let them down, too, by making the sunny bits on the map virtually undistinguishable from the cloudy ones.

Peter Black, a member of the Welsh Assembly, complained that the change showed "a cavalier disregard for Swansea."

Angus MacNeil, an MP from Scotland, said that the new map insulted Scotland by making it look too small. Bristling with indignation, Lord Pilkington, a peer from England, brought the matter all the way to the House of Lords, as good a place as any to discuss one's objections to the portrayal of weather patterns on television. A gale had been blowing outside his house for two days, Lord Pilkington blustered, "but I did not hear anything about it on the weather forecast." ("Believe it or not, ministers are not responsible for weather forecasts," responded Lord Davies of Oldham, speaking on behalf of the government.)

But on the bright side, the new weather map gave people a fresh weather-related issue to debate, other than whether or not it was likely to rain (a pointless topic, since it always is).

Britons are not just fond of talking about the weather; they are fond of talking about why they talk about it. The social anthropologist Kate Fox has a whole section on it in her book *Watching the English*. "In this spirit of observing traditional protocol," she writes, "I shall, like every other writer on Englishness, quote Dr. Johnson's famous comment that 'When two Englishmen meet, their first talk is of the weather.'" (In the same vein, everyone who has ever tried to write about England has also tried to write about the weather.)

Fox believes they use the weather as icebreaker, crutch, and filler. "English weather-speak is a form of 'grooming-talk'—the human equivalent of what is known as 'social grooming' among our primate cousins, where they spend hours grooming each other's fur, even when they are perfectly clean, as a means of social bonding," she writes.

In *Notes from a Small Island*, Bill Bryson says he can't understand Britons' obsession with weather that is so mild and relatively event-free, lacking the hurricanes, tornadoes, tidal waves, and blizzards that make it a serious issue elsewhere. But Jeremy Paxman, the anchor of the

BBC program *Newsnight* and the author of *The English*, believes that on the contrary, the weather is endlessly interesting on account of its moodiness and quick changeability.

They are all correct, in fact. The weather is all things to all people. The English do use the weather as a neutral topic, either to initiate intimacy ("I'm mentioning the looming black cloud because I am too repressed for normal chitchat"), or to repel it ("I will politely discuss the rain, but that is as far as it goes"). They are grateful for its presence as an available subject, because everyone has it in common and because it is uncontroversial, unless you are the sort of person who gets into fights about the chance of precipitation.

And they love to complain about it. In the London *Time Out*, Andrew Mueller, who is from Australia, marveled at how a mini–heat wave had sent the country into a collective fit of the vapors. "People, it's just not that hot," he wrote. "And by going on and on about how hot it is, you do nothing but reinforce the popular image of Britain as a nation of timid, whining knotted-hankie wearers who shun the sensual in favor of sandals with socks. Get a grip."

Britain officially has a temperate climate, benefiting from the Gulf Stream that sends relatively warm air its way, even though parts of it are pretty far north—but that doesn't explain the special nature of the winter cold and the mysterious damp that makes it worse. Even when it is above freezing outside, it can feel like it's below freezing indoors, particularly in old stone buildings in the country. A lot of people, whether by tradition, frugality, or perversity, fail to heat their homes adequately.

This causes cross-cultural distress. An American friend told me that she was at a loss as to how to deal with the situation in her mother-in-law's house, which is so poorly insulated that when the mailman drops the mail through the door, it blows around for a while inside the front hall before finally falling to the floor. Mary Killen, the *Spectator* advice columnist, once got a letter from a London resident wondering how to handle the weather inside a friend's country house. "There is a reasonably warm conservatory we huddle in during the day, but even in high summer last year it was so cold that birthday cards would not stand up because of the damp in the house and we could see our breath even in the bedroom, where my husband resorted to sleeping with a tea-cozy on his head."

What to do? Killen suggested that sleeping bags might be brought from home for use as "internal envelopes" in bed and as impromptu emergency shawls during cold afternoons. "Meanwhile," she said, "deep heat patches as used by rheumatics can be adhered to your clothing to give a good seven hours' back-up heat."

Even though Britons try to pretend otherwise, the weather has a huge influence on the national mood. Because so many days start bright and quickly turn gloomy, early-morning enthusiasm turns to late-morning glumness. "Our dispositions too frequently change with the colours of the sky," Dr. Johnson said, and writers from Shakespeare to Daphne du Maurier have written obsessively about the weather as instigator and mirror of their characters' moods.

The fog is a character in itself in Dickens's *Bleak House*. The extended Gothic melancholy that is *Jane Eyre* begins with a horrible November day and "ceaseless rain sweeping away wildly before a long and lamentable blast." It is no coincidence that when the American poet Sylvia Plath killed herself in February 1963, by sticking her head in a gas oven, England was in the midst of a sustained assault of snow, ice, and cold, its worst winter in a century.

I think one of the reasons Britons lack Americans' perky enthusiasm is lack of light. The moodiness makes for lovely landscape paintings, but the sun's failure to rise all the way in the sky brings on a natural melancholy. At its best the sun is large and cold, like the dying sun of an old dying planet in a science fiction story. The sky might be blue, but it is always pale blue. In the winter, darkness follows lunch. "The afternoons . . . slip away faster and faster and night cheats by coming shortly after 4," Plath wrote in her journal. The UK Seasonal Affective Disorder Association estimates that one in fifty Britons have full-blown SAD, a deep winter depression brought on by lack of sunlight, and that one in eight suffer the "winter blues" (that figure sounds low to me).

You would think that the British would crave light in all this shade, which in the winter gives London the feeling of dusk in a Bergman film about the unbearable nature of being. It makes me depressed. The gray covering the sky like an old sweater matches the gray in my heart. Having diagnosed myself with SAD (symptoms: you are sad all the time), I bought a special lamp that floods the room with artificial sunlight and tricks my body into believing that it lives in Miami, even when it is physically in London. I keep it in my office, turned on high, all year long.

My husband, however, has the native constitution of a mushroom, not so much impervious to the dank and moist as actively craving it. He so enjoys the dark that he shaves, showers, and dresses with the light switched off. Like old-school Britain, stoically soldiering on through all the slings and arrows of its long history, Robert keeps a fine stiff upper lip, effecting an insouciance about the elements and venturing into the storm-tossed street with neither raincoat nor umbrella. He thinks the inscription on the U.S. General Post Office in New York—"Neither snow nor rain nor heat nor gloom of night stays these couriers from the swift completion of their appointed rounds"—is a good rule of thumb, when it comes to walking around outside.

My children, good English girls, are schooled in the different gradations of rain—"spitting" barely counts; "chucking it down" is serious. When they have sports matches outdoors, I'd say it rains at least half the time, and unless we are talking about the Great Flood itself, the match goes ahead. The mother you see over there, huddled miserably under the trees, whining to the other mothers? That's me. ("When we try to cancel the matches, everyone complains," a school administrator once told me, when I called to ask whether my older daughter's hockey game was likely to be postponed by the freak storm that at that very moment was ripping the roofs off an entire street of houses in north London. It wasn't. "So we have a policy of not canceling.")

I have begun to make my own minor adjustments. I don't leave the house without an array of layered clothing that can be removed or reapplied as the day changes. I always take an umbrella. I have begun to get used to it, actually. All the gloom makes you grateful for what sunshine there is. A sudden flash of beautiful weather gives you something to celebrate in your heart in a way that people from, say, California, never can. And I feel tougher, hardier, more robust.

I even walked across Crib Goch—a knife-edged ridge leading to the summit of Mount Snowdon, in Wales—on a day when it rained, hailed, and snowed, practically all at once. Crib Goch is known for being challenging and sometimes fatal. Although I cried several times, and although I crept so slowly that my friends and I were passed repeatedly by hordes of hill walkers—hiking zealots whose requisite equipment includes maps hung around their necks and encased in waterproof covering, to show that they fully expect and indeed relish the prospect of a good drenching—I made it to the end, frozen hair and all. And then, on the drive home, we saw about eight spectacular rainbows, one right after the other.

Feeling hopeful, I once hauled the girls to St. James's Park, near my office, for a picnic on one of those days in June that can go either way. We left Robert at home, happily ensconced in his darkened study. It was a long walk, but the subways weren't working so well just then, and I wanted to catch the best of the day.

For some reason, the girls tend not to complain when British figures of authority force them to go outside in inclement weather; with me, they suspect that my motives aren't entirely sincere, and they tend to make a fuss. They acted as if I were dragging them along on the Bataan Death March. They did not want to go. But a British mother is not deterred by something as minor as her children's heartfelt objections, and go we did.

We laid out our picnic. The wind picked up, and we found that it was necessary to weigh the paper plates and napkins down with our bags. When the clouds blew in front of the sun, the temperature fell, and because we were wearing shorts and T-shirts, we folded the sides of the picnic blanket over our legs to make a kind of comforter. Soon we were lying on the ground, cocooned together, and it was quite nice and cozy.

Sensing that there was worse to come, the park's ducks were swimming as fast as they could to their island in the middle of the pond. It started to hail, and the hail hurt when it hit our heads. "I'm sure it will blow over," I said. But the children knew when to call it a day—we had reached the point where it was chucking it down—and we gave up and ran for cover.

Except for the frozen children, I didn't mind this experience. It was kind of fun. I had felt for a moment like an intrepid British person unflinchingly braving the elements with fortitude and cheerful good grace (and also, unlike, say Captain Scott, with the good sense to know when it was time to turn back).

We had some nice food that we had brought from a handy local sandwich shop. We made some tea and finished our picnic indoors. It wasn't the car, but you can't have everything, can you?

ACKNOWLEDGMENTS

Many people agreed to read all or parts of this book before it became a book, offering essential criticism cunningly disguised as friendly reinforcement. A huge thanks to Hilary Boyd , Dexter Filkins, Geordie Greig, Eric Lax, Ben Macintyre, Amelia Mendoza, Timothy Nation, Anne Goodwin Sides, Jacob Weisberg, and Lisa Wolfe. I am especially grateful to Michael Lewis and Margaret Marshall for their help with titles.

More people than I can say have provided friendship and distraction and listened with apparent interest to my tedious concerns, and since this is my first book, I'm going to mention some of them. Special thanks to Hillary Harmon, Lesley Cavendish, Flora Hood, Linda Lynch, Kathy Lette, Isabel Fonseca, Michael Specter, Deborah Needleman, Ian Fisher, Kirk Semple, Felicity Rubinstein, Justine McGovern, Nina Darnton, Natalia Schiffrin, Kate Figes, Maggie Mills, Alessandra Stanley, Jonathan Fielding, Mark Landler, Sophie Radice, Elizabeth Meyer, James Bird, Tim Golden, Victoria Hislop, Andrea Elliott, Peggy Edersheim Kalb, Maureen Dowd, Diana Phillips, Roxana Robinson, Vincent Meyer, Steve Myers, and Sarah Helmstadter for their kindness and patience.

In the *New York Times* London bureau, Marion Underhill, Sue

Nestor, and Pamela Kent demonstrate every day the sort of low-key stoicism that enabled the British to withstand the Blitz. John Darnton, Warren Hoge, Patrick Tyler, and Alan Cowell have been friends as well as bosses, and I especially thank Warren for his sensitivity and enthusiasm, Alan for his collegiality and amazing deadline skills, and John for his dry good humor (and his fantastic books). I am lucky in having had a collection of delightful colleagues at whom to yell things down the hall: Julia Werdigier, Eric Pfanner, Lizette Alvarez, Ray Bonner, Jane Perlez, and Heather Timmons. And especially Don Van Natta, who left me his bottle of whiskey when he moved back to New York.

Some of the reporting for these chapters comes from articles I've written for the *New York Times*, and I can't thank my editors enough for their indulgence, support, and alchemical talents with leaden prose. I especially thank Bill Keller, Rick Berke, William Schmidt, and Jill Abramson for help from above, and Susan Chira, Sam Sifton, Rick Gladstone, Ed Marks, Scott Veale, Chuck Strum, Kyle Crichton, Andrea Kannapell, Kathy Rose, Helen Verongos, and Marc Charney for day-to-day stuff. And David Rampe, brilliant editor and soother-of-egos, subversive management figure, and great friend, always. And also foreign editors past: Andrew Rosenthal and Roger Cohen.

My in-laws, particularly my mother-in-law, Christine McCrum, have been unbelievably nice about this whole thing. My mother, Susan Lyall, and my brother, David Lyall, have put up with a lot from me over the years and kept me to high standards. Benji Stanley provided crucial and thorough fact-checking help, and Sue Llewellyn is a copy editor with a golden touch.

I owe more than I can say to Bob Weil, unflappable editor with a sideline in therapy; to Lucas Wittmann, the calm voice of reason on the end of the phone; and to Louise Brockett, who knows everything but wears it lightly. And a million thanks to the wonderful, wise, and charming Kathy Robbins, who is far more than an agent, and her army of able lieutenants, particularly Coralie Hunter, Kate Rizzo, and David Halpern.

Nothing would have happened without Robert McCrum, husband and willing case study, and his unfailing support and surprising, under the circumstances, belief that someday it would actually get done.

I lost three people I loved while I was writing this book. Lily Metcalfe, whose wry opinions on everything from the mice in our college apartment to the Englishmen we married brought such joy to her friends. Connie Hays, my wickedest partner in crime, favorite writer, and oldest friend at the *Times*. And Josh Rosenthal, whose endless enthusiasm for the absurd was matched by the size of his heart, and who always appreciated a nice hedgehog story. This is for you, too.

FURTHER READING

Many writers have attempted over the years to wrestle the subject of England (or Britain, depending) to the ground. George Orwell's essay "England Your England," part of *The Lion and the Unicorn*, is as wise and pertinent now as it was when he wrote it, more than sixty years ago. More recently, Jeremy Paxman plumbs the nation's psyche in his rigorously researched *The English: A Portrait of a People* (London: Penguin Books, 1999), and Bill Bryson provides a humorous account of his experiences as an expatriate in *Notes from a Small Island* (London: Doubleday, 1992). A. A. Gill's *The Angry Island: Hunting the English* (London: Weidenfeld & Nicolson, 2005), takes as its thesis that the prevailing emotion in England is fury.

Julian Barnes looks at the matter from a novelist's perspective in *England, England* (London: Jonathan Cape, 1998), and Kate Fox takes a social anthropologist's viewpoint in *Watching the English* (London: Hodder & Stoughton, 2004). Roger Scruton makes the case for forgotten values in *England: An Elegy* (London: Chatto & Windus, 2000).

CHAPTERS 1—2

The dismaying British man—although he is often disguised as a hero—is a familiar figure in fiction. In her unfinished novel *The Buccaneers*, completed long after her death by Marion Mainwaring and published in London in 1993, Edith Wharton examined the allure of the British man (for American women) and the pitfalls of marrying one. The transplanted American Consuelo Vanderbilt Balsan provides an on-the-ground perspective in *The Glitter and the Gold* (New York: George Mann Books, 1953). Orwell describes the unremitting miseries of boarding school life in "Such, Such Were the Joys," an essay about his time at St. Cyprian's prep school.

The novelist Paul Watkins's memoir *Stand Before Your God* (London: Faber & Faber, 1993), is an eye-opening account of life at The Dragon and Eton in the late 1970s and early 1980s. Nick Duffell takes a grim view of British education in general, and boarding school education in particular, in *The Making of Them: The British Attitude to Children and the Boarding School System* (London: Lone Arrow Press, 2000). Unnerved by his experiences attempting to date women in New York, the British banker Robert Kelsey wrote about it in *The Pursuit of Happiness: Overpaid, Oversexed and Over There* (London: Bantam Books, 2000).

For an in-depth discussion of the travails of the women elected to the House of Commons in 1997, see *Women in Parliament: The New Suffragettes* (London: Politico's Publishing, 2005), by Boni Sones, with Margaret Moran and Joni Lovenduski. *Hansard*, available online, is an invaluable resource for transcripts of parliamentary debates.

CHAPTER 3

The satirical novel about journalism is one of the staples of British fiction, and two of the best examples are Evelyn Waugh's *Scoop* (first published by Chapman & Hall in London, 1938) and Michael Frayn's *Towards the End of the Morning* (first published by William Collins Sons & Co. in Glasgow, 1967).

Andrew Marr, formerly the political editor of the BBC and now the host of a Sunday-morning talk show, examines his profession in *My Trade* (London: Macmillan, 2004). In *The Blair Years: Excerpts from the Alastair Campbell Diaries* (London: Hutchinson, 2007) the former prime minister's chief spokesman describes the unhealthily symbiotic relationship between the media and the government. Piers Morgan, a former tabloid editor, looks at the same issue from the other side of the table in *The Insider* (London: Ebury Press, 2005), an account of his colorful and not always sober career, and John Lloyd takes the media to task in his stern *What the Media Are Doing to Our Politics* (London: Constable, 2004).

Angela Levin and the celebrity publicist Max Clifford talk about the tawdry deals behind the tawdry stories in *Read All About It* (London: Constable, 2004).

In *Only Correct: the Best of Corrections and Clarifications* (London: Guardian Books, 2005), Ian Mayes—who, as the first reader's editor at the *Guardian*, pioneered the corrections and clarifications column—offers his favorite examples.

CHAPTERS 4—6

British fiction is rife with accounts of people who get drunk and do mortifying things, but Kingsley Amis has one of the best such scenes in *Lucky Jim* (first published by Gollancz in London, 1954).

The account of the village cricket game comes from A. G. Macdonell's classic novel *England, their England* (first published by Macmillan in London, 1933). The well-known cricket player E. T. Smith deals with his own cultural dissonances in *Playing Hard Ball: A Kent County Cricketer's Journey into Big League Baseball* (London: Little Brown, 2002), in which he goes to America and joins the New York Mets for spring training. *The Faber Book of Cricket* (London, Faber & Faber, 1987), edited by Michael Davie and Simon Davie, is an invaluable anthology of cricket-related writing.

The implications of Kate Middleton's possibly middle-class family were thoroughly examined in the British newspapers when she and

Prince William briefly broke up and the press wondered why. Nancy Mitford's classic essay about class, "The English Aristocracy," appears in *Noblesse Oblige*, along with Evelyn Waugh's response, "An Open Letter to the Hon. Mrs. Peter Rodd (Nancy Mitford) on a Very Serious Subject." The book also includes a satirical poem, "How to Get On in Society," in which John Betjeman crams as many non-U words as he can into each stanza ("Phone for the fish-knives, Norman," the poem begins); and the essay that started the whole thing off in 1954, "U and Non-U," by Professor Alan S. C. Ross.

CHAPTERS 7—8

While the 1999 debates in the House of Lords over the abolition of hereditary peers are available from *Hansard*, the 1979 debate about UFOs comes in its own slender volume, *UFOs in the House of Lords* (London: The Stationery Office, 2000). Molly Dineen's film *The Lords' Tale* (2002), offers a poignant look at the hereditaries' waning days. John Wells's *The House of Lords* (London: Hodder & Stoughton, 1997), is filled with anecdotes about the chamber's history.

For a discussion of the unwritten constitution, nothing beats Walter Bagehot's *The English Constitution,* first published in 1867. In *This Time: Our Constitutional Revolution* (London: Vintage, 1997), Anthony Barnett advocates that radical alternative, a written constitution.

Alan Bennett's backhanded approach to his own talent shines out particularly in the essays compiled in *Writing Home* (London: Faber & Faber, 1994) and *Untold Stories* (London: Faber & Faber, 2005). Toby Young's desire to promote his own haplessness permeates *How to Lose Friends and Alienate People* (London: Da Capo Press, 2002).

For more about the strange forces that roil around the mind of Boris Johnson, read *Friends, Voters, Countrymen* (London: HarperCollins, 2001), his memoir about running for Parliament, and *Have I Got Views for You* (London, HarperCollins, 2003), a collection of his witty and stylish essays. A number of the weirdest ads to appear in the *London Review of Books* personals column are reprinted in *They Call Me Naughty Lola* (London: Profile Books, 2006).

Some bad report cards of famous Britons are excerpted in *Could Do Better: School Reports of the Great and the Good* (London: Pocket Books, 2002), edited by Catherine Hurley.

CHAPTERS 9—12

The inimitable Hugh Massingberd, who died in 2007, compiled his favorite obituaries from the pages of the *Daily Telegraph* into five volumes and then picked the most amusing ones for inclusion in *The Very Best of the Daily Telegraph Books of Obituaries* (London: Pan Books, 2001).

Pat Morris's *Hedgehogs* (Ipswich: Whittet Books, 1995) is a good introduction to a prickly subject. *The Tale of Mrs. Tiggy-Winkle* is perhaps not the most sophisticated of Beatrix Potter's children's books, but it is the only one with a clothes-washing hedgehog as its main character.

Writers like Orwell and Martin Amis have considered bad teeth—their own and other people's—in passing in a number of works, but William Leith tackles the subject head-on in *British Teeth* (London: Short Books, 2001), a cautionary tale that makes the reader want to whip out her dental floss and apply it immediately.

CHAPTERS 13—14

It's not about Britain, but Dave Barry's "Can New York Save Itself?" which appeared in the *Miami Herald* in 1987, is one of the funniest magazine articles ever written. *Austerity Britain, 1945–1951* (London: Bloomsbury, 2007), by David Kynaston, is an excellent account of a singularly difficult time in recent British history, while *The Age of Austerity*, edited by Michael Sissons and Philip French (first published by Hodder & Stoughton in London, 1963), contains a sharp collection of essays on the subject. Anne Fadiman's lovely piece "My Odd Shelf," which lays bare her obsession with books about failed polar expeditions, can be found in *Ex Libris: Confessions of a Common Reader* (New York: Farrar, Straus & Giroux, 1998).

Tina Brown's *The Diana Chronicles* (London: Century, 2007)

includes an incisive discussion of the emotional madness that followed Diana's death. Jonathan Dimbleby's *The Prince of Wales* (London: Little Brown, 1995) will tell you more than you probably want to know about the bad childhood and good works of the heir to the throne. In *Paranoid Parenting* (London: Allen Lane, 2001) and *Therapy Culture: Cultivating Vulnerability in an Uncertain Age* (London: Routledge, 2003), the sociologist Frank Furedi mourns the passing of the Enid Blyton meat-pie-scarfing, shin-scraping generation, arguing that Britons have become hopelessly risk-averse. Pat Barker's three Regeneration books—*Regeneration*, *The Eye in the Door*, and *The Ghost Road*—are exquisitely sensitive examinations of the price men can pay for their stiff upper lips.

INDEX

Fiennes, Ranulph, 151–53, 163
Final Test, The (film), 91
Financial Times, 53
Finnegans Wake (Joyce), 99
Fisher, Ian, 86
Fishleder, Paul, 97
Fitzsimons, Lorna, 46
Flather, Baroness, 138
Fleming, Ian, 17, 93
Flintoff, Andrew "Freddie," 88–90,
    91–92
"Floral Revolution," 233
Flying Saucer Review, 131
Follett, Barbara, 41
food:
    low expectations for, 214–16
    as necessity vs. pleasure, 214
Foot, Michael, 36
football, *see* soccer
Forbes of Craigievar, Ewan, 171
Forster, E. M., 109, 228
Forth, Eric, 47–48
Fortnum & Mason, 116*n*
Four Weddings and a Funeral (film),
    3, 20, 153, 154
Fox, 52
Fox, Kate, 83, 255
"fragrance," use of term, 44*n*
Franklin, John, 228
Frayn, Michael, 155
Freedom to Be Yourself Campaign, 164
fresh air, getting of, 249, 251
"frit," Thatcher's use of term, 124
Frith, David, 103–4
Frost, Alan, 243
Frost, Lisa, 186
frugality, 117–18, 213–14, 219
fruit stands, customers as enemy at,
    207–8
Fry, Stephen, 147, 148, 183
"fuck," use of term, 118–19
Furedi, Frank, 237, 340

Gainford, Lord, 133
Garrick Club, 23

Garter King of Arms, 129
gay marriage, House of Lords
    debate on, 144
Geddes, Baron, 140
Geldof, Bob, 66
Geller, Uri, 178
General Belgrano, 51
General Post Office (New York), 258
genitalia, 42
    euphemisms for, 16
    named for German chancellors, 149
Gerkan, Manon von, 177
Gibbens, Roy, 210
Gibbs, Peter, 254
Gibson, Peter, 250, 253
Gidley, Sandra, 48–49
Gilbert, W. S., 126
Gill, A. A., 119*n*
Gladwyn, Lord, 132–33
Glasgow, Earl of, 140
Glasper, George, 203
Glasper, Lillian, 203
glowworms, in World War II, 183
Glyndebourne opera house, 249
Glynn, Mr., 200
Godiva, Lady, 166
Gold Stick-in-Waiting, 129*n*
Gone With the Wind (film), 230
Goody, Jade, 175–76
Gordonstoun, 234–35
Gorman, Teresa, 44
Gourmet, 219
Grant, Hugh, 3, 153–54
Graves, Robert, 148
Great Brington, England, 108
Green, Stanley, 164
Greene, Graham, 207
Greer, Germaine, 21
Grey, Earl, 134, 142
Griffiths, Jane, 34
Grigg, John, 235
Guardian, 22, 54, 67, 104, 118, 178
    April Fool's hoaxes in, 59–60
    "Corrections and Clarifications"
        column of, 58–59

Sex Pistols, 195
Shakespeare, William, 17, 22, 71, 142n, 257
   hedgehogs and, 184
Shaw, George Bernard, 109
Shepherd, Gillian, 44
Short, Clare, 42, 52–53, 77
Shrewsbury, Charles Henry John Benedict Crofton Chetwynd Chetwynd-Talbot, Earl of, 134
Silver Stick-in-Waiting, 129n, 183n
silverware, proper use of, 109n
Simpson, Wallis, 11
Simpsons, The (TV series), 195
Simpsons, The: The Movie, 52
Sky News, 62
Sky People, The (Trench), 131
Sky TV, 52, 177
Smith, Delia, 214n
Smith, Judith, 175
Snapps, Grant, 218
snobbery, reverse, 122–24
snoek, Spam as preferable to, 212–13
"Snoek Piquante" (Cooper), 212
Snow, Jon, 58
Snowdon, Mount, 259
Soames, Nicholas, 36, 45–46, 49
soccer, 52n, 93, 97n
social grooming, weather-talk as, 255
Soderling, Robin, 248
Sones, Boni, 43
"sorry," use of term, 10, 119
Sound of Music, The (Rodgers and Hammerstein), 157–58
Sound of No Hands Clapping, The (Young), 162
South Uist, 181, 188
Southwark, Bishop of, 81
Spam, 213
spanking, 17–18
  see also beatings
Speaker of the House, 35, 36, 37–38, 46
Spectator, 46, 74, 113, 256
  Boris Johnson as editor of, 158, 159–60, 161

Spencer, Baldwin, 98
Spencer, Earl, 107–8, 118n
Spider-Man (film), 174
Spike's Dinner hedgehog chow, 186
sports days, 145–46, 238
Stafford, Earl of, 142
stag parties, Europe as preferred venue for, 84–85
Stanbrook, Ivor, 44
Stand Before Your God (Watkins), 13–14
Stanley of Alderley, Lord, 143
Starbucks, 220
Starkey, June, 210
Starkey, Phyllis, 43
Star Trek (TV show), 182
state schools, 239
Steiner, George, 83
Stewart, Potter, 108
stiff upper lip, 244–47, 258, 260
  see also reserve; self-denial
Stiff Upper Lip, Jeeves (Wodehouse), 24
Stone, Jennifer, 196, 202n
Stoppard, Tom, 99
Strabolgi, Lord, 133
Strange, Baroness, 137, 141, 143n
Strathclyde, Thomas Galloway Dunlop du Roy de Blicquy Galbraith, Baron, 134, 142, 143n
Straw, Jack, 169
strikes, 132, 215–16
Stuart, Gisela, 43
subways, London, 218, 222, 223
Sun, 50–51, 56, 66, 69, 121, 178
  Page Three Girls of, 52–53
Sunday hours, retail, 219
Sunday Mercury, 168
Sunday People, 67
Sunday Telegraph, 168
sunlight, Britons' unfamiliarity with, 254, 257–58
superheroes, 172–75
supermarkets, 209
Swayne, Desmond, 37, 42–43, 45

ABOUT THE AUTHOR

A native of New York City, Sarah Lyall has worked for the New York Times since the late 1980s, covering an array of topics including the New York City Police Department, book publishing, sports, and politics. From 1995 to 2013, she was a correspondent in the New York Times's London office. She now lives in Brooklyn and has two daughters who speak with English accents.